# SHADES

# SHADES

## THE SHORT LIFE AND TRAGIC DEATH OF ERICH SCHAEDLER

COLIN LESLIE

BLACK & WHITE PUBLISHING

First published 2013
by Black & White Publishing Ltd
29 Ocean Drive, Edinburgh EH6 6JL

1 3 5 7 9 10 8 6 4 2     13 14 15 16

ISBN: 978 1 84502 541 0



A CIP catalogue record for this book is available from the British Library.

Typeset by RefineCatch Limited, Bungay, Suffolk
Printed and bound by ScandBook AB, Sweden

# ACKNOWLEDGEMENTS

The many former teammates, friends and manager of Erich who took time to meet me or speak to me – anyone quoted within this book I thank for their input. Jim McArthur for the many contacts he shared with me, Alex Gordon, Alan Pattullo, Aidan Smith, Mike Aitken, Simon Pia, Martin Hannan, Stephen Kerr at Rangers, Charlie Taylor, Colin Smith, Kerry Black and Craig Nelson in *The Scotsman* library, Kenny Darling and Pete Mason on *The Scotsman* picture desk, Alistair Grant and Douglas Swan in Peebles, Tom Brogan (*State of the Games* blog) and Paul Forsyth (*Scotland on Sunday*) for the inspiring articles they wrote in recent years on Erich Schaedler, George Stewart and Sandy Jardine who gave up their time during what was a difficult time for them, Graeme Robertson and Robert Ryan for their invaluable Dumbarton information, Paul Kane, Jay Crawford, Sandy Macnair, Bobby Robertson, Janette Campbell, Bobby Sinnett for his excellent statistics website *ihibs*, Hibernian historian Tom Wright, Stirling historian Jim Thomson, Robert Inglis in Mönchengladbach, Michael Ahrens, Ted Brack for putting me in touch with all of the Tornadoes, Marcello Mega, my proofreader and pal Stevie Burns, Sharon for her patience throughout this project, the Schaedler family, especially John and Beryl, and all at Black & White Publishing.

# CONTENTS

# FOREWORD

by Pat Stanton

I consider it to be a privilege to have been Erich Schaedler's friend, teammate and manager at Hibernian.

When he first walked through the doors at Easter Road, Erich was a rather shy, raw laddie, and the transformation he underwent in the years that followed was truly remarkable. If you had said to me that first day I saw him that he would go on and play for Scotland I would never have believed it. But he did, and it was richly deserved. He epitomised how far hard work and determination can take you in sport. He was the ultimate driven professional. When he first came into the Hibs team, he looked a million miles off being good enough to play for Scotland. But he got there, and when he was picked and he earned his place in the 1974 World Cup squad he *was* good enough to play for Scotland. That was down to sheer application.

There were better, more skilful players in the Hibs team of the Seventies, but over a period of time, we saw the qualities Erich had, and he got a lot of respect for that. Willie MacFarlane, the manager who signed him for Stirling and Hibs in 1969, saw the potential within Erich and his successor Eddie Turnbull was the man who cultivated it. Eddie Turnbull and the other coaches at Easter Road spent hours on the training ground working with Erich – and he was always willing to put in that extra work. There was never a single grumble from him, he lived for his football. He recognised that the only way he was going to better himself was to listen and learn. His fitness, of course, was his other main asset – that and his long throw-ins. He was powerfully built and always worked tirelessly at improving his strength and stamina. At training throughout his career he was a shining example to the players around him.

The supporters loved him too. The guy who paid his money and stood on the terracing could immediately identify with someone like Erich. He never gave anything less than 100 per cent. When he came to Hibs he had rough edges, but my God, what a player he became. He worked hard and ended up a really good player. Erich forced it. He was always quietly confident in his own ability and used the attributes he had to maximum effect.

As a personality you couldn't fault Erich – he was quick-witted and a bundle of energy. He could be deep and had his quiet moments, but he was enormously popular with the rest of the team. Even Alex Cropley liked him! If you got the nod off Cropley you were all right because he was a really nippie sweetie! Erich was a quiet man on the pitch, he just got on with his game, and while we had moaners right through the team – Alex Cropley, Alex Edwards and John Blackley – Erich wasn't moaned at much. You didn't have to moan at him because he had that steely determination that everyone recognised. Nobody put that in him – he was born with it.

When we were back together at Hibs in the Eighties, he was a pleasure to manage. He was great with the younger players and I'm sure many of them will have picked up good habits from his professionalism that stood them in good stead for the rest of their careers. He had an aura about him and was universally respected.

I'm sure Erich Schaedler would have gone on to become a success at whatever he chose to do after football. I can imagine he would have made an excellent coach.

His death was a tragedy for his family and all who knew him, but he will never be forgotten by all of his friends and colleagues at

Easter Road, nor the fans. I'm sure that goes for those at Stirling, Dundee and Dumbarton too.

Whenever the remaining Turnbull's Tornadoes gather, Erich is never far from our thoughts. At dinners, we set a place for him. He was a wonderful guy and through his own commitment and hard work, a top-class footballer. We will always miss him.

# 1

# "ALL HELL LET LOOSE"

1985 had already been a year of horrors for British football. First, Millwall fans rioted on the pitch after an FA Cup quarter-final at Luton in February, prompting Prime Minister Margaret Thatcher and her government to adopt a contemptuous attitude to all football supporters and how they should be treated. In May fifty-six fans lost their lives in the Bradford disaster when fire ripped through an antiquated grandstand at Valley Parade. That was quickly followed the same month by the Heysel tragedy, in which thirty-nine fans were crushed to death after crowd violence triggered the collapse of a wall at the European Cup final between Juventus and Liverpool in Brussels. Heysel led to English clubs immediately being banned from European competition for five years. The death of Jock Stein at Ninian Park in Cardiff in September was yet another dark night for the game – the legendary Scotland manager collapsing and dying of a heart attack moments after his team had secured a World Cup play-off place with a tense 1–1 draw against Wales. The year 1985 had been a depressing spiral of shame, sadness and tragedy for the sport in Britain, and as the calendar entered its final days there would be one more terrible twist.

Christmas Day 1985. In his home in Peebles, in the Scottish Borders, John Schaedler receives the telephone call from Lothian and Borders police that will change his life and those closest to him, forever. Frantic follow-up calls are then made to Pat Stanton,

George Stewart and several other close friends of Erich Schaedler – the son of a German prisoner of war, who became a revered Hibernian hero and who had been to a World Cup with Scotland.

Erich was missing, and the police were concerned as to his whereabouts and his intentions. Early investigations had failed to reassure officers that this was a false alarm, and their instincts hinted that something tragic was about to unfold. What heightened their anxiety was that Schaedler had taken with him a 12-bore shotgun – not unusual for a skilled shooting enthusiast, but a major worry given that Erich had vanished without a trace and had failed to show up to collect his beloved Doberman Pinschers from the couple he had left them with. Erich was normally Mr Reliable and this no-show was wholly out of character.

John couldn't understand why Erich had disappeared. Nobody could. Twenty-four hours earlier John had seen him in their hometown of Peebles, larger than life. Fitness fanatic Erich, a publican and still playing professional football for Dumbarton at the age of thirty-six, had tried to persuade his brother, a year older, to come on an impromptu shooting trip with him, but John – a joiner – was busy re-fitting a local hotel, a job he was understandably keen to get out of the way in time for Christmas.

Erich, an ebullient, energetic character who could rarely stand still, eventually accepted that he couldn't twist John's arm and said he was instead heading to Edinburgh for the day. He had a flat in Musselburgh, but would spend a lot of his time in the city, either working in one of his pubs, socialising with friends or going to the gym. He said he would catch up with his brother for Christmas dinner along with their mother Leah and the rest of the family in Peebles the following day. While disappointed that he couldn't persuade John to spend the day with him, Erich gave absolutely no indication that he was troubled or that something was wrong. It was the last time John saw Erich alive.

The passing minutes and hours from that initial police phone call to John were accompanied by a mounting feeling of dread. John recognised that Erich's disappearance was inexplicable and that there were serious grounds for concern, especially with the added worry that he had a loaded gun in his possession. Together with his father-in-law, John jumped in a car and scoured the area surrounding Peebles, Innerleithen and Cardrona looking blindly for any sign of his missing brother. There was no clear information to suggest Erich would be in the area, but John had nothing other than gut instinct to go on.

As Lothian and Borders police escalated the search for Erich – not an easy thing to do with manpower stretched during the festive holiday period – John divided his time between frantic searches in his car and helping officers with their enquiries. He was at the police station in Peebles on 27 December when the call came through on the police radio. They had found Erich, and tragically the worst fears had been realised – he was dead.

"I was in the police station in Peebles when the call came through that the body had been found," John recalls. "My head was spinning. My mother was at my house and I had to go and break the news to her. Then all hell was let loose after that."

The "hell" that John refers to is the mystery and many unanswered questions that surround Erich's death to this day, and his search for a truth he still feels eludes him.

The bare facts show that Erich was found in his silver Volkswagen Passat car, in dense forest between Cardrona and Innerleithen. He had died from a single shotgun wound to the head. A straightforward suicide, one would assume. The official records say as much. But there was no suicide note and no obvious motive. In the years that followed Erich's tragic demise, John and his family have had to deal with countless rumours and theories why his brother had been found dead and an unbearable amount of gossip and tittle-tattle. This has only added to the layers of complexity and intrigue surrounding Schaedler's unexplained death.

Journalists frequently request death certificates from the Registrar in the course of their work. They are functional tools of the trade, providing an accurate method of establishing names, addresses, birthplaces and family links. Scrutinising the death certificate of Erich Peter Schaedler, however, leaves me with a heavy heart.

Erich Schaedler is a hero of mine, same as he was and still is to thousands of other football supporters. Even though I only saw Erich play in the twilight of his Hibernian career, I marvelled at a player fiercely committed to the cause – fearless, brave and admired by fans who knew a trier when they saw one.

The only face-to-face meeting with Erich that I recall came on a guided evening tour of Easter Road stadium which I had been invited to as a "Hibs Kid", around 1983. Erich was in his second spell with the club – a grim period for Hibs when compared to the dizzy heights they had reached during his first stint. Having been shown round the crumbling ground, our party had an added bonus when we unexpectedly stumbled upon one of the players, hours after the remainder of the squad had departed the stadium after the morning training session. In the spartan gym that sat underneath the old wooden staircase of the Centre Stand, there alone was the ever-dedicated Erich, pumping iron and putting in the extra work that had made him stand out during his long and distinguished career. His face broke into a broad grin when he saw us, and he stopped his workout to chat with the wide-eyed young fans and to sign autographs. Nothing was too much trouble for him. He made an instant impression on me, and in the course of researching this account of his life and career, it is clear that he made a similar effect on most people he met.

With that happy childhood memory at the forefront of my mind, analysing the official record of Erich Schaedler's death was a difficult task to perform. Erich Peter Schaedler, born on 6 August 1949. Occupation: Professional Footballer. Twice married, twice divorced. Name of father: also Erich Peter Schaedler. Name of mother: Leah Schaedler. When and where died: Found dead 1985 December Twenty-seventh, 1535 Hours, Cardrona Forest, Innerleithen. And then, underneath the column marked "Cause of

Death", the four words that make this extract from the Registrar of Deaths in Scotland particularly chilling: "Shotgun Wound of Head".

It was a grief-stricken John Schaedler who registered his younger brother's death in Peebles on Hogmanay 1985, although it would be weeks later before Erich's funeral could be held as police carried out and eventually concluded their enquiries.

John also courageously fielded questions on behalf of his numbed family as police broke the news of their grim discovery at Cardrona Forest to media outlets.

Coverage of a sensitive incident such as this in 1985 was far removed from the way the media would report the news now. In today's instantaneous news environment, the unexplained death of a high-profile footballer would doubtless command a front-page headline stacked up in decks of 100-point type print, as was the case when Wales manager Gary Speed died from apparent suicide in November 2011. Erich's death in 1985, however, was sombrely reported in small wing columns on the front of several Scottish newspapers. South of the border it barely registered a mention.

Police informed reporters that the formal identification had been completed and inquiries were continuing, but stressed, "It is understood that there are no suspicious circumstances." Almost thirty years on, that remains the police position on a case that was closed long ago.

The *Glasgow Herald*'s account of Erich's death recorded the final hours he had been seen alive: "Mr [Erich] Schaedler had gone to Peebles to visit his brother and mother. He was a field sports enthusiast and had a 12-bore shotgun with him for rough shooting in the Borders. He had been asking his brother John, 37, to go shooting with him on Tuesday (the 24th) but John, a carpenter, was unable to go because of work. Mr Schaedler had spent Tuesday morning helping John out at his work and had taken a cup of coffee at his brother's home before setting out for Edinburgh about lunchtime."

John told the *Herald*, "He seemed to be okay. Maybe he was a bit unhappy because I couldn't go shooting with him but he seemed generally fine. We often went 12-bore shooting together. When Erich left me he said he was going back to the town. I took that to mean he was going to Edinburgh. I don't know if he had any really pressing problems."

John never was able to get to the bottom of these "problems". Certainly, there were rumours circulating that Erich's pubs – Shades Bar at the foot of Easter Road, and the Victoria Bar on Leith Walk – had encountered financial difficulties in the months preceding his death. There were also rumours about a complicated personal life. Rumours of illness. Rumours of depression. There were rumours aplenty, but little if any hard facts to accompany any of them. Several past acquaintances have offered me theories why Erich might have taken his own life. One or two of the reasons suggested are theoretically plausible but far from conclusive. Others are based on hearsay and laden with urban myth, perpetuated by the "village" mentality Edinburgh is famous for when it comes to spreading gossip like wildfire. It's given me a glimpse into the torment John must have felt during the past three decades chasing up supposed "leads" into the circumstances surrounding Erich's death – only to be left no closer to the truth. To print these rumours when the man himself is no longer here to defend himself or give his side of the story would, in my opinion, be plain wrong. It would also be insult to a great footballer and a great man. A definitive explanation for why Erich would have reason to take his own life remains as elusive now as it was in 1985.

Erich's funeral was held in early 1986 and the chapel at Mortonhall Crematorium on the south side of Edinburgh was packed beyond capacity, with hundreds of mourners lining the pathways outside. Alongside Erich's devastated family and friends stood teammates from his final club Dumbarton, stunned members of the tight-knit Turnbull's Tornadoes Hibs squad of the early Seventies and countless other teammates and friends Erich had met during his spells at Hibs (1969–77 and 1981–85), Dundee (1977–81) and Stirling

Albion (1969). Iain Munro – twice Erich's teammate at Easter Road – gave a stirring eulogy. Munro's words eloquently captured Erich's character and the high regard in which he had been held, but still no one could understand why someone who seemingly had so much zest for life had been taken from them.

At the wake afterwards, mourners shared memories of the strong, handsome joker who would pounce on unsuspecting teammates in the dressing room and bear hug them into breathless submission; the flying full-back with the long throw who lifted trophies and played all over Europe as a key member of Eddie Turnbull's celebrated Hibs team of the Seventies; the raw lad who listened, learned and worked relentlessly on his game and fitness to became an international defender good enough to earn a place in the stellar Scotland squad for the 1974 World Cup; the man who would tirelessly work for charities and who displayed all the attributes and inspirational qualities that would have made him an ideal coach; the devoted father of a young girl; the popular, smiling publican who ran two pubs in Leith and was loved by his regulars. There were so many wonderful positive memories in the room that it made it impossible to fathom why he had died such a lonely death.

Twenty-seven years later, and I am accompanying John to Erich's final resting place, deep within the majestic, dense forests of the Tweed Valley. As we ascend the hill above the village of Cardrona – "Schaedler's Hill" they personalised and christened it as adventurous young boys – John points out the many wondrous places they would play together growing up together during a simple, happy countryside childhood in the 1950s. Eventually we reach a plateau near Wallace's Hill and make the short walk to a breathtaking viewpoint high above the valley. Directly below I can see the village of Cardrona, opposite lies Glentress, and to the east – further along the snaking River Tweed – are the outskirts of Innerleithen. Yards from the precipice of this vantage point stands a handsome lime tree, and this is where the ashes of Erich Schaedler were scattered by the family in 1986. It is a beautifully peaceful spot and one that John and his family visit regularly, whatever the weather. "We've had to wade through three feet of snow sometimes," says John, who will head up there each Christmas with his wife Beryl to lay flowers or bring a plant in memory of Erich and their mother Leah, whose ashes were also scattered here years later.

"From time to time I have thought about having a plaque erected here for Erich," he adds. "A lot of people have asked me where Erich's final resting place is so they can come and pay their respects. It's something I may look into, but for the moment I'd prefer it to remain private. It's a lovely spot though, isn't it?"

We're standing here on a mild mid-summer's night, and the fine rain up here in the clouds has spread a thick rainbow across the lush green valley, enhancing its natural beauty further. It would have been a very different landscape when Erich was found there in the depth of winter in 1985, but it's an uplifting experience to stand here on this fine evening and remember what made the late Erich Schaedler so special.

## 2

# BIGGAR AND BETTER THINGS

Most young men in Scotland in the 1960s and 1970s could say their father had fought in World War II. John and Erich were the same; their father too had bravely served his country. There was one major difference in the Schaedlers' case, though, as the surname suggests – their father had served on the side of the Germans.

Erich Peter Schaedler senior hailed from München Gladbach, as it was then, a city in the west of Germany close to the Dutch border. Erich senior had been an athletic youngster and a talented footballer who had earned a place on the books of the city's club Borussia Mönchengladbach. Football in Germany was exclusively amateur in the 1930s, and clubs played within district leagues. Mönchengladbach were one of the country's emerging sides and Erich senior had harboured realistic dreams of becoming a footballer. But war would dramatically alter his destiny, just as it did to millions around the world. Like every other able-bodied young man in the country, Erich senior was drafted into Adolf Hitler's Wehrmacht – the Third Reich's combined forces. Erich opted for the Kriegsmarine, the German navy, and on completion of his naval training he was sent to serve on board the *Bismarck* – together with her sister ship *Tirpitz*, the biggest battleship ever built by Germany, with a crew of 2,200.

Just weeks before the *Bismarck* was commissioned in 1940, a quirk of fate saw Schaedler switched from duty on the *Bismarck* to a fleet of smaller torpedo boats. The *Bismarck* was sunk following a dramatic chase and sustained bombardment by the British Navy in the North Atlantic in 1941. Only 114 men survived. Had Erich been on board, his odds against survival would have been in excess of 200-1.

While the *Bismarck* was perhaps the highest-profile maritime casualty of the war, the small boat Erich was serving on also came to grief. When it came under heavy fire, Schaedler was hit by a bullet in the foot and was captured off the coast of France. "He was picked up because he couldnae run," says John, adding that the wound left no lasting damage and no notable limp. Erich's active service was over. He was declared a prisoner of war and taken to mainland Britain.

With prisoner of war numbers rising to 400,000, hundreds of camps were set up across the United Kingdom to accommodate this enormous influx of unexpected visitors. Schaedler was taken to Happendon, within a complex of three camps at Douglas in rural South Lanarkshire. The camps were also known as Douglas Castle or Douglas Water, but during wartime the complex was referred to by its official name: Camp 19. These camps were closed and the structures torn down at the end of the war, but what remains of the site lies behind the Happendon Service Station adjacent to the M74 motorway.

These rectangular POW camps comprised rows of Nissen huts made of corrugated iron, along with an exercise yard and basic facilities. Locals have shared memories of seeing the prisoners – most of them German or Italian military men – being marched from their camp to the pithead baths at Douglas West for their weekly wash.

Supplies were scarce, food provisions especially, and prisoners were known to trade in scrap, clothes and even roadkill to source food and cigarettes. However, all evidence suggests that they were well treated by their captors and that the POWs lived harmoniously alongside the neighbouring communities.

As the war years passed, security was relaxed at the camp and the 300 or so prisoners who had been sent to work on farms and quarries in the area were occasionally allowed supervised overnight stays within the farms they had been labouring at.

Locals, to their credit, showed genuine warmth towards the incomers, who had demonstrated that they represented no threat. This peaceful co-existence must have had a major bearing on Erich Schaedler's decision to remain in Scotland rather than return home to München Gladbach at the end of the war. There was a further factor which would influence where Erich's future lay: he had met and fallen in love with a Scottish girl, Leah Bulloch.

"My mother worked in the chip shop in Biggar and my father used to go in there after he'd been working on the farms," says John. "He could speak very little English at first, so he'd just point and say, 'Chips!'"

Committing his future to Scotland, Erich Schaedler married Leah in 1948 and the newlyweds set up home at a cottage in the town of Biggar. Later that same year their first son, John, was born, joined the following year by Erich, who came into the world at 12.30am on 6 August 1949.

Erich was accepted into the community, made friends and found farm work. He also kept in touch with other German former POWs who had settled in the area. John has vivid early memories of his father entertaining friends in their cottage, sharing stories round a coal fire – sometimes in their native tongue but usually in English as they tried to improve their conversational skills. "He had picked up the language fast and his English was good," John says of his father. "He was a nice writer too, as I could see from his letters. My father was fluent but some of the others had only broken English. He was always happy enough to talk about the war – it wasn't something taboo that shouldn't be mentioned.

"I remember us sitting in the cottage with a big coal fire and gas lights hanging on the wall, listening to episodes of Dan Dare on the wireless. He had a pal named Hans who used to come down and they would talk about some of their exploits from during the war and their time on the boats, or some of the stories from the prisoner of war camp. I was only five or six so I wasn't taking it all in, but it was still interesting. Erich and I would sit in the corner listening to them talk, until we got spotted, that was, and booted off to bed!"

It was a bold move for Schaedler to gamble on making a fresh start in Scotland, particularly as Britain struggled to put itself on a firm financial footing after the war, but it had worked. He had found employment, a family and happiness in a foreign land.

It would have been easier to head back to his home city München Gladbach, which was changed to Mönchen Gladbach in 1950 and the Mönchengladbach that we refer to now, in 1960. But Erich had laid down new roots in Scotland, leaving family behind in Germany.

The Schaedler family made an emotional trip to Germany in 1954, as Erich senior returned home for the first time since the war. "We were only wee laddies but I remember it," says John. "We met cousins and relatives I barely knew we had. We got a wonderful welcome. It was Dad's first time back, and I suppose it can't have been easy for him."

During that visit Erich met his brother Wilhelm, a decorated war hero in Germany for the role he played in the evacuation of Stalingrad. Wilhelm had been in the Luftwaffe and his plane was one of the last out of the Russian city in one of the deadliest battles of World War II. It was a strange coincidence that Wilhelm had befriended a Scot who had made a move in the opposite direction to Erich, settling for a new life in Germany, Robert Inglis.

Robert had lived in Sherwood on the outskirts of Bonnyrigg before the war. After serving in the Military Police, Inglis met and married a German girl and they raised a family in Mönchengladbach – the reverse of Erich's move to Scotland. "I got to know the boys well over the years," says Robert, "and when I went back to Scotland to visit I paid them a visit in Peebles. I was a Hibs fan myself, so it was nice to hear how well Erich was doing later in his football career, and when he played for Scotland in West Germany, his uncle Wilhelm and I watched the match on television together. He was very proud of what his nephew had achieved. We also used to go to the Borussia Mönchengladbach matches together."

Inglis has been watching Mönchengladbach for more than sixty years, and remains an avid season ticket holder. He is also a neighbour of the famous former midfielder Günter Netzer, a two-time Player of the Year in Germany who starred for Borussia Mönchengladbach, won the World Cup with West Germany in 1974, and later played for Real Madrid.

While Borussia are his team now, Inglis retains a soft spot for Hibs. "I visited Easter Road a couple of years ago and spared a thought for Erich," he adds in a broad Scottish accent. "I went to the club shop and although they didn't have any Erich Schaedler T-shirts, they did have one which says, 'Gie the Ba' to Reilly', which I sometimes wear to the Borussia matches," says Inglis, who is still in touch with John and Beryl and who was able to fill in a significant portion of the family's German history for them.

Around the same time as the Schaedlers' 1954 visit to Germany, Erich senior had shown a particular aptitude for gardening and his green fingers landed him a gardening job which came with a family home in Cardrona. The cottage sat on the fringes of the Cardrona Forest and within a short distance of where the MacDonald Hotel and golf complex is located now. It would be the boys' home throughout their formative years, and they enjoyed a happy childhood there, walking to the train station whenever they had cause to make the three-mile trip to Peebles or Edinburgh, twenty-five miles north.

The boys had a ready-made adventure playground literally on their doorstep and they took full advantage, running, climbing, exploring and fishing whenever the opportunity presented itself. Erich senior was a strict disciplinarian, but he still encouraged his boys to expend their energy and allowed them a degree of freedom to roam the fields and hills – one of which the imaginative boys claimed as their own and christened "Schaedler's Hill".

The pair struck up lasting friendships with other children, including those of the forestry workers who often stayed nearby, but most of the time Erich and John were content enough in each other's company.

"The hills were really steep so we were both as fit as fiddles," says John. "Growing up in the country was great for us both. We would spend hours up there or playing up at the Roman fort. We just lived a nice simple country life, and I remember going away on camping holidays, usually with our collie dog Roy. My mother and father seemed happy enough too, and they would go away to the bingo together once a week in a wee Morris Minor."

It wasn't all sweetness and light for the Schaedler boys, however, and they knew that their father was not to be crossed. "Some of my memories of him were good and some of them weren't so good," says John with a laugh. "He was a strict man. You couldn't say boo to him or mess about with him."

It wasn't just the boys who occasionally strayed out of line. John remembers his father trying to pull a fast one by feigning illness with his employer so he could sneak along and watch Peebles Rovers play one Saturday. "He was football daft," says John. "He had said he wasn't well, but his boss spotted him at the game. He would have been hard to miss. You could always see where he'd been standing at the Rovers games because there would be a hole in the ground from where he'd been pacing back and forward. You'd hear him before you saw him anyway – he would shout loudly and his accent always stood out from the crowd."

Erich must have been a mighty fine gardener, because he survived this little indiscretion and got back to his job, making sure that he had authorised time off when watching his beloved Peebles Rovers in future!

The segment of Cardrona where the Schaedlers lived sat in the catchment area for Innerleithen rather than Peebles, so the boys went to school there, attending St Ronan's Primary School. Despite their heritage, John says that having a dad who had been a German prisoner of war was never a problem within an understanding community.

Peebles and the surrounding area had escaped any damage in the war and the only bombs dropped in the area had been dumped on Hamilton Hill, to the north of the town, by a German plane fleeing from an aborted raid on the Central Belt. German planes could be heard flying overhead on their way to bombing raids, but Peebles was left unharmed. While many men from the area had obviously gone off to fight in World War II, the fact the area had never come under direct attack must have contributed to the welcoming nature of locals towards the POWs and the new families of those who stayed behind at the end of the war.

"The only problem I remember was before Cardrona, when we moved to Peebles and I went to Kingsland Primary School when I was about six or seven," says John. "I did get picked on a bit, but that was because were seen as 'incomers', it had nothing to do with our background.

"I never came across any prejudice. There were only a couple of jibes about our surname, but I think that was more just because they couldn't spell it than anything else!

"We already knew a lot of the kids at school in Innerleithen anyway and had no problems settling in, but Erich and I always looked out for each other."

Erich was beginning to show signs of being a promising athlete at an early age, and as John ruefully recalls, "Erich was always picked first for football; I usually ended up in goals. A teacher, Mr Borrowman, took a shine to Erich and encouraged his football. He seemed to be good at any sport he tried, and he was a very fast runner."

Throughout school Erich's sporting prowess developed and he excelled at athletics, rugby and football. The main source of employment in the area was the textile industry and on leaving school, he got a job as a turner in the woollen mills of D. Ballantyne & Bros in March Street, Peebles.

The teenage Erich, playing as a winger or a centre forward then, was also attracting the interest of the local football clubs in Peebles. Tweeddale Rovers were a successful amateur side that played at Kerfield Park, while Peebles Rovers – who in the mid 1960s were making the transition from the East of Scotland League to the Junior football ranks – were the senior team in the town, based at Whitestone Park.

Tweeddale Rovers were the first to persuade Erich to turn out for them. The amateur ranks were a logical starting place for a raw inexperienced teenager. There was nothing fancy about the Rovers. They had the most basic of facilities until a pavilion was built at Kerfield Park in 1965, but they had a reputation as a formidable team in what was a very competitive local league.

Erich's arrival at Tweeddale coincided with a successful era in the club's history. From 1965 to 1968 Tweeddale won the South of Scotland Cup in three consecutive seasons, beating Kelso United in the first two finals and Gala Rovers in the third. In the 1967/68 season they also reached the quarter-finals of the prestigious Scottish Amateur Cup – no mean feat for a club in the Borders. It was around the 1967/68 season that Erich flitted in and out of the team. His appearances were not down to selection issues – more a combination of injuries and the fact that Peebles Rovers were keen on using him too.

Erich started off playing for Tweeddale as a forward, but as his teammate Alistair Grant recalls, Schaedler soon became an accidental left-back. "There's a funny wee story about why Erich became a full-back," says Grant. "Erich was one of the youngest lads in the team and when he first played for us I was the left-back and he was the centre forward. The problem was that while he had a fierce shot, he wasn't scoring too many goals. He did stand out as one of the few left-footed players in the team, and it was decided that we should switch as an experiment and see how we got in our new positions. He obviously never looked back."

*C'Mon the Dale*, the history of Tweeddale Rovers, written by Ian

Smith, confirms Erich's transformation from forward to full-back: "Schaedler's experiences on the Peebles footballing scene were erratic to say the least. He started off as an attacker, but during his first stint at Tweeddale Rovers there was a shortage of defenders and he was moved to the back of the field." In his new position, Schaedler started cultivating his long-throw. The monster distance he could hurl the ball became a big asset, as his natural upper-body strength made it almost effortless for the youngster. The long throw-in was a bit of a novelty then, and it helped Erich stand out. He was an easy-going teenager and a popular figure in the dressing room.

Grant recalls, "Erich was a nice lad. There was never any controversy with him; he was a just a pleasant fellow to meet and to speak to, and he loved his football. His ability was obvious – he was fast and he could really zip up the wing. I think he immediately enjoyed playing at full-back as it allowed him the freedom to make long runs forward." As well as Grant, some of Erich's teammates at that time were Ian "Ruff" Thomson, Norman Kilner, Jock Stewart, Colin Brown, Drew Fraser, Dougie MacDonald, Hugh Tulloch, Bert Brodie and Jim Bauchop.

Tweeddale Rovers were renowned for being one of the fittest teams in their league, and Erich would have enjoyed their training regime. Gruelling sessions sometimes included piggy-backing teammates up the stone steps of the Peebles Hydro Hotel.

Schaedler's burgeoning reputation quickly reached the Peebles Rovers committee room, possibly brought to their attention by his father, who was a Rovers regular and eventually served on their committee. Erich had grown up aware of Peebles Rovers' lofty reputation – as his schooldays coincided with one of the brightest periods on the pitch for the club. The main man for Peebles Rovers during that era was Renwick Sanderson, who had arrived after a spell at Hibs. Sanderson is recognised as the club's greatest player and he featured in several memorable Scottish Cup runs, notably the 1955/56 season. Peebles beat Inverness Thistle after a replay then spent four games locked in an epic battle with Brechin City. The pair drew at Glebe Park, then at Whitestone Park, then at Easter Road, and only when Sanderson was incapacitated by flu for the third replay did the gallant Rovers finally succumb, in a 6–2 defeat at Tannadice.

Sanderson's achievements at Peebles Rovers cannot be overplayed. He scored 539 goals for Rovers before hanging up his boots in 1964. He was the son of former Rovers, Celtic and Hearts player Bobby Sanderson, and if he had not been on the books at Easter Road when a certain Smith, Johnstone, Reilly, Turnbull and Ormond were around, then who knows what kind of name he could have made for himself as a Hibs player. Sanderson and other reserves, such as Andy Murray's grandfather Roy Erskine, could be performing wonders – but with no substitutes in those days and opportunities only presenting themselves when the first-choice players were injured, it was extremely difficult to make the breakthrough into the top team.

In the history of Peebles Rovers, Ian Smith, notes: "Sanderson had the bad luck to arrive at Hibs during a particularly strong period in their history – and also at a time when the club was unwisely neglecting the development of young players. With the first team stuffed with such big names as Ormond, Turnbull, Reilly and Johnstone, Sanderson was restricted to playing for the second or third team. Nor did he receive much in the way of constructive training or advice. 'If you weren't in the first team,' he said in hindsight, 'they had no time for you.'"

Despite his limited opportunities, Sanderson's record in Hibs' shadow teams was still hugely impressive. There can't be many players who are discarded by a club after thirty-nine games, sixty-three goals and eleven hat-tricks.

Hibs' loss was Rovers' gain, and he had a phenomenal record of scoring hat-tricks. In his Peebles career, he scored 539 goals in 338 games (eighty-one hat-tricks) and during a spell at Vale of Leithen he scored eighty-seven goals in seventy-three games (ten hat-tricks).

Sanderson's career totals are like one-sided cricket totals. He notched 689 goals from 450 games (102 hat-tricks, including three double hat-tricks). One black mark on his stats, however, is that he was in the Peebles team that infamously lost 15–1 to Hibs at Easter Road in 1960. Joe Baker knew a thing or two about scoring goals too, and Sanderson and his Peebles teammates had to watch a masterclass that day, as the great Hibs striker scored nine in that one game. Before the match, Peebles had actually headed to Easter Road with high hopes of causing an upset, as they had a little slice of history on their side – having famously held Hibs to a draw in the 1923 Scottish Cup. This time, history belonged to Hibs and that 15–1 thrashing is inked in the club's annals as their all-time record victory.

With Sanderson retired, Erich was joining Rovers at an uncertain time for Rovers and the town in general. The textile industry was already in decline and Peebles was still trying to recover from the hammer-blow it had been dealt in 1962 when its 107-year-old railway line ceased operations. With this major artery to the town cut off, locals now had to rely on cars and buses to get them to Edinburgh, Glasgow and other Borders towns. The number of visitors to the area also plummeted, hitting the economy hard.

Rovers themselves were strapped for cash and after a meeting in May 1966, the decision was taken, perhaps out of desperation, to adopt Junior status and opt out of the East of Scotland League. Joining the Junior ranks had its perks and must have looked an exciting new option at the time, but for Peebles it was a catastrophically bad call. Leaving the East of Scotland League not only deprived Rovers of their place in the Scottish Cup, it also meant they would miss out on the money-spinning local derbies with the other Borders-based sides playing in the East of Scotland League. Rovers began their new life in the Mid-East Junior League, but it would be a constant struggle and gates and interest dwindled. The club tried and failed to return to the East of Scotland League a couple of times, before they were finally granted re-entry around 1980.

Even Erich's time in the Peebles ranks seems to have been one of confusion. He was recruited as a full-back, and essentially as cover for Rovers established No.3, but was sent back to Tweeddale Rovers a couple of times when the regular left-back was preferred. Schaedler, naturally, took it all in his stride, and looking back on the experience in a 1969 interview when he had just signed for Hibs, he explained his unusual conversion from attacker to full-back and also the way he shuttled between the two Rovers.

"In my younger days I started off as an attacker," said Erich. "I used to be fielded regularly on the left wing because I had a pretty good burst of speed. In fact, I had to go a real roundabout route before I finally ended up at full-back.

"I was playing for Tweeddale Amateurs when I first had a go in defence. In emergency, they were so short of defenders due to injuries that I was moved back. I stuck there for a few weeks until Peebles Rovers spotted me. I actually signed for Rovers as a full-back – but that still wasn't me settled in the berth. For the left-back they had was playing so well I couldn't get my place. So it was back to Tweeddale for me, but not for long. The Rovers' left-back broke a leg and that was me doing an about-turn once more. I thought I was in for keeps this time. Some hope! I was just settling in when I was asked to make up the numbers in a friendly match arranged by a local amateur team. I played – at outside-right – collided with the opposing full-back, damaged a nerve in my neck and was out for weeks. By the time I was fit again, the Peebles left-back had recovered and I was out once more. But a friend recommended me to Melbourne Thistle. I played a trial and was signed."

In the history of Peebles Rovers, Erich is remembered as one of the club's most notable former players. Ian Smith says: "His father eventually became a member of the Peebles Rovers committee. The younger Schaedler's name appeared in Peebles Rovers team lists during those uncertain years in the 1960s when they were playing Junior football. It may have been a humble start, but Schaedler eventually joined Tommy Cairns and James Reid in that very small group of Peebles Rovers players who went on to don shirts and play for the national team."

Both these Scotland internationals played for Peebles in the early twentieth century. James Reid, who played inside-right or centre forward, was at Peebles before moving to Lincoln City. He signed for Airdrie in 1912 and enjoyed a long and distinguished career with the Lanarkshire club. He played for Scotland twice in games against Wales in 1914 and 1920 and against Northern Ireland in 1924. Tommy Cairns, meanwhile, started his football career at Bristol Rovers before arriving at Peebles Rovers. In 1913 he spent a few months with St Johnstone before signing for Rangers, which proved to be the making of him. He spent fourteen years with the Ibrox club. He won seven league titles, appeared eight times for Scotland and played until the age of forty-two, when he retired after a spell at his final club, Bradford City, in 1932. As Cairns was born in Lanarkshire and Schaedler born in Biggar, he was the only Peebles-born ex-Rovers player to be capped by Scotland at full international level.

The present-day player Kevin Thomson, who like Erich has had two spells at Hibernian, was born in Peebles and has followed in Schaedler's footsteps by representing Scotland at full international level, but he never turned out for Rovers.

# 3

# MELBOURNE IDENTITY

Scottish football in the 1960s was no place for the faint-hearted. Sure, there were plenty of gifted, skilful players around, but at the opposite end of the football food chain there lurked a hefty proportion of brutally physical journeymen only too glad to dish out the rough stuff and help separate the men from the boys.

Any aspiring young player wishing to make the transition from school or juvenile football to the senior game would be in need of "toughening up" – a necessary rite of passage which would help a developing youngster cope with the rigours ahead.

Skill alone usually wasn't enough to survive. With an in-built competitive streak and a healthy natural appetite for bone-crunching tackles, Erich Schaedler was not really a player who needed "toughening up". Schaedler's outings in Junior and amateur football with Peebles and Tweeddale had already equipped him well for the physical challenges he would encounter against stronger, faster and fitter players, but it was his association with the juvenile side Melbourne Thistle in Edinburgh which really nourished his will to win and offered him the springboard to becoming a professional footballer. The term "juvenile" is something of a misnomer given that Melbourne were playing football at Under-21 level. These were young, fully grown men, rather than juveniles – and most of them had already had a taste of life at professional clubs. The standard of the league Melbourne were playing in in the late 1960s was exceptionally high, and it was a fertile breeding ground for clubs, particularly in the Second Division of the old two-tier Scottish Football League set-up, who would cherry-pick the best players.

Erich was still only eighteen, and at least a couple of years younger than the majority of the Melbourne squad. Whereas most of the Melbourne team were inner-city boys who had signed schoolboy-forms with top Scottish clubs like Hearts, Hibs, Rangers and Dundee, only to return to juvenile football after failing to make the grade for one reason or another, Erich had not yet popped up on the radar of any senior clubs. Perhaps that was because the Borders lay outside clubs' regular scouting boundaries, or possibly because Erich at that stage was simply too raw technically to be considered a standout contender for professional trials. A spectacular, trophy-laden season with Melbourne Thistle would change that perception and present Erich with the opportunity to embark on a long and successful professional career, eventually decorated with medals and an international cap.

The success of Melbourne Thistle was no accident. While the team undoubtedly contained many talented, strong-willed players, crucially they also had the guidance, leadership and coaching that made them a semi-professional outfit in all but name and a cut above their peers. In manager Johnny Mochan and trainer/ secretary Sandy Brown they had patient, forward-thinking coaches, who recognised the importance of making the team a close-knit unit on and off the pitch.

David Ross, who played in front of Erich on the left side of Melbourne's midfield, never made it as professional footballer, but became a major success in Scotland's finance sector. He worked for Ivory & Sime for twenty-two years and rose to the post of managing director, and now works for the internationally respected unit trust management firm Aberforth Partners. Ross treasures many fond memories of his Melbourne days and is still in touch to this day with some of his teammates from the Sixties. "It was an exceptional team," he says, his eyes scanning a team photo of the Melbourne team – a row of trophies in front of the proud young men who had won them. "We had a few guys who had already had ties with professional clubs and had come back to Under-21 football because it hadn't worked out for one reason or another. Allan Munro had been at Hearts, while there were quite a few others who had been involved with top teams. Allan was right-back, Charlie Murphy was centre-half and Gus Henderson was a central defender too. In midfield, we had me and Lenny Young alongside Tam Cropley, and up front we had lads like Billy Blues, Denis Nelson and Charlie Morrison."

Erich, while still a little quiet and reserved, had no problem fitting in to a team predominantly made up of Edinburgh lads. His cheery demeanour and willingness to learn and give his all at training and in matches made him a popular and valued team member. "Erich was very shy to begin with," recalls Ross. "We had a lot of strong characters in the team, and it could be hard for some of the quieter guys to get a word in edgeways. Erich was one of those lads who came along, trained and played his football and didn't say too much. But that's not to say he wasn't sociable or one of the lads – he definitely was – he was just a quiet, unassuming guy at that age. But when he got on the park it was a different story. He became a different character. He was understated, though – nothing showy, he just got on with the job in hand, and was a very important part of the team, totally reliable and never any bother. He had pace, he was strong and a very good tackler. I played on the left with him and as pace was not one of my strong points, it was a big help to have him bombing past me up the wing when he was getting forward."

There were quality players sprinkled throughout the team – and some well-known names too. There was Alan Buchanan, brother of one of the greatest ever boxers Scotland has ever produced, the former world lightweight champion Ken Buchanan. There was Tam Cropley, elder brother of Alex, the mercurial midfielder who starred for Hibs in the 1970s alongside Erich, then Arsenal and Aston Villa. And there was team captain Allan Munro, who, like Schaedler, would play a role in Hibernian's history, albeit Munro's contribution has remained largely unsung.

Munro, a financial expert of renown in Edinburgh, was called in by Hibs in 1990 when their very existence was threatened by a hostile takeover bid audaciously launched by Hearts chairman Wallace Mercer. The club had been laid bare to a predatory bid during the wayward chairmanship of David Duff – later jailed for two years for a building society swindle. The parent company "Edinburgh Hibernian" had made a string of ill-advised investments, including a chain of pubs in the south of England, and saddled by bad debt, it had effectively become a sitting duck. The majority shareholder, venture capitalist and future Conservative Party Treasurer David Rowland had little if any interest in the football team and, keen to emerge from the debacle with a financial return, he was ready to strike a deal with Mercer. Duff, for all his shortcomings, did at least profess to care about Hibs, and salvaged an iota of honour by refusing to sell his personal block of shares to Mercer. Duff's refusal to sell was pivotal in repelling Mercer, but his legacy is tainted. In the aftermath of the takeover bid, it emerged that during his chaotic reign the club's debt had rocketed from a manageable £882,000 in 1988 to a perilous figure of £4.5 million in the days before Mercer moved in.

Mercer's misguided vision had been to merge Hibs with Hearts to create an Edinburgh "super team", but he and Rowland had underestimated the fierce resistance his bid would meet from fans of both clubs. The Hands Off Hibs campaign, headed by Kenny McLean, was created to battle Mercer's proposal head-on, and rousing rallies held at Easter Road and the Usher Hall gave the fight the public platform it needed to be a success. But behind the scenes, the financial battle for hearts and minds was equally important.

Munro and his colleagues mobilised and fought tooth and nail to first fend off the bid and then stabilise the club, which was ultimately rescued from Mercer's clutches by the investment of Sir Tom Farmer. It had been a desperately close call for the club. The vanquished Mercer had come within a few shares of completing his takeover before he finally backed off. Always one for a dramatic soundbite, the bombastic Mercer claimed at a press conference he had been sent a bullet in the post and had decided his "vision" simply was not worth the hassle. Hibs had lived to fight another day, and while Kenny McLean and the fans could celebrate a hard-fought victory, Munro and his team of financial experts could also be immensely proud of their efforts.

As a teenager at Broughton High School, Munro – a quick, versatile defender who played for both the Edinburgh schools select and Scottish juvenile team – may have harboured boyhood dreams of playing for Hibs, but it was city rivals Hearts who signed him when he was a fifteen-year-old. Only a small percentage of S-form signings made the grade, and Munro was deemed surplus to requirements and released by Hearts. He did train with Hibs for a few months, but as his blossoming financial career began to offer an attractive, more feasible alternative to professional football he made the decision to stay amateur and became a mainstay for Melbourne Thistle in the highly competitive Under-21 ranks. During the 1968/69 season that witnessed Erich's arrival at Melbourne, Munro captained them to seven trophies out of the eight available to them, including the big prize on offer, the Scottish Cup, which was habitually won by teams from the west rather than upstarts from Edinburgh.

Munro immediately took to Erich, who had come through a trial match for Melbourne with flying colours, after a friend had recommended the club to the Peebles lad. "When Erich first came he was a raw laddie, but he was unbelievably quick," says Munro. "He was the quickest guy I ever played with. I used to regard myself as being quite fast, but Erich was something else. In the shuttles at training, he was the only guy who could beat me. He was a natural athlete."

It also quickly became apparent to Schaedler's new teammates that their quiet new recruit could look after himself in the tackle and was able to use his pace to assist his powers of recovery. As he was still far from the finished article as a footballer, this was something Erich had to do quite often. He had a lot to learn in terms of awareness and positioning, but you could be sure that on the occasions a right-winger did manage to get past him, the full-back would soon be in hot pursuit and usually successful in retrieving the situation. "When Erich hit you it was like being hit by a ton of bricks," recalls Munro. "The winger might beat him the first time, but by the time he had looked up and thought to himself, 'Where am I going to put this ball,' Erich would have got back and dispossessed him – he was that quick."

George Young, the Melbourne goalkeeper who at the end of the season would make the move into the pro ranks together with Schaedler at Stirling Albion, was another admirer of Erich's all-energy, uncompromising style. "Erich had one style of playing, and he would use it whether it was in a match or at training," says Young. "He would hit someone really hard in the tackle, then before they had time to know what had hit them, he'd be over offering his hand and helping them to their feet with a smile on his face. But he was a good player – there was far more to him than simply being fast and a good tackler."

The Melbourne boys had a good attitude to their football, and it helped that they got on well with each other socially too. "We were a side that all loved each other's company," says Munro. "After training we would sometimes sit and have a cup of tea and a blether. Most of the boys were still staying with their parents but because I was getting married I had my own house at Bonnington Grove, and some of the lads would come back to my house with fish suppers or to have chip butties. The other big attraction my flat held was that I had a telly – a bit of a rarity in those days. If *Scotsport* was on they would all come round and it could be two or three in the morning before I got rid of them! Other times it would be late on a Saturday night or Sunday morning and I'd hear a knock on the door – and there would be Erich or one of the other boys asking, 'Can I kip on your settee for the night?' We were all good mates, it helped bring us closer together.

"Erich just enjoyed being there, being part of a team. You might have thought it would be more difficult for him to settle into an Edinburgh team because he was from the Borders, but I wouldn't say he was isolated in any way. He was quickly adopted. The piss-taking in the dressing room had to be seen to be believed but he used to love coming along and getting involved in the banter. Like all of us, we just enjoyed being part of that club and a lot of that was down to Johnny Mochan – 'psychology-wise' Johnny was way ahead of his time. He made us feel like a professional outfit and how to take pride in what we were doing together. Even if the game was cancelled on a crisp, frosty day, he would say we were going to have a bit of training, down to Portobello – the beach or the swimming baths. We would all be walking along the promenade, Melbourne boys on tour, chests puffed out, proud as punch."

In the league that season, Melbourne, who played and trained at Hunter's Hall in Craigmillar or at Sandy's Field near Peffermill, were unbeatable, and despite a hectic fixtures schedule, they were able to replicate that form in the cup competitions too. The main focus was, of course, the Scottish Cup, and Melbourne were soon shaping as serious contenders.

"We were having a great run in the Scottish Cup and I had got injured," remembers Munro. "We had reached the quarter-finals and had been drawn to play alongside a team called Rancel, a hybrid club made up of Rangers and Celtic supporters. They were a really good side and well respected and had started off that season as favourites for the Scottish Cup.

"With me not playing, Johnny Mochan asked me to come through and watch Rancel with him, so we headed west to watch them and make a few mental notes on their strengths and weaknesses.

On the way back, he turned to me in the car and said, 'Well, what do you think?'

"'I think the only fear we've got is their pitch,' I told him. 'I think we are a better side than them and if we play to our ability we'll beat them, but the one problem might be the cinder pitch they play on. They are well used to it, and we aren't.'

"The following Sunday we were training at Peffermill, which in those days had a cinder pitch, and we started off with a bounce game. Mochan, who had been an ex-Junior player and a pretty hard player by all accounts, came up to me just before we kicked off and said to me, 'I'm going to do something here and I need you to keep your mouth shut. What I'm going to do, I'm going to do for a good reason.' Literally, the game had just started when Erich got the ball and went on a run, then BOOSH, Mochan put him up in the air with a scything challenge. Erich being Erich got right up and kept on running. The reason Mochan had chosen to put the boot in to one of his own players was to show us that you could fall on the cinder surface and it wasn't a problem, you had nothing to fear. Many of us would have been writhing about in agony, but Mochan had deliberately chosen Erich to make his point. He knew fine well that Erich could handle it and he wouldn't complain, and nor would he harbour any grudges."

It was an example of just how much thought Mochan would put into his preparations for a game. David Ross agrees: "Johnny Mochan was an excellent coach, who was SFA qualified, and had a really good grasp of the game. He deserves a huge amount of credit for the success we had. He made sure we had no prima donnas, and did not have any favourites. He treated us all the same and that worked well."

Melbourne, brimming with self-belief, conquered both the unfamiliar ash pitch and Rancel to book their place in the semi-finals – the spying mission by Mochan and Munro had certainly helped. "We then played Dumbarton at Boghead in the semi-finals and beat them 5–0," recalls Munro. "It was one of those days that if you'd shut your eyes and kicked it, it would have gone in – everything came off for us. We were in the final."

Whitehill Welfare from Rosewell were the opponents in the final, and after the match finished a draw, a replay in front of a large crowd at Olivebank in Musselburgh saw Melbourne triumph 2–1 thanks to goals from Ross and striker Billy Blues. Melbourne had added the Scottish Cup to their impressive trophy haul which included the league title and Secondary Juveniles' Insurance Cup, in which they came from 2–0 down to beat North Merchiston in the final – which was decided on corners gained rather than penalties. The Edinburgh *Evening News* noted: "Melbourne finished the stronger side, a tribute to their training and staying power over a crowded season."

"We won everything that season," says George Young. "Erich and I had to miss one of the Cup finals because we were training with Stirling Albion by that time and being fixed up with trial games with a view to signing for them."

Mochan's side were almost invincible, missing out on only one of the eight trophies they competed for. In the spring of 1969, Royston Boys' Club did what no other team had managed to do and beat Melbourne in their final fixture of the season to halt a glorious unbeaten run of almost fifty matches. It was a mere blip in an otherwise perfect season, and the silverware plundered made an impressive sight at the club's presentation dinner dance in the Inchview Ballroom. By that time, Erich and George Young had been snapped up by Stirling Albion.

Mochan had ties with Stirling and the success his juvenile side were enjoying had brought curious Albion manager Willie MacFarlane down to watch Melbourne. The former Hibs full-back, who had joined Stirling after a spell as manager of Hawick Royal Albert in the East of Scotland League, managed to see beyond a rare erratic performance from the young Schaedler to recognise a player of enormous untapped potential. "The first time Willie saw him, he was having a real off-day. Nothing would go right for him," a 1969 article in *The Weekly News* reported. "But Willie, of course, is a bit of a specialist in full-back play, having been one himself at Easter Road in the not-too-distant past. So it was obvious to him that the boy had what it takes. After forty-five minutes he had made up his mind to sign him for Stirling Albion."

Gordon McDougall, who would become a good friend of Schaedler when he later moved to Hibs, remembers MacFarlane describing to him the moment he knew he wanted to sign Erich for Stirling: "Willie told me: 'I was watching this juvenile game and I saw the winger beat his man. I looked away for a second and by the time I looked back the full-back had recovered, won the ball and played it to a teammate. I was wondering, "How the hell did he get back from there? He's got a bit about him, this boy."'"

Schaedler wasn't the only player to catch the eye of MacFarlane, and goalkeeper George Young was also invited through to train with Stirling – no easy task for boys who were already training at least twice a week with Melbourne, playing on a Saturday and holding down full-time jobs: "We would have two nights training with Johnny Mochan at Melbourne and two at Stirling, so we were practically training full-time – four nights a week – and also had our day jobs to do," says Young, who went on to play for Rangers after Stirling. "I was an apprentice lift engineer at the time. It wasn't just a quick scoot along the M9 either – there was no motorway then and we had to wind our way through the back roads and places like Winchburgh and Linlithgow before we got there. It was hard going, but when you want to make it as a footballer you're willing to do whatever it takes."

Young believes any one of the Melbourne squad could have been picked up by professional clubs and doesn't know why he and Erich alone were targeted by Stirling. "There were no great individuals that stood head and shoulders above the rest at Melbourne – we just had good players throughout the team, who were prepared to work hard at training and in games, and more importantly, were winners."

While George and Erich were destined for long careers in the professional game, amassing more than 800 senior appearances between them, others went on to enjoy great success in their chosen careers, including Munro, who served in a string of high-profile boardrooms, including the Scottish Rugby Union. He also became a regular attendee at Easter Road and looked on with pride as he saw his former Melbourne teammate Schaedler mature into one of the finest left-backs ever to wear a Hibs shirt.

"Once he settled down and had a bit of tactical awareness about him, he became a massively improved player," says Munro. "It wasn't until he had had a couple of years at Hibs that you really saw him start to develop. He had that great ability to get forward that Willie MacFarlane then Eddie Turnbull had instilled in him. He was also able to take his game on to another level because he was playing with such good players. Our paths crossed from time to time over the years. I went on to play a year with Hawick in the East of Scotland League and had a year or two with Bonnyrigg Rose in the Junior league, but my job was starting to take off so I stopped playing. I used to watch Turnbull's Tornadoes regularly and you could see he had developed tremendously well, playing alongside great players like John Brownlie and John Blackley. Generally it was Brownlie on the other flank that was known for bombing forward, but over the course of his development Erich started to develop the same habit of getting forward with some confidence. His distribution was never the best, he didn't have the eye for a pass the way some players did, but his tackling and his powers of recovery plus his speed were his big assets and he used them very well."

There was no doubting the Melbourne left-back was a work in progress, but his move to Stirling – a snip at just £25 – and his association with MacFarlane had a big bearing on his football destiny.

# 4

# THIS IS ANNFIELD

Like most clubs in Scottish football's old Second Division, Stirling Albion were a team operating on a shoestring budget. The part-timers of Annfield relied heavily on the well-trained eyes of dedicated scouts to replenish their playing pool and stay competitive against better-resourced rivals. Edinburgh was an area rich in up-and-coming talent, and while Hearts and Hibs maintained a relatively tight grip on recruitment from the juvenile sides within the city, there were still a few left-over gems to be mined from the boys' clubs and local leagues.

George Rankine, who played for Airdrie and St Johnstone, was a scout for Stirling at that time and he was responsible for bringing through a few promising lads from the east. It was reputedly Rankine who steered Willie MacFarlane's attention towards Erich, and the Stirling manager liked what he saw. "Erich was invited through to train with Stirling and he and the goalkeeper George Young – who were teammates at Melbourne Thistle – both trained with us and played a few trial matches for us in 1968 before they were signed early the following year," recalls Stirling Albion's club historian Jim Thomson.

While Rankine was one of the men charged with identifying signing targets, MacFarlane – and the board of directors – had the final say. In the case of Schaedler and Young, there was little need to deliberate. Clearly, both teenagers had all the attributes to be thrown straight into the first team to see if they would sink or swim. They played initially as trialists, before they were registered with Stirling as part-time players. Closer to home, Rab Duffin was recruited from Stirling Boys Club, and he too was considered ready to mix it with the hardened professionals. Stirling had made a conscious decision to freshen up an ageing squad, and injecting some youth was considered the best strategy.

Duffin was given his maiden first-team outing as a trialist in a 1–1 draw against East Stirling, one week before Schaedler and Young made their Stirling Albion debuts together in a match against Clydebank at Kilbowie on 19 April 1969.

It was not a case of Stirling simply opting to give youngsters a run-out in meaningless fixtures at the end of a mid-table season – their promotion hopes at that stage were very much alive. Motherwell topped the table and Stirling were still involved in a tussle with Ayr United and East Fife for second spot. So the pressure was firmly on Stirling at Kilbowie that spring day that the Melbourne Thistle pair made their debuts, and although Albion creditably rallied from two goals down to claim a draw, a victory for Ayr meant that their promotion hopes were hanging by a thread. The *Stirling Observer* match report of the 2–2 draw viewed the result as a disappointment but noted that "there were a few redeeming features – the promise of teenagers, goalkeeper George Young, and left-back Eric Schaedler, both formerly of Edinburgh juvenile team Melbourne Thistle. Young brought off several smart saves and Schaedler's headwork was good and he remained calm under pressure." It was the first mention of the young Schaedler in the pages of Stirling's local newspaper, and an "h" had been dropped from his Christian name. Throughout his time at Annfield he would always be referred to as "Eric" rather than Erich. The teenager was well used to people having difficulty correctly spelling either of his names and press cuttings show that it was a recurring theme throughout his career.

The following week Schaedler retained his place in the Albion team, again acquitting himself well in a match which saw Motherwell demonstrate why they were deserving champions that season. There was no place for Young that day, but it had nothing to do with his performance the previous week. He had to make way for goalkeeper Willie Murray, who was emigrating to Australia, to enjoy a swansong. Murray captained Albion that day as a gesture of his long service to the club, but as one old pro bade farewell to the game, at the other end of the spectrum the teenage left-back in the team was desperate to again make a good impression. Erich managed to do just that – the *Observer* noted "the youthful Schaedler had quite a useful performance" – despite the team going down 3–0 to superior opponents on their way up to the First Division.

Schaedler and Young had both revelled in the unexpected taste of Scottish League action they had been given at the end of the 1968/69 season, having just expected to attend training and play the occasional bounce match before perhaps signing for the club in time for the 1969/70 season, then having to fight for a place. They enjoyed the training and being part of a well-run football club.

"Yes, they were exciting times for us," says Young. "When we trained with Stirling, there was quite a group of us that had to travel through from Edinburgh. We'd meet in a cafe at Haymarket, then split up into two or three cars. Erich and I were only nineteen when we signed for Stirling, who had not long been relegated from the old First Division. We'd been taught some good habits at Melbourne, but the Second Division was a good place for us to continue our football education. It was a bit of a test for us to be thrown straight into it from juvenile football, but we both lapped it up."

Schaedler and Young had both sufficiently impressed as trialists and they signed on the dotted line as fully fledged Stirling Albion players in time for the beginning of the 1969/70 season. Both continued to catch the eye. The traditional curtain-raiser was the old League Cup, split into sections, and Stirling were grouped with local rivals Falkirk, as well as Forfar and Arbroath. In their opening fixture, Albion won 3–2 at Gayfield against Arbroath thanks to a last-minute winner from Joe Hughes, and the *Observer* match reporter noted: "Schaedler's speed in recovery and fast-tackling at left-back looks promising."

When Stirling won the reverse fixture against Arbroath 4–1 a fortnight later, the writer showered praise on Newtongrange newcomer Bobby Grant and enthused, "Albion's other star was left-back Schaedler. This youngster, if he maintains this form, seems destined to go far in the game." These were prophetic words, written by a reporter who knew a good player when he saw one.

A disappointing home defeat to Forfar snuffed out Stirling's hopes of progressing from their League Cup group, but Willie MacFarlane was keen to give Schaedler plenty of game time, and he gave him a run-out in the reserves in a 5–2 defeat against Celtic, with stars like Danny McGrain and Bobby Murdoch giving Erich experience of testing himself against top-class players.

Erich was still raw and prone to the occasional misjudgment, but if he was ever taken aside by the manager, a coach, or even a senior teammate he had a propensity to listen and absorb the advice he was being given. Terry Christie was one of the older members in the team, having been brought to Stirling by MacFarlane from Hawick Royal Albert. He already knew of Erich before he signed and he recalls that Schaedler may have had a lot to learn – but learn it he did. "There's no doubt Erich owed a lot to Willie MacFarlane for giving him his break as a footballer, as it was him who took him to Stirling Albion, along with George Young from Melbourne Thistle," says Christie, who went on to become an excellent manager himself with lower-division sides like Meadowbank Thistle, Alloa and Stenhousemuir.

Even in his early twenties, Christie was a keen student of the game and he would watch a lot of football as well as playing. Melbourne Thistle were the kind of the team that attracted along plenty of neutrals and Christie had been impressed any time he watched them, although he admits at that time Schaedler was not one of their stand-out performers. "They were an exceptionally good team, and I remember that they'd actually won the Scottish Cup the same year Erich signed for Stirling," adds Christie. "They had a super team, which included guys like Alex Cropley's brother Tom in midfield, and Davie Ross, and they were run exceptionally well by John Mochen and Sandy Brown.

"So I'd watched a bit of Melbourne Thistle by the time Erich and George Young joined me at Stirling and I have to be honest and say that Erich was not a player you would have pounced on at that time. He had great physical fitness, but he wasn't naturally skilful and had a long way to go to develop his game. But credit to Willie MacFarlane, who had tremendous knowledge of football and a good gut instinct. He had obviously spotted the massive potential that Erich had – that huge physicality that he offered – even as a teenager. He was very powerful and very quick but very raw as a footballer.

"He wasn't at Stirling for long, but you could see him improving with each game. He was as raw as you can get, but if he made a mistake he had the pace to get back and do something about it. I saw him up close because he played left-back and I played left midfield – and some of the passes I got were horrific! He made a few errors, but he usually made up for them with his other attributes. The underlying qualities he had were his great strength and a determined will to succeed as a footballer.

"Off the field Erich was a nice, nice lad – always keen to please. I used to see him socially as well and I always got on really well with him. You wouldn't want to be in a car with him when he was eighteen or nineteen though, as I had the misfortune to be. I remember him giving me a lift through to Stirling for a game, and it was terrifying – a real white-knuckle ride. He was as fearless and fast behind the wheel as he was on the pitch, a maniac. After that hair-raising experience there was absolutely no way I was getting back in the car with him driving, so I fixed up a lift with someone else on the sly to get me back home in one piece and gave Erich some lame excuse why I wouldn't be returning with him."

In the Second Division meanwhile, Stirling had developed an irritating habit of turning victories into draws, and they had to settle for a share of the points in five of their first six league fixtures. It was nevertheless good experience for the Albion new boys. Young and Schaedler were fast establishing themselves in a youthful and exciting team. They were also being afforded plenty of patience from supporters as they found their feet in this grade.

The local newspaper, which usually would not hold back when results were poor, preached the need for the young team to be given adequate time to gel. "It has to be recognised that Albion have a good number of young players in their team and must be given time to settle and develop," the *Observer* commented after a 1–1 draw at Montrose. "The talent is obviously there. Two first eleven regulars in that category are goalkeeper Young and left-back Schaedler, both of whom are fast establishing themselves."

MacFarlane's effervescent character had rubbed off on the club and with so many young players being given their chance to shine, these were exciting times for Stirling Albion. Coach Tom McLaren was delighted to see Schaedler and Young establish themselves in the team and he says their youthful enthusiasm was uplifting. "Erich was a great guy and he got on well with everyone," says McLaren, who used to give him a lift through to training in 1969. "He was only three or four months at Stirling as a part-time player, but he made a big impression in that time. I would pick him up at Broughton Road and take him through to training. The Melbourne Thistle team had a close link with Stirling Albion at the time, an arrangement that worked well for both clubs. Willie MacFarlane was pally with Johnny Mochan and the secretary Sandy Brown, and he would invite Melbourne players through to train with us and ask one or two of them to play in friendlies. They had an excellent team that year and I remember them winning seven cups, including the Under-21s Scottish Cup. Half that team could have signed for Stirling – they were all good enough. They had ability and they had the attitude to match, they were all good trainers.

"The main thing I remember about Erich was that he was a 100 per cent player – he would run into a brick wall if you asked him. He never gave less than 100 per cent, he was so enthusiastic. He had pace and plenty of stamina and as a guy he was tremendous.

"Willie's links with the East of Scotland League were another big factor in us building a team at Stirling. He had been manager at Hawick Royal Albert and had a lot of good contacts. I remember him signing Jimmy Logan, who later moved to Partick Thistle; George Brough; Terry Christie; Walter Lourie; Malcolm Bogie; and Billy Armstrong – all of them arrived from Hawick and all of them fitted in well."

Like Schaedler and Young, manager Willie MacFarlane's reputation was growing by the week, and the former Hibs full-back – who was retained by Stirling on a part-time basis, combining evening training sessions with his day job as a plant transport manager – was about to be offered his dream job, as manager at Easter Road.

The affable MacFarlane, whose father had played at a senior level for St Bernard's and Leith Athletic, had been a miner at Newcraighall before joining Hibs, and he played alongside members of the Famous Five, enjoying the club's glorious run to the semi-final of the European Cup in the 1955/56 season. A move later in his career to Morton had whet his appetite for coaching and he was shown the ropes by the Greenock club's extrovert manager Hal Stewart. It took an extrovert to know one, and MacFarlane himself was a funny, flamboyant, outgoing character, never slow to deliver a one-liner or a strong opinion.

Before finally getting his break as a professional manager at Stirling, MacFarlane had patiently worked his way through the coaching ranks, first at Gala Fairydean and Hawick Royal Albert in the East of Scotland League. In the short time he had been at Stirling he had made a good name for himself, and his promise had not gone unnoticed in the Easter Road boardroom. When the Hibs job was offered to him in September 1969, following the departure of

Bob Shankly from the Easter Road hot seat, he did not hesitate for a second to grasp the golden opportunity to return to his old club.

Within days of him taking the Hibs job in September 1969, the whispers began that MacFarlane planned to return to Annfield for the signature of his prodigy Schaedler. These stories quickly found their way into the pages of the national newspapers, and soon these rumours took on substance. MacFarlane had certainly inherited a promising Hibs team, but he knew how he could make it better, and a quick appraisal of the squad he had inherited left him convinced that Schaedler would be a shrewd acquisition – if not for immediate first-team action, then definitely for the future. As MacFarlane spectacularly began his reign as Hibs manager with a 2–0 win over Hearts at Tynecastle, a result which took his new charges to the top of the table, the *Stirling Observer* fretted that Albion's erstwhile boss could soon prise their promising young full-back Schaedler away from Annfield. "Manager MacFarlane hasn't been away much more than a week and already there has been some comment in the national sporting press that he might be interested in taking with him to Easter Road one of the players he brought to Annfield," commented the *Stirling Observer.* "Eric [sic] Schaedler, the Albion's lively young full-back, is the player being listed as a possible for Easter Road. He is one of the Albion staff with great potential, who has given the Annfield faithful hope for the future, and we wouldn't like to see him move just yet."

Albion fans were wary of the club selling any more of their up-and-coming players. They had endured a bad experience when they let Henry Hall join St Johnstone for a negligible fee. He would go on to become a Scotland international and a prolific goalscorer, and with the harsh lesson of his sale fresh in mind, the *Observer* – adopting a dose of realism to the prospect of losing Schaedler – added, "If the Albion's directors, however, do decide to sell – let's hope that it won't be a case of bargain basement. Remember a player named Hall!"

With MacFarlane gone, the Stirling Albion board dithered

somewhat in their search for a replacement. Being minus a manager seemed to have no effect whatsoever on the vibrant young Albion squad and they went on a run of four consecutive victories, thanks in no small measure to the goalscoring form of centre forward Joe Hughes. After a 5–1 win at home to Stranraer, fans' favourite Erich was singled out for praise again, with the *Observer* commenting, "Schaedler was outstanding again."

A hard-fought 1–1 draw at Hamilton in mid-October was attributed to the back four and goalkeeper Young. "That Albion did get a draw was due to the sterling work by their defence," raved the *Observer*'s correspondent. "Young, Schaedler, Carrigan and Logan baulked the home forwards time and time again." That draw at Douglas Park coincided with the arrival of a new manager, some three weeks after the departure of MacFarlane. Albion may have taken their time to find the right man, but in Frank Joyner, chairman Alex Hamilton and his board had appointed a fascinating character.

Either side of distinguished wartime service in which he rose to the rank of Army captain and fought in Burma and behind German lines in France, prolific goalscorer Joyner had played for fourteen clubs in Britain, including Raith Rovers, Sheffield United, Dundee and Stirling Albion during the early days of the club's existence. If that CV wasn't remarkable enough, Joyner was making his return to management straight from the press box, having worked as a sports writer covering matches – including some of Stirling Albion's fixtures – so he was no stranger to Annfield and seemed to have a grasp of the squad he had inherited when he said on his arrival: "I think the present Albion team has great potential."

Joyner's understanding of the media took no time at all to manifest itself. In his first game in charge in late October, a 3–3 draw at home to Berwick Rangers in which a point was salvaged thanks to a late equaliser from Billy Armstrong, Joyner introduced a "news from the dressing room" feature prior to kick-off over Annfield's public address system. It was a novel idea, but you can only imagine how it would have gone down with the cynical

Terracing Tams of 1969! A week later Erich got himself on the scoresheet – but not for Stirling. In a game at Glebe Park, Brechin, Schaedler sent the ball flying past Young. Even the *Observer,* which hadn't printed a word of criticism of the young full-back, couldn't disguise this *faux pas*. "There was a touch of panic in the Albion after Erich Schaedler had inadvertently sent an own goal flashing past his keeper, George Young. It wasn't Erich Schaedler's lucky day when, harassed by a couple of Brechin players, he fairly whipped the ball past George Young when he tried to send it wide of the goal as a safety measure." The OG was not to prove costly, though, and Stirling rallied from this setback to win 3–1.

The talk of the town was now a question of *when* and not *if* Schaedler would leave the club and join MacFarlane at Easter Road. According to well-informed sources, Hibs had tabled a "four-figure bid" for Erich, which had been rebuffed by the Stirling board. The door had not been closed on Hibs, however, and it seemed that their initial bid was just an opening salvo for a player who had his price.

Erich could easily have been unsettled by the talk of moving to join such a high-profile club, but he wasn't showing any sign of nerves. He lined up as usual at left-back at home to Forfar in early November and was one of the stars of the show as Joyner's side thrashed their visitors 6–0. The icing on the cake for Erich was a goal of his own – at the right end this time. With Albion already five up and with two minutes on the clock, Erich wrapped up the scoring following a tenacious run and shot. The Albion fans rose as one to acclaim Schaedler, especially as all the talk beforehand was that this would be his final game in the red shirt of Stirling. The word was that the board had met with their counterparts at Easter Road and agreed a deal in principle to take the youngster to the capital. The rumour mill was spot-on. Just hours after scoring for Albion, Erich was putting pen to paper on a life-changing deal with Hibernian.

The *Stirling Observer* ran a heart-warming opinion piece about Schaedler's departure, expressing resignation at the loss of one of the club's most popular players, but describing Erich in glowing terms and wishing him well for the future. The report, in its edition of 11 November, said, "When a promising young Second Division footballer wants to become a full-time professional with a First Division team there is nothing much the lower league can do about it. That's how it's been with Erich Schaedler, Albion's nineteen-year-old left-back, signed by Hibs on Saturday night after the Forfar game at Annfield.

"The representatives of the two clubs met at Linlithgow on Saturday night to complete the formalities after an agreement had been reached earlier in the week. And so Erich, who was brought to Annfield by manager Willie MacFarlane, goes to Hibs to serve with him as one of the Easter Road player pool.

"The fee has not been discussed, but it is reckoned to be considerably more than the £5,000 originally offered by the Edinburgh club. It might be, of course, that the Albion directors, remembering Henry Hall, have had included an 'extras' clause if Erich becomes a first-team regular within a certain period.

"Sorry as Stirling folk are to see Erich going, for the Albion defence is settling into a compact unit, all wish him well in his future playing career. His Sammy Cox-like speed in recovery is an outstanding asset, and in these days of the fast overlap strategy in attacking full-backs, he has much to offer in this direction too."

His teammates were sorry to lose Erich too. As Rab Duffin says now: "It was a no-brainer for Erich – he had to jump at an offer like that, to get full-time football and full-time wages. Our wages at Stirling were £7 basic, plus £3 appearance money and an extra £5 for a win. He must have been on a lot more than that at Hibs, even when he went there as a teenager. He was gone from Stirling, but never forgotten. Erich was a very fit boy. His fitness was supreme, he always gave 100 per cent at training and in games, and he was also a very talented player – a great left foot and a strong tackler. Erich was the best left-back the club ever had by a mile and one of the best players we have ever seen at Stirling."

Club historian Jim Thomson concurs: "When Erich left it was a real shame, but I think the board and the supporters knew that when you've got a young player as good as that he is going to be hard to keep hold of. It was obvious to everyone that the guy had talent; he was a fantastic player. We had hoped to keep him a bit longer, though. I remember at the time, he was about to get married, and there were plans for him and his new wife to move into one of the houses alongside Annfield. It was a blow to lose him, but that was the norm in those days. Stirling had books to balance and if a club came along and made a decent offer then it was practically impossible to refuse."

MacFarlane was delighted that he had managed to land Erich for a second time in the space of a year, and he hoped they would have a fruitful future together at Hibs. The manager also intended to take Schaedler's former Melbourne mate George Young with him, but the goalkeeper was in no rush for a move to the top flight, choosing instead to stick with first-team football, which was guaranteed as long as he continued his impressive form.

Young says, "When Willie MacFarlane got the job at Easter Road he quickly took Erich with him. I nearly went too, and Hibs did make an approach to sign me, but it never happened. I didn't know all the facts, but the word was that Hibs were planning to build a gym at Easter Road and because they had already splashed out a few quid on Erich they didn't have the money Stirling were looking for. It wasn't something I ever regretted – I knew I had a better chance of playing week-in, week-out at Stirling, especially when I was younger, and there was always a chance I could go to Hibs then have to wait a long time before I even got my chance. I wasn't scared of the competition, but it just seemed more sensible to keep my feet on the ground a bit and stay at Stirling.

"It was a shame that I couldn't join up with Willie again, but there was a new manager at Stirling and I was happy enough to stick around and play under him. Willie MacFarlane was certainly a charismatic manager and he was quite the motivator. It was easy to respond to him, and he was good at keeping team spirit high. It had probably helped that he'd been a manager at Hawick Royal Albert in the East of Scotland League, it kept him grounded, and he brought in a few guys from there that were tried and trusted. Erich and him were a good match, he certainly brought out the best in him.

"Erich was a good lad and a good teammate of mine, both at Melbourne and Stirling. He was a winner through and through, he had one style of play and it was full-blooded. He had a good career and I was really pleased to see him do so well at Hibs. He was a fun-loving guy and very focused on his football career. He was also dedicated to training and looked after himself. It was a pleasure to play behind him." Young's decision to stay with Stirling was wholly vindicated. He was the regular Albion No.1 for a decade, making 438 appearances for the club before he left to join Rangers in 1979, and is regarded as Stirling's greatest ever goalkeeper.

Erich's decision to leave Stirling was also vindicated. His transfer to Hibs was to signal the start of something special for the young, enthusiastic left-back.

# 5

# MENTOR MACFARLANE

At the age of nineteen, Erich Schaedler's main ambition in life was simple: to make himself a better footballer. Getting the chance to turn full-time at a club as big as Hibs after just a few months playing part-time at Stirling Albion represented a meteoric rise for the teenager. And the added bonus for Schaedler was that he would get to work once more with his mentor, Willie MacFarlane, who had taken him to Stirling and who had already been an important influence on guiding the precocious youngster.

MacFarlane, or "Packy" as he was known to his friends, was one of football's larger-than-life characters. Quick-witted and brimming with anecdotes, he was the type of manager players had no trouble warming to. It helped that he knew a thing or two about football too. Self-confidence wasn't an issue for MacFarlane either, and when he went back to Hibs as manager he would have done so with a spring in his step. He had left behind a big impression on the players he had worked with at Stirling.

As well as Erich Schaedler, there was another member of MacFarlane's Stirling Albion team who was a star in the making – but not in football. At around the same time the Melbourne hopefuls Schaedler and George Young were making their trips through from Edinburgh to train with the club in early 1969, Stirling signed George McNeill – one man Erich could not beat in a sprint. McNeill, who hailed from Tranent, was a multi-talented sportsman and he was lightning quick. He was also intelligent and articulate, and combined his early football career with training to become a quantity surveyor. McNeill started off as a right-winger with Tranent Juniors and was then picked up by Hibs. Despite a string of eye-catching displays in Hibs reserves, he only managed one first-team game. A brief spell at Morton followed, and then MacFarlane, always a fan of pacey players in his teams, snapped him up for Stirling Albion at the tail end of the 1968/69 season.

McNeill hit the ground running, scoring in a 3–1 win against his former club Morton, but football was just a hobby for him. He had his heart set on a career in athletics – something that was not going to go down well with MacFarlane. "Willie was a real character," laughs McNeill. "I remember the way he couldn't help but get involved at training. Because we were only a part-time team, when we trained time was precious. Willie was one of these guys who hated the fact he was retired from playing. He particularly enjoyed crossing balls, so the first half-hour of training could sometimes end up devoted to him pinging crosses in and standing back admiring them. Meantime, we'd be standing around wondering when the proper training was going to start. It could become the Willie MacFarlane show. He still thought of himself as a player, I think, and he just wanted to get as involved as possible.

"Although I had signed for Stirling, my athletics career was starting to take shape and I had already decided that I was ready to call it a day with football and concentrate all my time on sprinting.

"The way it was in those days, it was usually the last game of the season before you would discover who was going to be retained and who was going to be freed. I remember Willie marching up to one player after the final game, shaking his hand and cheerily saying to him, 'Goodbye!'

"He told me near the end of the season that I was a lucky bastard because he'd just paid £2,000 for me from Morton, so he had no option but to keep me to get his money's worth. But I was already planning to pack it in. I was studying to be a surveyor and had also started training for the Powderhall Sprint. I had to keep my plans to run at Powderhall top secret, because you weren't able to say anything that might let the cat out the bag and influence the bookies' odds.

"I wanted to be as up front as I could with Willie and told him that I didn't want to come back for the 1969/70 season, but he told me to think it over, over the summer. With pre-season approaching, I arranged to meet him in the Quaich, a place in Shandwick Place at the West End of Edinburgh. He said he would buy me a steak dinner and we could talk about it. He spent the whole dinner desperately trying to persuade me to stay at Stirling, but I stuck to my guns. Eventually he saw he was banging his head against a brick wall and snapped. He wasn't happy and said, 'I'm sick of footballers with too much brains – from now on I'm signing tatty-howkers and miners.' I saw him again later in life and we made our peace. He saw the funny side. I had a lot of time for Willie."

McNeill had got his wish and, free of his Stirling contract, he set about preparing for the New Year Sprint – training under the name of "Bob Gray" before his official entry was announced. He had a close escape to his identity becoming public knowledge in the build-up. "I remember one of the lads coming down with a copy of the *Evening News*. They had carried a team picture of Stirling Albion from the season before and he said loudly, 'I didnae ken you were a fitba player!' My coach Jim Bradley managed to convince him it wasn't me, and I got on with training."

McNeill, running off a generous handicap mark of 5.5 yards, streaked home in a time of 11.61 seconds over 120 yards in the 100th running of the New Year Sprint in 1970. His athletics career would run into major red-tape complications, however. Because he had signed professional forms as a footballer, he was banned from running as an amateur, ruling him out of any Olympic or Commonwealth Games, and he could only run on the professional circuit. McNeill's reputation soared as he continued to clock a number of world-class times. He was soon being hailed as the "unofficial fastest man in the world" and in 1972 he won the world professional sprint crown, defeating legendary Olympic gold medallist Tommie Smith over a four-race series. McNeill continued running into the 1980s in the highest-ranking events open to him, and in 1981 he won the biggest professional race in the world, the "Stawell Gift" in Australia. And did Erich maybe get the better of him once or twice at training? "No chance," says McNeill, ever the competitor.

McNeill was in high demand among football clubs for sprint training, and he worked with Erich four or five years after they had played briefly at Stirling together. "I was there around the time John Brownlie broke his leg, to help with his recuperation," says McNeill. "I went down to Easter Road to work the players, employing the speedball method I used. When it came to fitness work, Erich was a maniac – it was almost an obsession for him. If I asked the guys to do five hundred on the speedball, he wanted to do a thousand, if I asked them to do one hundred sit-ups, he wanted to do two hundred. He was so fitness conscious.

"He was a very bright character, very sparky, so it came as a big surprise when I heard of his death. He was a really enthusiastic character and a good guy to have around the place, from my point of view, because he didn't lack any motivation whatsoever – and his determination would help spur other, less committed guys on.

"I was one of the first fitness coaches around and asking players to come back for a couple of hours' extra work in the afternoon could go down like a lead balloon with some of them in those days. It could be a shock to the system for them, but Erich was such a fitness fanatic that it was a never a problem. The only problem with Erich was trying to stop him doing more."

MacFarlane may have claimed that he planned to only sign "tatty-howkers and miners", but it was a throw-away remark. He was a shrewd judge of a player and made many good signings, both at Stirling and at Hibs. He also had an eye for spotting a young player who could be nurtured. He kept an open mind, and in

Erich's case he obviously felt there were the makings of an exceptional player there.

Terry Christie believes the influence of MacFarlane – and later Eddie Turnbull – was an instrumental factor in turning Erich Schaedler into a potential internationalist. "I was a Hibs fan and after Willie signed him you could see him coming on leaps and bounds. He was a lad who owed a lot to Willie Macfarlane," says Christie. "Willie MacFarlane liked to have athletes in his team and Erich was the ultimate athlete. If it wasn't for Willie spotting something in him then he may not have got his chance.

"Erich is a great example of a player who may not be the most naturally gifted with skill, but through sheer guts, will and hard work can go a long way. He also had the benefit of working under some wonderful coaches during his formative years too, and was part of a great Hibs team. Where Erich was blessed was that he was a wonderful athlete and he maximised that because he had a winning attitude. He was brave and he was strong. He made himself a footballer.

"Eddie Turnbull also recognised his strengths and assets – Erich was the type of intelligent footballer who responded well to coaching. And with Alex Cropley playing in front of you, it helped. When Eddie Turnbull was manager after Willie MacFarlane had been and gone, I had ambitions of my own to move into coaching or management, and I would go along to Hibs training to watch, even if it meant hiding behind the bushes. There were no fancy academies then, and they trained at the Jack Kane Centre in Niddrie. Erich would spot me having a deek at them from the bushes and come over and say hello and we'd have a chat and a catch-up."

Mention of MacFarlane also raises a chuckle from Rab Duffin, who played alongside McNeill, Christie and Erich in his Stirling team. "Packy MacFarlane was a hell of a character," says Duffin. "When he became manager he was able to get a lot of Edinburgh boys to the club. There was a good healthy mixture of players from Stirling, Edinburgh and Glasgow. I remember on the bus to a game taking about thirty or forty quid off Willie at cards – he never said a word to me, but I could see he was raging. I never played again for three or four weeks after that!

"When Willie went from Stirling to Hibs, he must have thought he'd hit the jackpot – it was the perfect job for him. He never wasted any time coming back and getting Erich. He could not take Erich to Easter Road quickly enough.

"After we'd played together I kept an eye on his career and it was good to see him go on and do so well with Hibs, although I never doubted for a second that he would make it."

Schaedler was Willie MacFarlane's first signing as Hibs manager and his arrival at Easter Road in November 1969 was big news. As the *Stirling Observer* had speculated in the week the deal was done, the fee was indeed well over £5,000. The figure £7,000 widely quoted seems to have been an accurate reflection of the fee paid by Hibs. A decent return for Stirling on the £25 they had paid Melbourne Thistle!

As his name moved seamlessly from the local newspaper in Stirling to the national dailies, his mother Leah proudly started compiling a scrapbook chronicling her son's rise to fame. Erich also had an admission to get off his chest before he wore the green-and-white of Hibs . . . he was a Rangers fan! Leah Schaedler's scrapbook shows that the *Daily Record*'s Alister Nicol broke the big 'Closet Rangers Fan' scoop, telling readers: "Hibs' latest recruit Erich Schaedler was a Rangers fan – until Willie MacFarlane signed him on Saturday night. And yesterday, nineteen-year-old Schaedler joined his new teammates in training at Easter Road in the morning before returning to his job as a TV mechanic in the afternoon. Later, Erich told me: 'I'd always been a Rangers fan, but now it's Hibs all the way for me. It's great to be joining a club who are right up there at the top.'"

Erich also alluded to his former Ibrox allegiance in an interview with the *Scottish Daily Express*. The Easter Road new boy, who was in the midst of tying up the loose ends that would allow him to quit his day job and become a full-time professional with Hibs, said, "For the rest of this week I'll be training with Hibs in the morning and working in the afternoons. But I'll be full time as from next week. I've always wanted to be a full-time professional and could not, I'm sure, have joined a better club. Not even Rangers."

Another one of the early cuttings pasted in the pages of Leah Schaedler's well-tended old scrapbook is a report by the legendary ex-Hearts striker-turned-journalist Jimmy Wardhaugh of Terrible Trio fame, complete with a picture of a beaming Erich standing precariously on a roof adjusting the TV aerial of his mother-in-law's home in Rosewell. Wardhaugh wrote: "Erich Schaedler, Hibs' new signing, bid farewell to Second Division football on Saturday when he scored Stirling Albion's sixth against Forfar at Annfield. It came just thirty seconds from full-time and the nineteen-year-old full-back didn't touch the ball again before the whistle. If Schaedler turns out to be half as good as manager MacFarlane predicts then he may in the future have to decide between playing for Scotland or West Germany. For his father was a German prisoner of war who remained in this country and settled in Peebles after marrying a local girl. At the moment, however, Erich, who at one time worked in the Border mills, is concentrating on making the grade in the First Division. He will be a full-timer with Hibs and will have a talk with the boss of his engineering firm today to see if he can be released immediately to join his new colleagues at Easter Road.

"Schaedler is manager MacFarlane's first buy at Easter Road – but it is the second time in three months he has fixed up the teenager. Said the Hibs boss last night: 'I know what this young boy can do and he has a very bright future.' Schaedler, who is fast in recovery, is also a long-throw specialist, will add extra depth to Hibs' penetration as an overlapping full-back. Added the Easter Road manager: 'I have been looking for backs with striking power. I think I have the right man and given time to get used to First Division football, he will be an asset to the side.'"

Erich himself was quick to pay tribute to MacFarlane for working on his technical ability, along with his manager at Melbourne, Johnny Mochan – who would help out at Stirling with coaching sessions. "I didn't realise I had so much to learn until I joined Stirling," Erich said the week he joined Hibs. "At that time, my idea of a full-back was a guy who got the ball then belted it as far up-field as he could. Mr MacFarlane soon put me right on that score. He and coach Johnny Mochan took me aside. Between them, they taught me the techniques of modern full-back play.

"Apart from polishing up the defensive aspect of my game, they concentrated on teaching me how to overlap and knowing the right time to do it. It was hard work, but it certainly paid off for me."

Those comments demonstrate Schaedler's willingness to learn, but according to Pat Stanton – one of the biggest names at Hibs when Erich arrived – the defender still had a long way to go before he could be considered the finished article. "I first heard about Erich Schaedler when Willie MacFarlane was the manager at Hibs," says Stanton. "Willie had come to the Hibs from Stirling Albion and spent weeks telling us, 'Wait till you see this full-back I'm bringing.' Willie knew the game inside out, but he was prone to exaggeration and sometimes the more he spoke on a subject the more outrageous he got. By the time Erich was ready to arrive from Stirling we all thought we were getting a cross between Giacinto Fachetti [the famous Inter Milan left-back] and Tam Gemmell. But when Erich arrived, he was a raw young laddie. We were all thinking Packy had got a wee bit carried away with himself again. But when you think back to when Erich first arrived and compare it with what he was like when he got to the peak of his career, it was remarkable how far he had come."

Erich could not be joining Hibs at a better time. In his early weeks in charge of the 1969/70 season, MacFarlane had been a revelation, starting his tenure with a 2–0 win at Hearts, and keeping his team at the top of the table with a run of seven wins and two draws from his first ten league matches in charge, including a 3–1 win away to Rangers. With MacFarlane probably regarded as some kind of messiah in those early days, it is little wonder that his first plunge into the transfer market had generated so much interest.

Although Hibs were riding high, chairman William Harrower and his directors had some difficult choices to make financially. They had already controversially sold Colin Stein to Rangers for £100,000 – the first six-figure transfer in Scotland – and by the end of the 1969/70 season they transferred Peter Marinello to Arsenal and Peter Cormack to Nottingham Forest. Vice-chairman Alex Pratt made a thinly veiled reference to the fact the onus would be on MacFarlane to produce results and keep tempting the paying punters through the gates. "Our financial reserves have been more or less drained by our attempts to produce an attractive team," he said. "There's only one way to get the money back and that's through the turnstiles." Hibs had let some star names leave, but the board also backed wheeler-dealer MacFarlane's efforts to rebuild the team with transfer market bargains. In his first year in charge, MacFarlane was allowed to sign Johnny Graham (£20,000), Jim Black (£32,000), Arthur Duncan (£30,000), Jim Blair (£30,000) and Erich Schaedler (£7,000).

A week after signing, Erich pulled on a Hibs shirt for the first time – in a reserve match at Easter Road against Dundee United on Saturday, 15 November 1969. While the first team were at Tannadice, winning 1–0 thanks to a goal from Peter Marinello (the last he would score for Hibs), Erich had to suffer the embarrassment of scoring an own goal in his first match. Having scored in his final match for Stirling a week earlier this was a unique feat! The match report, which Hibs lost 2–0, shows Erich was unlucky to put through his own net, having been standing in the wrong place at the wrong time. Other than that unfortunate blip, he played well enough to suggest he would soon feature in the senior team. Describing the own goal, the report said a "shot from Wood that looked like going past struck the full-back and rolled over the line. Otherwise, Schaedler performed well enough to suggest it won't be very long before he is challenging for a first-team place."

The Hibs reserve team for Erich's first match was: Baines, Jones, Schaedler, Brownlie, Wilkinson, Pringle, O'Rourke, Hunter, Newman, Murphy, Cropley. Sub: McPaul.

Erich's first appearance had been a mixed bag, and when he got his chance to play in the first team, it was truly a debut to remember.

# 6

# DEMOLITION DEBUT

You have to hand it to Erich Schaedler: as memorable debuts go, he raised the bar! Erich announced his introduction to first-team football at Hibs by stepping off the bench as a substitute, hurtling into his very first tackle and crocking teammate Peter Cormack, who happened to be in the way – an incident which left the fans gasping and the dazed Cormack exiting the pitch on a stretcher.

The bizarre incident on 8 December 1969 has become the stuff of legend. In a glamour friendly match Hibs were hosting Górnik Zabrze, the Polish side who had torn Rangers apart in the European Cup-Winners' Cup, and MacFarlane had listed Erich as a substitute. Friendlies are ten-a-penny now and rarely pull in much of an attendance, but in 1969 they were still a rarity and MacFarlane hyped up the visit of Górnik to Easter Road. "The last big friendly match here was against Real Madrid and I remember well how Hibs won comfortably," wrote MacFarlane in his programme notes ahead of the game. "I mention the Spanish club for I firmly believe that Górnik are streets ahead of that Real side. Depending on how the game progresses, I may bring in two or three of my reserve players. Those in mind are Erich Schaedler, the full-back we signed from Stirling Albion; Mervyn Jones, who looks more of a right-back than a left-back to me; and goalkeeper Roy Baines, who has never had a first-team chance. At any rate, I'm sure it's going to be outstanding entertainment."

Outstanding entertainment it was, although not for poor Peter Cormack. On a bitterly cold midweek night, Schaedler sat like a coiled spring on the bench for the first half as Hibs fell 2–1 behind against their slick Polish visitors, but he was summoned by MacFarlane at half-time and told to get stripped. Itching to make an impression and with adrenalin surging through his veins, the unleashed Schaedler tore into a challenge within moments of the whistle sounding to get the second half underway – and with his eye straying from the ball, he clattered into his unsuspecting teammate Cormack.

"Schaedler went in over-anxiously into his first tackle and clashed with Cormack," *The Scotsman* reported the following day. "Cormack was carried off on a stretcher and he did not return. It was an unfortunate start for the young boy but he quickly forgot about it. It was learned later that Cormack's leg was badly swollen but the injury did not seem that serious." Schaedler's former Stirling teammate Terry Christie was at Easter Road as a spectator that night and winced as he watched through his fingers as Erich's enthusiasm got the better of him. "I actually saw his debut for Hibs, a so-called friendly, and he injured Peter Cormack," says Christie. "He was so determined to get the ball that he went bulldozing into one of our star players and took him out the game. I was groaning because I was a big Hibs supporter and I thought Peter might be out for weeks. That was Erich though! He had certainly announced his arrival at Easter Road."

Pat Stanton also laughs at the recollection of Cormack becoming Schaedler's first Easter Road "victim". "He was only just on the park when he clattered Peter," says Stanton. "You could see the Polish boys didn't know what to make of it all. They were probably thinking to themselves, 'If that's what the guy has done to his own teammate then what on earth is he going to do to us?' To be honest, if you'd looked at Erich that night and said, 'That boy is going to play for Scotland one day,' people would have thought your were mad. But Erich had great enthusiasm and he was a terrific trainer, you could see that much right from the very start. I liked him straight away as a guy and as a teammate, and his approach to the game was admirable. He wanted to do well, to improve himself any way he could, and when you get a player with that honesty and commitment then it can be very refreshing.

"On the other side of the park you had John Brownlie – one of the best full-backs we have seen in a long, long time. Even Alex Ferguson still talks about his ability. His skill, his pace, his vision was incredible – what a player he was, and that's why he was capped by Scotland when he was just eighteen. Brownlie had so many natural attributes, whereas Erich was a raw laddie. But what Erich had, he used. He was never going to be a John Brownlie or an Alex Cropley, but he could make a name for himself as Erich Schaedler, and the truth is he could do things that they couldn't do."

Other than his clumsy challenge on the unfortunate Cormack, the teenager acquitted himself well on his debut against Górnik, watched by a crowd in excess of 15,000. The tackle on Cormack was the talk of the pubs afterwards, and the name Schaedler was certainly not going to be forgotten by anyone who attended the game.

Sandy Macnair, the author and long-standing Hibs fanzine contributor aka "The Hibbie Hippie", instantly took a shine to the rough diamond his team had uncovered. "I have perhaps more reason than most to fondly recall Erich Schaedler's formative days at Easter Road – after all, we both started making appearances there around the same time," he says. "Erich broke through into the first team in the dying days of Willie MacFarlane's reign, just as I was becoming a regular on the terracing.

"It wouldn't be unfair to say Shades initially looked a rough and ready prospect – one of his first *faux pas* in Hibs colours was to injure teammate Peter Cormack with a wildly mis-timed tackle during a 'friendly'! However, anyone could see that he had the potential. He was strong as an ox and brave as a lion – if that's not one animal metaphor too many."

Hibs had also recently lost Peter Marinello to injury in a friendly match against Aston Villa, and as MacFarlane was quizzed by the press about Cormack's well-being after suffering at the boot of Erich, the manager was forced to defend his wisdom in arranging the Górnik match in the first place. "Our match against Górnik was well justified," insisted MacFarlane. "It kept our players in trim and while Peter Cormack was hurt he will be fit to play against Ayr United on Saturday."

There was no denying the Górnik match had helped Hibs gain some much-needed game time, as a particularly harsh winter had resulted in a number of postponements and idle weekends. This effectively slowed down then snuffed out any pretensions Hibs had of mounting a serious title challenge. The sale of the club's most exciting player, Marinello, to Arsenal at the turn of the year didn't help their cause either.

MacFarlane had been happy to let Erich ease himself into his new surroundings, content to let his young recruit find his feet in the reserves, but a defensive crisis over Christmas 1969 saw him pitched into the fray. Regulars Chris Shevlane and Billy McEwan both came down with the flu and the twenty-year-old Schaedler was handed his competitive debut for Hibs at left-back in the league fixture away to Dundee on 27 December, with another youngster Mervyn Jones playing at right-back. It was only Hibs' second match in four weeks, and their rustiness was evident as they went down 1–0 to a goal from Doug Houston. The young debutant still managed to catch the eye, with *The Scotsman* singling both he and John Blackley out for praise in its match report. Erich had done enough against Dundee to retain his place in the New Year derby against Hearts, and the Edinburgh rivals ushered in the new decade with a 0–0 draw at Easter Road in front of 36,421 fans – a drab, unremarkable game other than the red card shown to Cormack midway through the second half for taking a wild kick at Hearts' left-back Peter Oliver. Perhaps Cormack's crazy turn was down to first-hand experience, having been on the receiving end of a wilder kick himself against Górnik a few weeks earlier! Cormack at least redeemed himself by scoring in a 3–0 win against Raith two weeks later, with Erich at left-back contributing to a second consecutive clean sheet.

Two more first-team outings followed in January 1970 – against either half of the Old Firm – as Schaedler continued to accumulate some useful experience. Unfortunately for Hibs, both of these games resulted in defeats – a 2–1 loss to Celtic in the league at Easter Road, which heralded a scoring debut for Arthur Duncan, followed by a 3–1 Scottish Cup exit to Rangers at Ibrox. These matches pitted Erich against a couple of the finest wingers Scotland has ever produced, and this Old Firm double-header gave the *Daily Record* the excuse to again trot out Schaedler's former soft spot for Rangers.

"Few players have faced a tougher baptism in senior football than Hibs' twenty-year-old left-back Erich Schaedler," wrote the *Record*'s Alister Nicol. "After only a handful of games the youngster, who joined Hibs from Stirling Albion for £7,000, was pitched in last Saturday against the world-class skills and wiles of Celtic's Jimmy Johnstone. This week he's up against another wonder winger, Rangers' Willie Henderson. And although he enjoyed his game last week against the Celtic red head, he admitted to me yesterday, 'I was really very nervous before the game . . . and I'm no less nervous at the prospect of playing against Willie Henderson.' The speedy left-back, whose German father was a former prisoner of war in this country, was a Rangers supporter before he joined Hibs.

"'But it was not because I admired their play so much,' he went on. 'It was simply that they were one of the big successful teams. I don't suppose I've seen them more than half-a-dozen times. And in any case, that's all changed now. I'm an out-and-out Hibs man.'

"Schaedler has grounds for feeling nervous about meeting Willie Henderson just seven days after coming up against the dazzle of Jimmy Johnstone, but manager Willie MacFarlane is sure the boy won't let him down. The man Schaedler replaced at left-back, eighteen-year-old Billy McEwan, quickly regained a first-team place – as a midfield man. He too did well against Celtic and could keep his place against Rangers in Saturday's Ibrox Cup tie. MacFarlane also has a high regard for Mervyn Jones, John Greig's nephew, who had a run at left-back earlier this season. So the Hibs boss is well off for full-backs, although he reckons that the best of the lot might be Erich Schaedler, the man who in the space of a few days will have faced two of the greatest wingers Scotland has produced. He's certainly having to learn the hard way what top-grade football is all about."

Facing players as gifted as Henderson and Johnstone provided Erich with invaluable experience and he closed out a satisfying debut season for Hibs by playing in a low-key 1–0 win at East End Park against Dunfermline – a result which confirmed a respectable third place in the league for MacFarlane's side.

After a short break, Erich got his first full pre-season as a Hibs player under his belt, and MacFarlane must have been delighted to see his recruit blossom into the first-team player he had envisaged when he brought him to Easter Road from Stirling. Hibs headed to Europe for a three-match tour against German side Schalke 04 and Dutch pair NEC Nijmegen and MVV Maastricht. Already christened the "Mad Kraut" by his teammates, it was Schaedler's first trip to his father's homeland representing Hibs, and his nickname was at the root of a diplomatic *faux pas* from the excitable MacFarlane during the match against Schalke in Gelsenkirchen.

Teammate John Blackley explains, "It may have been a pre-season game but there was a big crowd and they were all excited because Stan Libuda was playing. He was the big local hero and he'd just come back from the World Cup in Mexico where West Germany had finished third, so they were out in their numbers to pay tribute to him.

"It was a horrible night, but the crowd were still in World Cup party mode. They were pretty vocal and animated, and it was a decent atmosphere for a pre-season friendly. Packy MacFarlane was patrolling the touchline in front of the German fans, and when Erich was needing a bit of encouragement over on the far side, he tried to get his attention by shouting over to him at the top of his voice – 'Kraut! . . . KRAUT!'

"He was only trying to get his message to Erich but the Germans thought he was insulting them and started going mental behind him. Thankfully, it didn't get out of hand, but for a while they were going bananas. Packy didn't even know what the problem was, he was totally oblivious to what he'd done until someone pointed it out to him in the dressing room afterwards."

With diplomatic relations preserved, but only just, Hibs returned to Scotland for the traditional curtain-raiser, the League Cup sectional matches, and Schaedler was an ever-present in six unbeaten group games against Aberdeen, Airdrie and St Johnstone. That booked Hibs a place in the quarter-finals, but Rangers snuffed out their interest with 3–1 wins home and away.

Erich also made his European debut in the Fairs Cup – the forerunner to the UEFA Cup – having precious little to do in a crushing 6–0 home victory against Malmo as Joe McBride banged in a hat-trick. The Swedes put up more resistance in the return leg on their home turf a fortnight later, but Hibs, handing a debut to the teenager Kenny Davidson, still won 3–2 for a resounding 9–2 aggregate win. Ironically, Malmo gained ample revenge when the clubs met again in the Europa Leaque at the start of the 2013/14 season, beating Hibs 7–0 at Easter Road to win 9–0 on aggregate.

Schaedler, now twenty-one, was holding down a regular place in the early months of the 1970/71 season, but injuries were making life difficult for MacFarlane and a lot of chopping and changing in personnel was reflected in some erratic results, perhaps typified by a dismal 4–0 thumping at Motherwell. Europe at least offered some respite from the domestic difficulties, and Hibs put themselves in a strong position to advance past Vitória Guimaraes by defeating their Portuguese visitors 2–0 in the first leg at Easter Road, thanks to goals from Pat Stanton and Arthur Duncan.

Before the return leg in Oporto, Hibs secured their first silverware of the Seventies – the East of Scotland Shield. They beat Hearts with a late penalty winner from John Blackley, who volunteered to take the crucial spot-kick, having won a penalty competition at the club's summer tour HQ in Germany, banging in ten in a row. It was Blackley's first competitive penalty and his first Hibs goal. "I had no worries about taking the kick," he told newspapers at the time. "I remembered how successful I had been in Germany and I volunteered for the job. I was delighted to get my first goal." Hibs scraped into the third round 3–2 on aggregate after losing the return 2–1 in stiflingly hot conditions in Portugal after Johnny Graham grabbed a vital away goal. It had been a close call, but the reward was substantial: a glamour tie against Bill Shankly's Liverpool.

Schaedler then experienced his first victory over an Old Firm side, Jim Blair scoring two in a rousing 3–2 home win over Rangers. But just twenty-four hours before the eagerly anticipated first leg with Liverpool, Erich and his teammates (average age at that time twenty-two) were left bewildered by the abrupt and unjust sacking of his mentor MacFarlane. MacFarlane may have been a single-minded, strong-willed character, but he more than met his match in new chairman Tom Hart, who would lock horns with anyone if he thought he was in the right . . . which happened to be most of the time. It is always an uneasy situation when a director feels he can meddle with the manager's team selection, and Hart was more than keen to have his say. On the day before the Liverpool game, he overstepped the mark when he ordered MacFarlane to drop Joe McBride and Johnny Graham. MacFarlane was initially ready to do as his chairman wished, but then – perhaps fearing he was making a rod for his own back and setting a dangerous precedent – he chose instead to defy Hart.

"Thinking things over, I have decided to restore the two players and also Hamilton to my party," MacFarlane explained to reporters, who scented that serious trouble was brewing behind the scenes at Easter Road. MacFarlane added, "It is the only logical thing I can do to keep my self-respect. At the moment I will be picking the team for tomorrow night. I am not in the slightest bit interested in the political situation at Hibs." An incandescent Hart was having none of it and sacked MacFarlane on the spot. Tommy Younger, the legendary Hibs and Scotland goalkeeper, was employed by the club at that time as a "public relations officer", but when pressed by newspapermen for a comment on the spiralling controversy, the genial Younger declined to comment and told them he "didn't want to become involved". MacFarlane had lost his job, but he at least kept a strong grip on his dignity, saying, "The chairman has every right to sack me, but no right to interfere in team selection."

The haste in which Hart had axed MacFarlane took everyone by surprise. The programme for the big match had already been printed, with an unsuspecting MacFarlane innocently declaring in his manager's notes: "Tonight's match with Liverpool rates as the most important Hibs have undertaken in my time here and I'm sure it will be a memorable occasion." In truth, the writing would seem to have been on the wall for MacFarlane for a few weeks before the Liverpool encounter. Hart was increasingly at odds with the teams MacFarlane was picking and was fidgety with the team's form as they languished in sixth place in the league. The chairman's recruitment of coach Dave Ewing from Sheffield Wednesday just a week before the Liverpool match had only served to weaken his manager's position and fuel speculation that Ewing, a former Manchester City stalwart who played alongside Famous Five great Bobby Johnstone in two FA Cup finals, had been lined up to take MacFarlane's job, although the manager didn't see it that way – publicly at least.

As Hibs headed for a short training camp at Inverclyde Recreation Centre to prepare for the Liverpool match, the *Glasgow Herald* reported, "Willie MacFarlane said that everyone at the club – and that included the present training staff of Tom McNiven and John Fraser – were very happy with Mr Ewing's appointment. Mr MacFarlane went out of his way to emphasise that the new appointment would mean a sharing of the coaching ideas." MacFarlane added, "We all believe that this will be to the benefit of everyone at Easter Road." On the face of it, he would seem to have been in the dark that Ewing was set to take his job days later.

With MacFarlane ruthlessly sacked by Hart, Dave Ewing was thrust into the spotlight and put in charge of the team for the Liverpool match. Hibs, with McBride on the bench and Graham conspicuous by his absence, lost 1–0 as John Toshack scored the winner. It was to be Schaedler's last game for four months, as he made way for Jones in the new manager's side. The return leg at Anfield, three days before Christmas, saw Liverpool finish the job – goals from Steve Heighway and Phil Boersma ending Hibs' brief resistance. In a high-quality tournament, Shankly's side would reach the semi-finals before losing to eventual winners Leeds.

In truth, Hibs had simply been outclassed over the two games by one of the leading teams in Europe. Erich, by his own admission, had one of his poorest games for the club in that first leg at Easter Road and the off night saw him banished by Ewing to the reserves – ending an unbroken run of thirty top-team games. When a new boss comes in he is entitled to chop and change a side as he sees fit, but it did seem unreasonably harsh to make the left-back the scapegoat for what, after all, was a narrow defeat against strong opponents. Schaedler himself believed he had been victimised and that Ewing had listened to stories that he had only held down his place for so long because he was MacFarlane's blue-eyed boy.

Schaedler was seething and he claimed he had lost his place, not simply because he had had an off night at Easter Road, but because of a whispering campaign behind his back. Erich was an easy-going lad and very rarely allowed his emotions to be captured so explicitly in print, but he gave a hard-hitting interview to *The Weekly News*, in which he claimed he had been the victim of some harmful tittle-tattle. Erich was struggling to come to terms with being frozen out, and according to his interviewer, he had been transformed from "an easy-going guy into a very angry and resentful young man."

His quotes backed up his simmering discontent: "What chokes me is the fact that my demotion stems directly from a whispering campaign that has been carried on against me for months and months," said Schaedler, speaking weeks after the defeat to Liverpool. "According to the wise guys, I never really got into the team on merit, but merely because I was 'in' with the boss. They even called me 'Packy's Boy' [MacFarlane's favourite]. Sure it might have seemed to some folk that there was some truth in the stories when I was dropped after just one game – against Liverpool in the Fairs Cup – under our new boss Dave Ewing. But the simple truth is that I had my worst ever ninety minutes in a Hibs jersey in that game and fully deserved to be dropped.

"Believe me, I have no complaint whatever on that score. But when I heard people muttering, 'I told you so,' my blood began to boil. I even had the feeling, rightly or wrongly, that some of my teammates were of the opinion that I was the boss's favourite. It's true Mr MacFarlane took an interest in me even when I was a juvenile and signed me for Stirling Albion and Hibs, but I never had any special favours from him. I'm sure that when he put me in the Hibs first team he honestly thought that at that time I was the best man for the left-back position. Actually, it's a bit of a relief to be cooling off in the reserves. I'm desperate to get back to the first team and I'll play my heart out to get back, for my one aim in life at this moment is to demonstrate to the knockers and scoffers that I can make the grade on merit alone."

Another player who was frozen out by Ewing and was eventually allowed to leave was the goalkeeper Thomson Allan, whose career curiously intertwined with Erich's on several occasions. Allan was on the books with Schaedler at both Hibernian and Dundee, played alongside him for Scotland in Frankfurt in 1974, and that same year joined him in the twenty-two-man Scotland squad for the World Cup finals in West Germany. Allan – an agile, but somewhat vertically challenged keeper at 5ft 10in – does not harbour any lingering grudges against Ewing and if anything admires the honesty he showed during their time together at Easter Road. "He came in after Willie MacFarlane and told me, 'I don't know you and you might be the best on the books for all I know, but I like my goalkeepers to be six foot and you're not.' So I was freed for an inch-and-a-half! Sometimes, it's better just to move on than beat yourself up by trying to prove a point. If your face doesn't fit with a certain manager, then it can be better to accept it and move somewhere where you are appreciated."

Allan did just that and demonstrated what an excellent keeper he was at his new club Dundee, winning the 1973 League Cup (where they beat Jock Stein's Celtic in the final) and coming close in the Scottish Cup that same year. He left Easter Road with more than 100 appearances to his name, and while most of them were during Bob Shankly's reign, he also has fond memories of MacFarlane's influential year in charge at the club. "When Willie came to Easter Road he was a breath of fresh air. I didn't get many games while he was there, but I went back and played for him years later at Meadowbank Thistle. He was always the joker and a good lad that the players liked and respected. Erich was the first signing he made at Hibs."

After stewing away in the reserves for a few months, Schaedler was true to his word and battled his way back into the first team. With his struggles against Liverpool a distant memory, he finally made his top-team return in April in the penultimate league fixture away to Dunfermline – but not in his usual left-back slot. Instead he was bizarrely deployed as a replacement for the great Joe Baker, brought back to the club in January but sidelined at that time with a poisoned foot. While Mervyn Jones continued to wear the No.3 shirt, Erich was thrown in up front wearing Baker's No.9 jersey alongside strike partner Jimmy O'Rourke. Ewing's thinking was that Schaedler would be the perfect foil for nullifying the physical threat posed by Dunfermline's classy centre-half John Cushley. To an extent his plan worked. While Shades went to work on softening up Cushley with some meaty challenges, the industrious O'Rourke was left to his own devices and banged in two goals in a 3–3 draw.

Schaedler had done well enough keeping Joe Baker's shirt warm to earn a place in the starting XI for the season-ending match at home to Clyde, back in his familiar role of left-back. It showed how disillusioned Hibs fans had become during the Ewing reign that the match was watched by a paltry 3,310 crowd. Those that stayed away missed a thumping 5–1 win, but the emphatic victory was scant consolation for a rotten league campaign – soured by MacFarlane's departure – and Hibs limped home in an embarrassing position of twelfth in the eighteen-team top flight.

While the Hibs players would probably have been glad to put their boots away for the summer and recharge their batteries, the season was prolonged by a series of friendlies in England and in the Highlands. Chairman Tom Hart at least tried to revive morale by flying the team out to the Balearics, where Hibs lost 2–1 in a friendly to Real Mallorca on 20 May. It would prove to be Ewing's final game in charge. He left with a less than impressive record of just seven wins in twenty-six competitive matches – those stats suggesting that the sacking of MacFarlane had been unduly hasty. It had been a draining, tumultuous campaign, and the club faced an uncertain future.

The Fates were about to smile on Hibs, however. Within weeks, a determined, forward-thinking manager would stride through the doors of Easter Road and revolutionise the club. He had been there before, he knew what was required. In fact, he was a ready-made hero. There was only one Eddie Turnbull.

# 7

# JUMPERS FOR GOALPOSTS

Erich Schaedler's professional attitude and keen approach to football had helped him to settle in remarkably well at Hibs. Being dropped for a few months by Dave Ewing may have dented his pride, but it had also strengthened his character and resolve. It was all part of a learning curve and, generally speaking, he was living the dream – playing full-time professional football in a team genuinely capable of challenging for honours and making a name for themselves as regulars in European competition. In 1971, Schaedler had another big responsibility in his life: he had become a father to a baby girl, Tracey. But Erich, in his early twenties, was still a big kid at heart and his adventurous streak was never far from bubbling to the surface.

Aside from football his other big passion was cars, and Erich was always popping into the garage of local mechanic Gordon McDougall at Spey Street Lane, a two-minute walk from Easter Road stadium. McDougall was a big Hibs supporter himself, took adverts out for his business in the match programme, and pretty much dealt with the motoring requirements of the entire squad. He has particularly fond memories of Erich – by some distance the biggest car enthusiast in the team – and the two men developed a long and lasting friendship. "He absolutely loved his cars," says McDougall. "He used to bring a big bag of steak rolls round at dinner time from Easter Road – all the ones that hadn't been eaten by the players and coaching staff – and we'd sit and have a blether.

"When I first knew him he was married and living at Penicuik and he had a Ford Cortina Mark 1 – I remember the engine was away and we ended up having to tow it into Penicuik. He also had a dark green Mark 2 Jaguar and I had to go and get it out of a field after he'd driven it right off the road coming up from Peebles – he'd absolutely destroyed it. It was just past Eddleston coming north, on the bend, and we had to go and dig it out. He also had a Cortina, then an Austin Princess, then he had a bright green Capri. There were a few more too – it's safe to say he was into cars in a big way!"

McDougall is now chairman of Livingston FC and before that held the same post for many years at Cowdenbeath, combining his interest in football with his other big sporting passion, stock car racing. Unsurprisingly, this was something that appealed to Schaedler too. "Yes, he was fascinated with stock car racing as well when I became involved," says McDougall. "He would come along to Newtongrange, then he would come to Cowdenbeath to watch. I remember him being at the 1976 World Final at Cowdenbeath. We managed to keep him from having a go himself – I don't think it would have sat too kindly with his football career, or Eddie Turnbull – but if you'd given him a helmet he would have jumped in the car no problem. Speed appealed to his nature."

Schaedler and McDougall remained good friends until his death, and Erich would pop in regularly to visit his family. "He'd come round to my house at Christmas time and he'd either be playing the Subbuteo or the Scaletrix at two or three in the morning – he was just that type of boy. He had a great sense of fun."

That Peter Pan side of Erich was one of his many endearing qualities. McDougall reveals how Schaedler and his best friend at the club, the goalkeeper Bobby Robertson, used to sometimes finish training, then take a ball down to Pilrig Park and play there for hours. Just the two of them, the inner child in them bringing out a wonderfully innocent side to their characters. "Boaby and

Erich used to play down at Pilrig Park – the pair of them diving about like overgrown schoolboys, oblivious to any risk of injury or getting noticed by passers-by," says McDougall. "Imagine that now. You're walking past a public park and you see two professional footballers having a kick-about! It says a lot about their enthusiasm, though."

Robertson was Erich's sidekick in those early years at Easter Road. They had known each other through football before Robertson joined Schaedler on Hibs' books, and they quickly became best mates. "I was at Whitehill Welfare Under-21s and Erich used to come along and help train us. That would be around 1970/71. Occasionally we would meet up and got to know each other, but when I signed for Hibs I became really good pals with him," explains Robertson. "Erich was just a year older than me, so it said a lot about his attitude that even at that age he was willing to give up his time to coach others. I'd been down at Burnley and I'd also been at Ibrox, but I got my break with Hibs. Erich was a very effervescent guy – you instantly took a liking to him."

And can Robertson confirm that their kick-abouts in Pilrig Park, with jumpers for goalposts, took place? Yes, and that wasn't the only parks they would play! "Aye, we would be there with the ball," he says, half-laughing, half-cringing with embarrassment at the memory. "We would go down to the park or the garages in Pilrig and muck around there for a while. Kenny Taylor was our big pal too. He played with St Mirren at the same time as Archie Gemmill and Whitburn Juniors, and we all used to pal about together. When training was done we'd be either kicking the ball about or hanging about the garages. We would play in Pilrig Park with the ball and in the Meadows, because I was from Tollcross. When I was at Hibs I actually used to play on a Sunday for the Royal Infirmary at centre forward. I went under another name to avoid detection, but Erich couldn't do that because his face was too well known. We used to go down to Peebles and play in the park there too, just muck about with the ball, taking shots and playing keepy-uppy. Some of my pals would come down with us and we'd make a day of it. Looking back, it was all great fun.

"I used to really enjoy those trips down to Peebles. It wasn't all just mucking around though, because sometimes we would do some tough training runs while we were down there. Erich was a strong, strong guy and he was always keen to improve his strength and fitness. Sometimes he didn't realise his own strength. I remember a time at Easter Road when he got the groundsman there – a big guy, Charlie from Newtongrange – in a bear hug and cracked one of his ribs.

"During those trips down to Peebles I also got to know Erich's parents quite well – his dad was crazy! His mum was a lovely woman, and Erich's father was a well-known character in the town. We used to meet sometimes on a Sunday night, a group of us, in the Cross Keys or the Tontine, and Erich's dad would come along and join us. You just knew it was going to be a lively night when he was there. He was larger than life, everyone knew him, and Erich and him were obviously very fond of each other. There was respect, but there was some father-and-son banter going back and forward too. I mind him going out on the street one day, goose-stepping up and down outside the Cross Keys! Erich never made any bones about his German background. It must have been hard for his dad settling into a community as a former prisoner of war. The sort of job he did as well, being on the *Bismarck* and the torpedo boats, it shows what strength of character he must have been. It moulds you for the rest of your life and the people you're bringing into the world."

Robertson and Schaedler's mutual love of cars also got the two petrol heads into a few scrapes. "We were always doing mad stuff with cars. Erich was crazy about cars and so was I," adds Robertson. "I mind Erich driving off the road into the woods down near Peebles and Gordon McDougall having to come down in his pick-up and fish his car out.

"One time there was a guy, 'Mad Jim' – a real character – and he asked me and Erich if we could help him out and run a wee errand for him. It was simple, he said, all we had to do was collect a car. The pair of us were still a bit naïve and wet behind the ears and what we didn't know at the time was that we were actually being sent to steal it! It was in Davidson's Mains – near the church there was a row of lock-ups, and he told us that's where the car would be. He said there would be keys in the car and so there was, so thinking nothing more of it we drove it back to Leith and went and had a couple of drinks. A couple of days later the car was in bits and it was all cut up – it must have been some kind of insurance job. We had been unwitting accomplices to a crime. Honestly, we didn't know any better, we didn't have a clue at the time what we were doing was a little bit shady!"

Cars were far from being Schaedler's only outside interest. He also adored dogs, having grown up around a few family pets in the countryside, and he would own several throughout his career. Robertson remembers one time that dog lover Erich bit off more than he (or rather his new puppy) could chew. "He bought a dog from Bertie Auld, who was on the coaching staff at Easter Road. It was a really weird-looking thing," says Robertson. "Bertie sold it to him as a Yugoslavian hunting dog, but it was a Heinz 57 – mixed breed. It was the weirdest dog I ever saw, it just ate everything in its path! Eventually Erich moved into a flat at Sciennes, near Newhaven, and he had all these nice leather jackets. He came back one day and the dog had shredded the lot – he'd eaten his way through the leather jackets and had started on the rest of his wardrobe. Bertie had literally sold him a pup!

"One time when I had borrowed his car, a Jaguar, to take Chris, the girl who would become my wife, out for the night. I took the Jag down to Prestonpans and picked her up. So we're sitting there talking, me doing my best to impress her, and when I looked in the mirror there is this same gormless dog looking at us both. It must have been having a kip in the back of the car when I took the car!"

Erich's marriage had run into trouble around that time and he was separated from his wife. He left the marital home in Penicuik and took a flat in Edinburgh, not far from Robertson, who was living with his parents in Tollcross. The pair of them socialised a lot, although Erich was never a heavy drinker and more often than not would draw the line at a couple of shandies. While he enjoyed the atmosphere of pubs and clubs, drinking did not appeal to him. "Erich was always up for a night out but he wasn't a drinker, he just liked being out and about," explains Robertson. "He had split from his wife at that time and the women were usually flocking round him. He was a good-looking guy. The rest of the boys were usually left to fight it out over Erich's cast-offs! We would go out all over town. I remember going regularly to a dance hall in Grindlay Street near the Lyceum, which was usually full of gangsters, and Valentinos was another one of our haunts. We also used to drink in the Golf Tavern at Bruntsfield before it underwent its metamorphosis into the trendy student place it is now. It used to be great for all the medical profession to gather. We used to drink in another place up in Marchmont, owned by one of the Hearts directors. We would go to a few parties too and before he had his flat he stayed with me quite a lot in Home Street. There was one party at John Blackley's place in Grangemouth that we went along to together and Rod Stewart was there.

"We had some crazy nights, but one in particular sticks in the mind. We were in Morningside for my twenty-first birthday, a whole crowd of us, and we ended up in a restaurant. But when I came out of there at the end of the night my car was gone. I thought somebody had pinched it and had no option but to report it stolen. It was only later that I found out my mates had nicked it. They had taken the handbrake off and rolled it round the corner into another street. But the police had got involved by that stage and we were panicking that it would make the news with Erich Schaedler being there. Thankfully, there was nothing made of it, but it could have been a bit embarrassing for us both. A lot of players get a tough time in the press now for relatively minor indiscretions – we used to do some far crazier things and we didn't have to worry about being recorded on YouTube or phones like they do now. We got away with everything."

Erich's Hibs career was thriving, but Bobby always found himself in fierce competition for the goalkeeper's shirt. When he first arrived he had to battle it out with Jim Herriot and Jim McArthur, and although he made a handful of appearances under Eddie Turnbull, injuries blighted his progress. Nevertheless, the "Goalkeepers Union" ensured that despite their rivalry, he and McArthur were good pals. "I left Hibs in 1975," says Robertson. "I got a back injury and had discs taken out. When I woke up from the operation in the Princess Margaret Rose Hospital, the first thing I clapped eyes on was Jim McArthur sitting by the side of my bed, playing my guitar! There was I, laid up in bed with tubes sticking out of me, and Jim's there chirping away, saying, 'I just came here to make sure you werenae getting my place on Saturday!'

"Even though I only got a few first-team games at Hibs, I absolutely loved my time there. The dressing room was full of brilliant guys and the camaraderie was excellent. I played a lot of games for the reserves or the Colts, who used to play in the East of Scotland League. In the reserves we would play the first team on a Tuesday at training, but some of the games would go on for a long time until the first team was winning!

"I was pleased to see Erich do so well. I saw him scoring against St Johnstone with his right foot, which was very strange. Erich thrived working under the great Turnbull system of the overlapping full-back. It was a sad day for me to leave the club, but I had some good times and featured in a few European games," adds Robertson, who went on to play for Bonnyrigg Rose. "The end-of-season trips at Hibs were legendary too. One trip to Spain I can remember Erich started going from balcony to balcony of the high-rise hotel! Then Dessie Bremner was cajoled into doing the same. It was crazy stuff, not advisable. Maybe Dessie was getting a free drink for doing it, but Erich wasn't even getting that – he just did it for the thrill.

"Erich remained a good mate, and he was at my stag do and wedding. When I packed in football in 1980 we would still catch up from time to time. We always had a lot in common."

# 8

# READY, EDDIE, GO

The 1970/71 season had been one of great upheaval for Hibs, and the club's future sat uneasily at the crossroads. After the sacking of Willie MacFarlane and the turbulent months under Dave Ewing, it was vital for Hibs to appoint the right man to stabilise the club and allow the squad to realise their undoubted potential. Luring Eddie Turnbull back to the club he had served with such great distinction as a marauding inside-left in the Famous Five forward line was a masterstroke by chairman Tom Hart. Turnbull was no managerial novice. He had already been a trainer at Easter Road in the Sixties before heading to Queen's Park to cut his teeth as the boss. Next stop was Aberdeen, and in his six years as manager at Pittodrie he not only produced stunning results on the pitch, but built the firm foundations on which the club's glory years were built under Alex Ferguson in the late 1970s and early 1980s. Turnbull's crowning glory at Aberdeen had been leading the Dons to a triumph in the 1970 Scottish Cup – the trophy which still eluded Hibs. He had also guided Aberdeen to second place in the league the following year. He ticked every box and was the ideal candidate for Hibs – the right man at the right time if Hibs were ever going to produce a side which could come anywhere close to the illustrious side of the late 1940s/early 1950s in which Turnbull himself had shone so brightly.

With a nimble coaching brain and a gruff, dictatorial but

ultimately effective approach to "man-management", Turnbull was quite simply born to be Hibs manager. He would also prove to be the perfect man to harness Erich's development as a footballer. Eddie worked best with players who would listen to his methods and advice, not question them, and in Schaedler he had a willing student who would absorb every morsel of tuition he was given. Erich's pal Bobby Robertson says, "As a coach Eddie was outstanding, but as a manager he could be harsh when it came to man-management. It could have gone either way for Erich, because he had been Willie MacFarlane's signing, and when Eddie came in he could have decided to keep another left-back on at the club and dispensed with Erich. But Erich was perfect for Turnbull's way of playing. He had one amazingly skilful full-back on one side in John Brownlie and one hard and committed, do-or-die type in Erich on the other side.

"Eddie was fantastic at imparting his knowledge of the game, but he was a hard man, not to be crossed. We were training at Muirhouse one time when Jim McArthur dived for a shot and got glass in his hands, but Turnbull made him carry on. When Jim got back from training he needed stitches, but Eddie was not for apologising. I think that hard, uncompromising personality was perhaps because Eddie had served on the Arctic Convoys and seen people die in the war – it made him a hard man."

Martin Buchan, Turnbull's young captain at Aberdeen and later a Scotland teammate of Schaedler, believes his former mentor Turnbull was peerless as a coach. "Eddie made every player better that he came into contact with – even cynical old pros could learn a thing or two from him," said Buchan, who went on from Aberdeen to become an FA Cup winner in a long and distinguished career at the heart of Manchester United's defence. "To me, Eddie Turnbull was the best coach that ever drew breath. It was no surprise that Shades eventually got into the Scotland squad, having benefited from Eddie's touch on the training ground.

"I remember at Aberdeen there were a few players who won

international honours under Eddie. Some of them had been very average players and may never have got to that level, but they improved enormously after learning from Eddie to the point that they fully deserved international recognition. Eddie made the game simple for them and uncomplicated. He would spend hours walking them through situations. He was incredibly thorough. I also think that Shades, as a full-back, would have learned even more from Eddie, as one of his specialties was balancing a back four – having full-backs who knew when to stay back and when to go forward, and how to complement each other. Erich would have had a huge understanding of how a back four works best because of what Eddie taught him."

John Blackley agrees: "Erich did work hard at what Eddie taught him. He knew what he had and he knew what he could give to this squad of players. He gave us solidity on the left side because John Brownlie was bombing forward on the other side, so we were always kind of open on that side. John Brownlie's natural ability to go attacking was unbelievable, it was such a big part of that team, but Erich's influence on the other side was another big part. He would sit most of the time but on occasion he could romp forward, and when he did he was effective."

Looking back at his early days at Easter Road, Turnbull himself said, "John Blackley, Jim Black, John Brownlie and Erich Schaedler were impressive talents to work with, and soon the defensive organisation began to take shape. Brownlie was all skill and flair, and one of the best attacking full-backs I ever saw. By contrast, Erich Schaedler was all speed and strength. He had not been rated by the previous administration at Easter Road, but I took him under my wing and he prospered as a result, largely because he was a good listener and prepared to learn lessons. The subsequent success of Turnbull's Tornadoes stemmed from that early work with the defence."

Balancing a back four was just one of umpteen tasks Turnbull was faced with when he arrived at Easter Road. In his opinion, the players were a long way off optimum fitness and they were disorganised. He quickly got to work. "I had heard on the grapevine that there had been a certain amount of slacking under the previous manager," added Turnbull in his 2006 autobiography *Having A Ball*, as he reflected on his arrival at Easter Road. "Above all, I demanded fitness from players, and I knew some of them were lacking in that department. The players were about to get a rude awakening. It was not plain sailing at all. There was a lack of discipline about the establishment. I was not prepared to compromise in any way at Easter Road."

While Erich was steadfast in his approach to training, he was still one of the first to learn that the new manager had an unwavering approach to discipline. Schaedler breezed in after his summer break, proudly boasting a voluminous beard for pre-season training. When he returned twenty-four hours later for the second day of training, he was conspicuously clean-shaven. "I had a quiet word with Erich," Turnbull explained to the *Evening News*. "I don't mind long hair, as long as it is tidy."

A revival at Easter Road was not something that would happen overnight, whether the players were fitter or not, and Hibs failed to win any of their pre-season friendlies ahead of the 1971/72 season. However, with Erich restored to the team after his period of inactivity during Dave Ewing's last few months, they did showcase Turnbull's early influence in no uncertain terms in the League Cup. In their section, they impressively romped to five straight wins then rounded off the batch of games unbeaten with a 0–0 draw at Kilmarnock when top spot was already assured.

Turnbull was not the type of manager who felt he had to be loyal to players already on the books just for the sake of it, and he made it known that if he felt it was necessary to bring in new faces to improve the team then he would do just that. Building from the back, one of his first signings was the goalkeeper Jim Herriot. The former Dunfermline and Birmingham City No.1 had been capped nine times for Scotland, but was now in his thirties and playing in relative obscurity in South Africa for Durban City. Turnbull had long been an admirer of the big keeper and, feeling that he still had a lot to offer, he brought him back to Scotland. International clearance was secured and Herriot – famous for smearing black grease paint under his eyes to protect against the glare of floodlights – began the season as Hibs' first-choice goalkeeper.

The new-look Hibs had quickly clicked and under Turnbull the sleeping giant was stirring. Rejuvenated and improving with every outing, Hibs proved they were no longer the disjointed team that had stuttered through the previous campaign when they went to Tynecastle for their opening fixture of the new league season. It had looked a very tough assignment to begin the season, but Turnbull already had his team fit and organised and they deservedly beat Hearts 2–0. It was Erich's first taste of derby success in the league and he played his part as Hibs defended resolutely then took an eighty-fourth minute lead thanks to a twenty-five-yard screamer from Alex Cropley. Substitute Johnny Hamilton put the icing on the cake with a second goal in the final minute and Turnbull made sure his squad savoured every moment – teaching them how good a derby win in the backyard of their greatest rivals felt. The experience stood them in good stead, as they would go on to dominate the fixture throughout the Seventies.

A 2–1 aggregate defeat to Falkirk in the quarter-finals of the League Cup proved a mere hiccup as Hibs set about their league fixtures with relish and new-found belief. It wasn't all plain sailing for Erich, however. While Eddie Turnbull was delighted with the progress his young full-back was making, he clearly still had a lot to learn, and after a 2–1 defeat against Aberdeen – which would have severely dented the manager's pride on his first visit back to Pittodrie, particularly as Hibs had been leading 1–0 at half-time – Schaedler was dropped. Erich sat out five games before he was restored to the first team, and reacted positively to the lesson – playing his part in three consecutive league wins, Hibs boasting clean sheets in all three.

It may seem incredible to younger football fans, but matches could and would be played on Christmas Day in these austere times. Whether it was right or wrong to be wreaking havoc with family plans and playing on Christmas Day, the fixtures still proved popular enough with supporters and a crowd of 25,000 descended upon Easter Road for the 1971 festive meeting with Rangers. There was little Christmas cheer for Hibs fans though, as they watched their former hero Colin Stein return to almost inevitably score the only goal of the game for his new club. Hibs' coffers must have been overflowing as another 36,000 crammed in to the old ground a week later to watch the 1972 New Year's Day derby. The home fans again left the ground disappointed after a stuffy 0–0 draw, but little did they know that 365 days later they would be celebrating the club's greatest ever result.

Erich was getting his best run of games so far, and another landmark was just round the corner – his first goal as a Hibs player, against Partick Thistle in the Scottish Cup on 5 February 1972. Schaedler was not the only Hibs legend in the making to get on the scoresheet for the first time that day – elegant centre forward Alan Gordon also notched his first Hibs goal at Firhill, with Erich the provider. Erich's friend Gordon McDougall was on the terracing to see the momentous goal. "Erich wasn't exactly a regular scorer down the years, but I do remember him scoring a crucial goal in the win against Partick in the Scottish Cup run of '72," he recalls. "It came from his own long throw, and when the ball was played back out to him, he hit it first time and it flew into the net. It was normally his teammates who would benefit from the long throw, which was such an effective weapon for Hibs. The first player I remember doing the long throw was Ian Hutchinson of Chelsea, but Erich's throw was as good as anyone's – it must have been all in the shoulder muscles."

Pat Stanton was as surprised as anyone, not only to see Erich score but to smash home a goal-of-the-season contender: "Erich took this throw himself and somebody cleared it right back to him out near the touchline. Without breaking stride he just cracked it first time and it flew into the net from thirty yards. I remember speaking to big Roughie [Alan Rough] about it afterwards, and he says he never even bothered moving. He said it was like playing against Superman!"

Ted Brack, author of several acclaimed books on Hibs, has watched the team for more than fifty years and also remembers Erich's breakthrough strike well. "Hibs won this Scottish Cup tie 2–0 against a very good Partick team which had just beaten Celtic 4–1 in the League Cup final and Erich scored Hibs' second goal. He took a long throw and when the ball was headed back in his direction, he smashed it on the volley back past Alan Rough, who could only stand and look at it as it flew past him."

*The Scotsman*'s John Rafferty was less convinced about Erich's intent as he surveyed the incident from the press box. "It was a shade fortunate," he reported. "Schaedler had a long throw-in knocked back to him. He was out at the corner of the penalty box from where he lobbed the ball without stopping it, presumably aiming for the far post, but as the Thistle defence stood as if hypnotised, the ball curved into the goal. It might have gone anywhere."

Eddie Turnbull didn't care how the goals were scored. "That's us in the hat for Monday," he said, sensing a Cup run was on the cards.

Erich's delight at scoring his first goal for Hibs was tempered a few days later when he had to endure the embarrassing experience of seeing his name in the newspapers for a different reason, as he faced up to a potential driving ban at Peebles Sheriff Court. Schaedler had been caught driving without insurance following a minor collision in Peebles three months earlier. He admitted the offence, but his solicitor revealed that Erich had only jumped in his car because he was trying to do a favour for his mother. "Mr W. Goodburn, agent for Schaedler, said he had bought the car and was repairing it in his garage at Penicuik," *The Scotsman* reported. "He had been training at Easter Road when his mother phoned to say that a friend of hers had been taken to hospital. Schaedler went by bus to Penicuik and, without thinking of insurance, which was not due to come into force for another few days, drove his car to the hospital. He was later involved in a minor collision. Sheriff Isabel Sinclair QC said she normally disqualified drivers for this type of offence, but she accepted the mitigating circumstances." Shades was fined £20, which would have wiped out his Firhill win bonus, but he at least escaped with his licence intact. Losing his right to drive would have been a massive blow to the car addict so, negative press coverage apart, it was a decent result!

The following Saturday a rousing 3–2 win against Falkirk at Brockville, capped by a brilliant winner from substitute Joe Baker, was marred when key midfielder Alex Cropley was stretchered off with a broken ankle, an injury which kept him out for the rest of the season. Eddie Turnbull blamed Alex Ferguson – sent off that day – for his role in Cropley's injury, and the resentment he felt towards the future Manchester United legend for that tackle was something that simmered deep within Turnbull for the rest of his life.

Hibs, without Cropley, were back on Scottish Cup duty a week later and Baker was on the mark again, along with Gordon as Hibs beat Airdrie 2–0 at Easter Road to book their place in the quarter-finals. Next up were Aberdeen at Easter Road, and Turnbull's side came flying out the blocks, taking the lead within twenty seconds through Jimmy O'Rourke and then marching on to the semi-finals when Baker added a second. Turnbull's team were now evolving into something close to the "Tornadoes" team that would sweep majestically to League Cup glory months later, and a week before the Scottish Cup semi-final against Rangers they demonstrated their firepower by dismantling St Johnstone 7–1 at Muirton Park. Hibs were riding high, and with a run of consecutive games under his belt, Schaedler was already showing signs of vast improvement under the careful guidance of Turnbull.

The Scottish Cup semi-final draw had been made, and Hibs were paired with Rangers, who had come through a replay with

Motherwell. In the other semi-final, Jock Stein's Celtic would face Kilmarnock. In the build-up to the match, Hibs captain Pat Stanton lavished praise on his young teammate, describing Schaedler as the "most improved player in Scottish football". Stanton explained: "Erich has made great progress this season because he has played to his limitations. He has not tried to do anything beyond him and so has become a very good player for us."

Stanton's opinion was endorsed by Turnbull, who agreed: "Erich had certain qualities when I came to Easter Road – good in the air, a strong tackler and speedy. It is to his credit that he has developed and learned during the season, and no effort is spared by him. I left him out of the team for a few weeks, but he returned against Partick in the league game at Firhill and hasn't looked back."

Buoyed by their monster 7–1 win in the league against St Johnstone, Hibs should have been heading to Hampden brimming with confidence, but they looked edgy on the big stage in front of a 76,000 crowd and Rangers punished their vulnerability by taking the lead through Alex MacDonald. Stung by a typically fiery Turnbull team talk at the interval, Hibs were far more assured in the second half and they forced a replay, thanks to an equaliser from Jimmy O'Rourke. Nine days later, Hibs didn't afford Rangers the same respect and goals from Pat Stanton and Alex Edwards sent Hibs into their first Scottish Cup final since 1958.

Hibs warmed up for the final against Celtic by beating Rangers again in the league at Ibrox to claim a highly respectable fourth spot, only missing out on third spot to Rangers on goal difference. However, the 1972 Cup final was a chastening experience for Hibs. Celtic ran riot, scoring six goals in front of a mammoth Hampden crowd of 106,000. Erich and his teammates were devastated, although Jim Herriot insists Hibs were "quite unlucky", and the reports show that the margin of victory was harsh. Trailing 2–1 at half-time, Turnbull refused to abandon his attacking principles and ordered his team to keep attacking. It left gaping holes at the back, and Jock Stein's Celtic brutally punished Hibs – Dixie Deans scoring a hat-trick and Lou Macari scoring two in the 6–1 rout. There are pictures from the annihilation of an anguished Erich looking on as Herriot is beaten time and time again, but none of the goals were down to his shortcomings – Celtic were just too clinical on the day.

Despite the Cup final thrashing 1971/72 could be viewed as the season Hibs had won back their pride, and fans had been given a glimpse of a bright future under Turnbull. There was another silver lining to the humbling Hampden defeat: Hibs would have the consolation of playing in the 1972/73 European Cup-Winners' Cup as Celtic had already assured themselves a place in the European Cup as league champions.

# 9

# WHIPPING UP A TORNADO

When he joined Hibs in November 1969 Erich Schaedler, by his own admission, still had a lot to learn. He had the raw ingredients of strength, pace and determination, but all of these attributes needed fine-tuning if he was going to dramatically improve as a player. Willie MacFarlane taught him how to exploit his speed as an overlapping full-back, but it was during Eddie Turnbull's time in charge that Schaedler really came into his own, learning how and when to charge forward and how to execute a very specific role within a highly organised team. Turnbull worked tirelessly on Schaedler's positional sense, his awareness, and how to use his superhuman long throw-in to maximum effect.

Turnbull and Erich enjoyed a relatively smooth teacher-pupil relationship, while the middlemen in the equation were coach John Fraser and physio/trainer Tom McNiven if either man wanted to let off steam. Following Eddie Turnbull's death in 2011, Fraser has now become the father figure to the Tornadoes and he has a central role in the thriving association for former Hibernian players. Fraser, a right-winger, had joined Hibs in the 1950s from Edinburgh Thistle, a juvenile club who were run by Harry Rennie, the Easter Road groundsman, and wore the same green and white strip. Thistle served as a production line for Hibs, and graduates from their ranks included great players like Lawrie Reilly, Archie Buchanan and Tommy Preston, as well as Paul Kane's father, Jimmy. Fraser returned to the club as a coach and he remembers Erich's arrival well, and his subsequent transformation from raw teenager to disciplined international: "I had not long returned to the club to become a coach when Willie MacFarlane became manager. I had been a player under his predecessor, Bob Shankly, and when it came time to get a free transfer, Shankly said, 'If I ever get a chance to bring you back I'll bring you back as a coach.' I thought he was just trying to let me down gently. But no, I was sitting one day in the house when he phoned and said, 'I'd like you to come back and take the young boys for training.'

"Then Willie MacFarlane arrived after that and it was Willie who signed Erich Schaedler – the first player he brought to the club. From a coach's point of view, Schaedler was ideal. You would say to him, 'Erich, do this; Erich, do that,' and he would do it. He would listen and learn, which is rewarding for a coach because there is nothing more frustrating than when a player doesn't take in what he's been taught.

"Willie did well with Erich, but there was a big difference in his game when Eddie Turnbull got hold of him. Erich Schaedler and Arthur Duncan used to get into great positions down the left-hand side of the park, but between the pair of them nines times out of ten the ball would finish behind the goal – their last ball could be shocking! So, we used to bring the two of them back in the afternoons and work on the overlapping full-back system. Erich sending Arthur to the bye-line, or getting past Arthur to do the same. We would work on cut-backs, near-post balls, far-post balls and we did that for months, to the extent that the two of them became internationalists. I think Arthur was an Under-23 international and played for the Scottish League, whereas Erich won full honours, but there's no doubt Eddie Turnbull made them far better players. Erich was already a good defender – he was pacey and hard as nails, but once you got a wee bit of composure from him he was international-class."

Turnbull and Fraser marvelled at Erich's ability to propel throw-ins from the touchline and while the "long-ball game" was not in keeping with the generally swashbuckling style of Turnbull's Tornadoes, it was a useful weapon that the manager was happy to utilise. Turnbull would work on Erich's range of throw-ins and his accuracy, and soon teammates would know exactly where the ball would be coming and how to get on the end of these Howitzers.

Goalkeeper Jim McArthur recalls, "We used to do a lot of training on the long throw. We got so many goals from that, including the first goal in the 7–0 game against Hearts. We worked so hard on functional training. People used to say to us, 'You guys are telepathic,' but we used to work at it every morning with Turnbull. In training, we used to do the long throw with Alan Gordon at the front post. I had my back four in front of me trying to defend it, but if it was done right it was virtually impossible. Erich could launch it to the back post too – it wasn't like a corner, it was better than a corner. Erich's accuracy was frightening; he could put it right on a spot. It's a weapon that hasn't changed – look at Rory Delap."

Jimmy O'Rourke, the prolific striker in the Tornadoes team, says, "We would work at throw-ins, which was Erich's specialty. When we got throws on the left Erich could launch the ball to either post, but when we got throws on the other side it was usually thrown straight up the line by John Brownlie. We knew when to peel off, where to run to, who would make the runs, and how to adapt to a Plan B if our opponents got wise to our methods. We would just keep at it – each day, a half-hour here, a half-hour there, until it became second nature for us to get on the end of Erich's throws."

"The long throw was something Erich brought with him to Hibs, but I think it became even better with some coaching," agrees John Fraser. "Erich was like an Adonis when he was stripped, so it wasn't a shock for him to be a long-thrower. When we did any of the physical stuff it was a piece of cake for him. Medicine balls, press-ups, step-ups – Erich was the leader in every exercise. Arthur Duncan was known as 'The Flyer', and he was the only one who could match Erich for pace. We used to do what we called interval running back and forward, timed, but at the end of that we would have a race – the whole length of the park. I remember before the race everyone was saying The Flyer will win. But Schaedler could always beat him over the length of the park. Arthur was probably faster over a shorter distance and in terms of acceleration, but over the length of the pitch, Erich's determination would usually get him there first. These sprints were competitive and everyone wanted to win it, but Erich would win more often than not.

"Erich and Arthur were funny lads, extremely nice and polite, both of them. Like Erich, Arthur could be quiet sometimes, a bit of a loner. Erich and Arthur Duncan were sometimes roommates when we went away for European games or short breaks. They were the odd couple. You could pair them off quite easily, but they were the odd couple – they were well suited together. The rest of the lads were maybe a bit more street-wise and they would come in and say to me, 'What day this week is going to be the hard day at training?' I would tell Eddie Turnbull some things, if it affected the team in any way, but there were things I saw and heard that went no further. I had to juggle the trust of the manager with the trust of the team.

"Eddie would ask me, 'What are they saying today?' I would say, 'They're asking me which day it will be this week that they are going to get hammered,' and Eddie would say, 'Tell them fuck all! They only want to know so they can organise their bevvy day.'

"Pat Stanton and I had been roommates when I was a player so I knew what was going on, all the dodges. Half a dozen of them, the Edinburgh boys, were very close-knit, but even though Erich and Arthur were a bit different, they were still highly popular guys within the dressing room."

Jimmy O'Rourke, the prolific goalscorer in that Tornadoes team, laughs at Turnbull's efforts to try and discover what his players were doing and saying behind his back. "Turnbull used to say to us, 'I know what you do, I know where you go,' but he'd been a player himself and we'd heard a few stories about him too, so there was an understanding there, even though we knew who was boss."

O'Rourke agrees that Schaedler and Duncan were individuals, and different from the Edinburgh-born players. "Erich was a bit of a loner in some ways. He had his own interests," says O'Rourke, who was later his assistant manager when Erich returned to Hibs for a second spell with the club. "He was the fittest player I have ever seen – both training with him and training him as a coach. He was ultra-fit. Wee [Alex] Edwards used to turn to you at training, with Erich miles ahead, and say, 'Look at that ****. Tell him to slow down.' And I would say, 'You tell him!'

"At the far side of the pitch at Easter Road, in front of the Cowshed, we used to set up a head tennis court where the eighteen-yard box is. There was a player Denis Nelson – who had played for Melbourne as well – and Erich broke his leg by accident. They were just going for a ball and they collided. Erich was so hell-bent on getting the ball that he smashed into him accidentally. He just had an incredible will to win, even if it was head tennis.

"Tom Hart would take us away for end-of-season trips to Spain and Erich would sometimes wander away himself, he just had different interests to us. But he was one of these guys you would far rather have with you than against you. He'd still have a laugh and a joke, but he had different outlook on life. Most of us were a bit daft. My wife's brother Rory has got a pub in Peebles and Erich's dad used to drink there – and he seems to have been the same type of character as Erich. It was probably that he came from the Borders and was more used to the country life than we were. Erich always had beautiful dogs with him. The only dugs that we kent were running at Powderhall!"

For Turnbull and Fraser and the rest of the coaching team, it must have been immensely satisfying to see Schaedler and Duncan make such giant strides as footballers. It was a just reward for all the hard work they were willing to put in on the training ground, as well as the players. While the coaching ethos was all about keeping football simple, Turnbull and his staff nevertheless went to considerable lengths to study the strengths and weaknesses of their team, eke out improvement and get them all working within an intelligent and considered attacking tactical system. "That was Eddie Turnbull's forte – coaching players, being there with them, and walking and talking them through their game," says Fraser. "He was always working on it from week to week, he never stood still and thought his work was done with a certain player.

"Erich was the one player who benefited from functional training. He didn't know so much about the functional, technical side of the game at first because he was so raw when he came to Hibs. But, my God, he was willing to learn.

"The training routine was broadly similar most weeks. Sometimes the players would be given a Monday off, on Tuesday they would get hammered with the physical stuff. On the Wednesday and Thursday we would concentrate on what we called coaching sessions, then Friday was a case of sharpening up for the game on the Saturday. We would work the back four continually, and do waves of attack, six against four, repeat, repeat, repeat. It's amazing how you could sometimes put eleven players against a back four, and if the back four is properly balanced and coached it's hard to score against them."

It wasn't just the defence who benefited from these training drills. Looking back, Jimmy O'Rourke appreciates how Turnbull's methods improved his game too. "When Willie MacFarlane was manager I felt he was too fond of the long ball. I used to complain to him, 'Why are we playing forty-yard balls – they are World Cup balls – just play short passes!' But Eddie Turnbull did things differently. He would work a lot with the back four and Erich was a quick learner. He worked out how to play in tandem with John Brownlie, and soon they had the awareness when it was time to bomb forward and when it was right to stay – especially John Brownlie.

"In these defence v forward training sessions we used to play with six against four and there were days that, whatever we did, we just couldn't score against them. They were so well drilled.

Football is all about repetitions. The dimensions of the pitch are always the same, the size of the goalposts is always the same; it's about finding different ways to exploit space and getting beyond opponents, and Eddie would work us hard to do that.

"We would also work on something Eddie called 'waves of attack' – six forwards against four defenders in waves of attack. Erich use to excel in these drills, he had so much pace and his powers of recovery were excellent. Erich had qualities to compensate for other areas that he wasn't so hot. If he ever got exposed, he had the pace to recover.

"We used to train at Hunters Hall in Niddrie and Tam McNiven was the best trainer I ever had – we were always well warmed-up before every session, before we then got down to the hard stuff, then down to the small-sided games. We would break down into three v one in small boxes. We would also work on 'give it and go'. Turnbull would come up to you and say, 'What are you admiring the pass for, give it and go!' Boom, boom, boom – passes had to be played fast. The defenders were taught to shut you down quick. It was hard training, but with just rewards. All that hard work produced some spectacular results on the pitch, so there was no grumbling – we could see it was working

"Turnbull was a stickler for discipline too. He wanted you to look good as well as play well. He wouldn't let you wear the strip over the pants. I would stick on a pair of training shorts instead of the regular ones and he would go mad. Turnbull got the best out of players. He made everyone a better player, including me."

Turnbull's carefully structured pre-season training was another reason for the team's great success. "First day was always up Arthur's Seat to do the hard, lung-bursting, cardiac stuff, then we would beat at Hunters Hall," says O'Rourke. "We would also be down at Marine Drive, that was our base. I liked it down there, there was lots of room, and we did a lot of hard stuff down there too. Then we would move on to ball work and then pre-season games."

John Fraser agrees: "Eddie Turnbull used to do pre-season training that was better than anyone, so much so that we won the Drybrough Cup two seasons running. That was organised before the season started and Hibs were always the fittest team. They ran over Celtic twice in Drybrough Cup finals at Hampden because they were fitter.

"No other club did this, but at Christmas and New Year we would have another mini 'pre-season' – really hard sessions for about three or four weeks. We gave them another hammering, but it was all done with Tom McNiven's supervision, we didn't go over the top. After all the hard work was done we would always give them the ball at the end, give them a game so they leave the training ground quite happy. Once they were fit, we would then think about the technical stuff.

"Tom McNiven, the physio and trainer, was a great guy to have around the place – his methods were fantastic and, like Eddie, he was ahead of his time. He was on the receiving end of a few practical jokes, mind you. On the day of big European games we would come in in the afternoon and just do some light stuff, walking through moves and so on. The back four would be myself, the other coaches Wilson Humphreys and Bertie Auld, and Tom McNiven. We lined up as a back four just to let things happen for the players and to walk them through a few moves, with Eddie coaching from the sidelines.

"Tom McNiven used to love that, feeling like a player and getting involved. Tom would come out and he would just have a pair of what we called flatties [trainers] on and Tam would be sliding about all over the place. So Eddie said to him, 'Next time, make sure you have your fuckin' pingers [your boots] on.' All the players loved that, Tam getting a row from Eddie. So the next time Tam came in wearing his flatties but under his arm he had his pingers. He put them on top of the dugout while we were doing the warm-up, so Ned said, 'Right, let's get down to business then.' So Tam went over to get his pingers and they weren't there – Erich Schaedler had taken them and hid them away somewhere. Everyone realised what was happening, everyone except Tom! This was right before a big European tie, so it was great to relax the players; they were all pissing themselves laughing as Tam searched high and low for his missing boots with Eddie barking at him. He was in and out the dugout, away into the dressing room, all over the ground, looking for his missing pingers. They were good times, and that's the type of guy Erich was – he was up for fun all the time."

Erich had impressed his coaches with his attitude and application to training and when it came to match days, he was similarly easy to instruct and motivate. Turnbull also liked the steely side to Schaedler and the way he complemented the silkier qualities of his fellow full-back over on the right, John Brownlie. Erich knew his job in any given game and he usually carried it out to the letter. "There wasn't much that needed to be said to Erich," says Fraser. "You couldn't alter the physical side of his game. You didn't need to say to Erich, 'Sort him out' – whoever played against Erich got sorted out. That wasn't a problem. His biggest problem before we really started to coach him intensively was when you got him on an overlap.

"Alex Cropley and Alex Edwards were great passers of a ball. Edwards could switch play from right to left and it was either Arthur or Erich who would benefit from that. Alex Edwards could ping a ball from one half of the park to the other and put it right on your toe, so these two would get clear many, many times, but it was the end product that was sometimes the problem. Arthur scored a lot of goals, but Erich only scored a handful – although from what I remember, the goals that he did score were usually quite special. He was never known as a goalscorer, though. When he did score it would usually be the result of a rampage into the box rather than him being involved in classical moves. Wee Cropley and Edwards were the creative players in the team and Erich wasn't involved so much in the intricate build-up play. But he was always encouraged to go forward.

"John Brownlie was the class act on the other side of the pitch, the opposite to Erich in some ways. John wasn't a physical guy the way Erich was. He was very classy, though."

Striker Tony Higgins says Erich was one of the great examples of the magic Eddie Turnbull could work with a player. "Eddie was a magnificent coach way beyond his time. What Eddie recognised in Erich was the raw talent he possessed," says Higgins. "He wasn't as naturally gifted as Brownlie on the other side, but he worked both of them equally hard. With Brownlie he worked on his defensive technique and his ability to link up going forward. With Erich he worked on his overall awareness of how to defend, because Erich had all the natural attributes – he could get up and down the pitch all the time with his phenomenal energy, so that was not a problem – but he worked on his game awareness. He would spend endless hours on him and it worked: he got a cap. If you had seen him at Stirling Albion he had come a long, long way. Erich had been at Easter Road a year or two before I arrived in 1972, but during my time the development in him as a player was absolutely incredible. You could see him improving before your eyes. Eddie and the coaches would have him back in the afternoon for extra work, but Erich was always willing. Most players in those days almost saw that as punishment, but Erich lapped it up.

"Turnbull worked and worked on Erich, and eventually made him an international player. I'm sure Erich would have recognised that he would not have got near playing for Scotland without Eddie's influence, particularly at that time because you looked at that team in 1974, arguably our best group of players ever. Erich was immensely proud of that. We used to wind him up saying the 'international team must be bad if you're getting a cap' but he was so proud. He always had the chest puffed out, but that made him puff it out that bit further. It was incredible because for a guy with limited ability to get that far, I put that down to Erich's hard work and Turnbull's hard work. Erich already had that incredible athleticism, but Turnbull made him a player. Turnbull believed what has been proven in the modern game: the fitness has to be right and players have to be athletes. Erich was a player coached from very basic standards to an international player – Turnbull recognised the raw ingredients he was working with and added to that, adding game awareness and his idea on how to defend properly.

"In later years, Eddie did something similar with Jackie McNamara. His injury had maybe slowed him down a little, but Eddie worked on Jackie's game and allowed him to adapt as a sweeper. Eddie coached Erich to be a specialist in his chosen position. That was Eddie's forte though, looking at the raw material and then saying to himself, 'I can make this boy a better player than he is.' I'm sure Erich appreciated what Turnbull did for him and I know the respect he had for him."

Fraser said Erich was the perfect professional to have around – at training and on match days. "Before the games Erich was good for the dressing room, full of fun, giggling and laughing. You know how some players take the piss out of each other – you didn't want to go too far and take the piss out of Erich! They knew not to step over the line with him, everyone was very respectful. He was full of fun, but well respected among the players. If they were going out for a pint and there was any trouble, Erich would sort it out. He was like their private security guard! He wasn't a drinker and I never heard of him getting into any trouble."

10

# SEASON OF WONDERS

Eddie Turnbull's exciting Hibs team had emerged as serious challengers to the domestic dominance Celtic had enjoyed in the early 1970s, and although the capital side had been firmly put in their place in the 1972 Scottish Cup final, that lopsided result only served to make the Easter Road squad mentally stronger. They had tasted a Cup final at Hampden, and they wanted more. To a man they were determined that the M8 would become a well-worn road for them in their quest to bring back some silverware.

They did not have to wait long. Turnbull's meticulous fitness regime ensured Hibs' stamina and sharpness was superior to many of their rivals. After doing the hard yards up Arthur's Seat, Marine Drive or Portobello beach, the back four of Brownlie, Schaedler, Black and Blackley pleasingly kept three clean sheets in five days on their pre-season jaunt to Ireland against Home Farm (2–0), Waterford (2–0) and Cork Hibs (0–0) and when they returned to Scotland for the curtain-raiser to the 1972/73 season, the Drybrough Cup, they were hungry for action.

Montrose were brushed aside 4–0 in the opening round then Hibs over-ran Rangers days later, Alan Gordon scoring two in a 3–0 win to set up a Hampden final with Celtic – just weeks after their humbling experience in the Scottish Cup.

An astonishing game unfolded in the 1972 Drybrough Cup final between two teams hell-bent on attack. An experimental relaxation of the offside rule – where players could not be offside unless they were inside the eighteen-yard box, led to a glut of goals. Hibs came flying out the blocks and raced into a 3–0 lead through a double from Alan Gordon and an own goal from Billy McNeill. A drunken pitch invasion by Celtic supporters broke Hibs' concentration, and they then contrived to squander their lead – McNeill scoring at the right end, and Jimmy Johnstone netting a double to take the final into extra-time. The outstanding levels of fitness Hibs had already built up from a typically sharp Turnbull pre-season came to the fore in the thirty additional minutes of play, and goals from Jimmy O'Rourke and Arthur Duncan settled a rousing final 5–3 in Hibs' favour. True, it was "only" the Drybrough Cup, but the competition carried plenty of prestige and the 50,000 attendance at the final proves it was a Cup well worth winning. The victorious Hibs team were delighted to take the trophy back to Easter Road and there is no doubt it fuelled their desire for further success.

Spurred on by their confidence-boosting Drybrough Cup success, Hibs won five out of their six matches in their League Cup section, but to Turnbull's irritation the only match they lost was at his previous club, Aberdeen. The manager's mood darkened further when Hibs returned to Pittodrie for their opening league fixture of the season and again lost, Dons striker Joe Harper scoring the only goal of the game. The stocky match-winner perhaps prompted Turnbull to make a mental note of his capabilities, as the pair would before long be working together at Easter Road. Hibs quickly made amends for their slip-ups in the North-East with a solid derby win over Hearts, Alex Cropley and Pat Stanton scoring in a 2–0 win at Easter Road.

Hibs were back on an even keel in the league, but another campaign was starting – the European Cup-Winners' Cup – and the first round draw had not been kind. Powerful Portuguese club Sporting Lisbon were the opponents, and playing in a new away kit of purple shirts with white sleeves, Hibs lost 2–1 in the Alvalade Stadium. Arthur Duncan's away goal at least allowed a measure of optimism for the return leg. Some observers had tipped Hibs to edge through narrowly, but there was nothing slender about their win over the Portuguese – wearing natty all-green "European" jerseys, they romped to an astonishing 6–1 victory, Jimmy O'Rourke scoring a hat-trick in one of his finest displays for the club.

Just after Sporting had been put to the sword, Hibs again showed their appetite for cup football by progressing past Dundee United in the League Cup, 5–2 on aggregate. Hibs were becoming a joy to watch, goalkeeper, defence, midfield and attack all contributing to an all-action style of play and working together like a well-oiled machine. The League Cup quarter-final first leg saw Hibs hit another team for six – Airdrie this time, then just for good measure the dazed Diamonds were punished again 5–2 in the league days later, thanks to another O'Rourke treble. In the Cup-Winners' Cup Albanian side Besa were never likely to pose the same threat as Sporting Lisbon, and Hibs destroyed their bewildered visitors 7–1 at Easter Road. Goalscorer supreme O'Rourke was in the form of his life and bagged his second successive European hat-trick and his third inside a month. Supporters quickly coined a catchy song in his honour, to the tune of the "Rupert the Bear Song" ("Jimmy, Jimmy O'Rourke, everyone knows his name"), and he was one of the firm favourites on the terracing.

The second leg of Hibs' European tie against Besa may have been a formality, but the trip to impoverished Albania proved to be a real eye-opener for the squad. The country was under the fierce grip of leader Enver Hoxha and the Albanian people had grown used to a desperately harsh regime where secret police reported back to the communist state and political opponents disappeared. This iron rule meant the Hibs travelling party – a group of long-haired footballers from the "West" – was viewed with a mixture of fear, curiosity and suspicion when they arrived in the city of Kavaje on the coast of the Adriatic Sea.

Erich's best friend Bobby Robertson was in the squad and the goalkeeper has colourful memories of a unique trip. "The trip to

Albania was like no other," he says. "Most of the time we were confined to the hotel because Albania was still quite a dangerous place, but we were allowed to go for out a walk. Me, Erich and a few of other lads couldn't wait to get out and went for a wee stroll. Just as we were coming back up the road towards the back of the hotel, there were a couple of armed guards standing in booths with big machine guns strapped to them. They didn't speak English but they were gesturing to us that you weren't allowed to walk on the road, you had to stick to the pavement. So as we got close to them Erich walked right up to one of them and started to talk to him. The guard's face was absolutely deadpan, and he stuck the gun in Erich's stomach, trying to order him away, but instead of being freaked out by it Erich was just laughing and joking – he wasn't fazed in the slightest. Thankfully, the guards let us get on our way and get back to the hotel. I didn't fancy going back and trying to explain to Eddie Turnbull that Erich had got involved in an argument with a machine gun."

Robertson was handed a surprise first taste of European football when Jim Herriot picked up a leg injury during the match and was forced to come off. Besa were playing for pride and they took the lead, but Alan Gordon ensured Hibs salvaged a draw on the night. "After the game we ended up in a nightclub in the hotel, down in the basement," says Robertson. "I say nightclub, but it was unofficial, and we just stumbled in, really – myself, Erich and Derek Spalding. When we went down the steps there was a band playing – a guy with a squeeze-box and another guy on the drums – and there were lots of locals up dancing. But the moment we walked in everyone stopped and the place fell silent. I don't know if it was because they thought we were secret police, because we found out later that the gathering was illegal and they probably had every reason to be frightened and suspicious. But they soon realised that we were no threat to them and they took to us.

"I used to play the guitar, so the guy allowed me to play. I played 'House of the Rising Sun' by The Animals and all the locals got up and started dancing again. Erich got this old woman up and he was dancing away as well. It was bizarre, playing 'House of the Rising Sun' in an illegal Albanian nightclub, with Erich dancing to it with an Albanian pensioner!"

Back in Scotland, whipping boys Airdrie, no doubt sick of the sight of the green and white shirts of Hibs, turned up at Easter Road for the second leg of the League Cup quarter-final, and lost 4–1, meaning Hibs had put fifteen goals past them in three quick-fire games. By thrashing Airdrie 10–3 on aggregate, Hibs were in the semi-finals of another major competition, where they would face the stiffer challenge of a clash with Rangers at Hampden. In a dress rehearsal the weekend before the semi-final, Rangers won 2–1 at Easter Road in the league. But when it came to the League Cup, Hibs defended magnificently and found an unlikely match-winner in John Brownlie, who grabbed the only goal of the game. Turnbull's side were the talk of Scotland. They already had the Drybrough Cup in the trophy cabinet and were now mounting a serious challenge on three fronts – the league, the Cup-Winners' Cup, and the League Cup – with the Scottish Cup still to come.

Excitement in Edinburgh was at fever pitch as Hibs again squared up to Celtic at Hampden. On the day of the Cup final, the *Pink News* handed Erich the honour of stepping into the spotlight as their weekly "Sportsman on Parade". The Q&A feature gives an insight into Erich's personality at that time, and interestingly and perhaps out of deference (or fear) to his current manager, he opted for Eddie Turnbull rather than Willie MacFarlane as the "biggest influence" on his career. On the brink of glory in a national Cup final, who could blame him?

Here's how Erich responded to his list of questions:

*Height:* 5ft 8in
*Weight:* 11st
*Age:* 23
*Date of birth:* 6/8/49

*Married:* Yes, wife's name is Isa. Daughter Tracey (18 months)
*Car:* Vanden Plas
*Favourite player:* Pat Stanton
*Most memorable match:* Winning the Drybrough Cup final
*Biggest thrill:* Signing for Hibs
*Biggest disappointment:* Losing the Scottish Cup final to Celtic
*Best country visited:* Germany
*Favourite food:* Steak and chips
*Miscellaneous likes:* Driving and shooting
*Miscellaneous dislikes:* Smoky rooms, long bus journeys
*Favourite TV show:* Colditz Story
*Favourite singer:* Rod Stewart
*Biggest influence on career:* Eddie Turnbull, Hibs manager
*Best friend:* My brother
*Biggest drag in sport:* Losing
*International honours:* None
*Personal and professional ambitions:* To be a better player, and to help Hibs win some honours

Erich's stated ambition of winning some honours was being realised just as the *Pink News* was hitting the newstands in Edinburgh. Despite their blistering early-season form, Hibs were still rated underdogs against a Celtic team desperate to atone for their embarrassing 4–1 defeat in the 1971 League Cup final against Partick Thistle. But Hibs had a score to settle of their own. And a much bigger one. The 6–1 thumping in the Scottish Cup final might have left some teams quaking in their boots at the thought of facing the same team responsible for handing out such a hiding, but Eddie Turnbull had shrewdly used that bitter experience to his advantage. He instilled in every one of his players that this was their chance for revenge. Fail to take it and that 6–1 defeat would haunt them forever. Take it and they would be Hibs heroes forever. They did not let him down.

After a keenly contested but goalless first half, Hibs made the breakthrough on the hour mark. Alex Edwards showed great awareness to flight a quick free-kick for Pat Stanton to score, and then Stanton turned provider with a wonderful cross for Jimmy O'Rourke to head home. Kenny Dalglish pulled a goal back for Celtic, but Hibs fought like tigers to ensure the cup would be theirs. Footage from the match shows animated captain Stanton, at the final whistle, first sportingly shaking hands with the Celtic team and then ordering his teammates over in front of the Hibs end to salute their supporters. It was that kind of selfless gesture that makes Stanton one of the greatest to have ever graced the club.

It was Hibs' first win in a national Cup competition since 1902 and their first at the present-day Hampden Park. It was truly a momentous achievement. The Hibs heroes that lined up that day were: Herriot, Brownlie, Schaedler, Stanton, Black, Blackley, Edwards, O'Rourke, Gordon, Cropley and Duncan. Ted Brack remembers that Erich was partly to blame for the Celtic consolation goal, but true to his character, it only made him even more determined to see out the final stages. "Hibs were well on top in the League Cup final when Erich made an error with eight minutes to go which allowed Kenny Dalglish to run through and make the score 2–1. Shades was clearly annoyed with himself but he kept his composure and defended brilliantly for the time remaining, and Hibs saw the game out comfortably. A lesser player and weaker character would have let his mistake get to him. Erich didn't."

*The Scotsman*'s John Rafferty, who always championed Eddie Turnbull's admirable brand of attacking football, also lauded the Hibs back four for standing firm against Celtic: "In the end, the merits of Hibs as a team brought the cup to Easter Road. Nowhere did this show more than in defence. Hibs' organisation there far surpassed that of Celtic. Right across the back through Brownlie, Black, that happy competitor Blackley and the under-rated but staunch Schaedler, there was good covering."

Keeper Jim Herriot agrees that Erich and his fellow defenders were immense that day, but for him Pat Stanton was the dominant hero. "When I look back at the video now, I didn't have to do too much," he says. "I think I only had one real save to make in the second half and a couple of crosses to deal with. What a game it was though. Celtic were in it all right, but we just annihilated them. They were a great side, but that day we surpassed them. That was Pat Stanton's final – he was all over the place, running, running, covering every inch of the pitch. When we went back to the North British Hotel in Edinburgh afterwards, I had severe stomach cramps, probably because of all the nervous tension, and I had to go out for a walk. But we had a nice meal and all the wives and girlfriends were there. It was one big party."

Before setting off back along the M8 with the cup being passed around on the bus, an elated Eddie Turnbull held court with the press, and told them, "I'm very happy for these players. They have worked hard and they needed this cup to show them there was reward in work. Now they can look at it and feel it and know it's theirs. They won it by their own efforts. It will be a great thing for them. They can start from here. They have no tie in the European Cup-Winners' Cup till March and they will be striving to be at the top of the league by that date. There is much more to them, and this cup will bring it out."

Turnbull was bursting with pride, and so too was the man who appointed him, Tom Hart. Rafferty made generous reference to the unsung hero, a hands-on chairman who had made it his ultimate goal to return Hibs to the forefront of Scottish football: "Tom Hart, the managing director, moved around with remarkable composure and restraint. His must have been the ultimate in satisfaction. He had supported the club like a fanatic in the great days of the Famous Five and suffered in the bad days since. He had taken over the club and reorganised it. Seldom can such satisfaction have befallen a supporter."

Some teams may have rested on their laurels after such a result. Some might even have been slightly affected by over-indulging in a week of celebrations. But Turnbull made sure his team kept their feet on the ground and made them focus on the job in hand. Their first match after the Cup final – with the same eleven Hampden heroes starting – was an exhilarating feast of football. Ayr United were the unwitting victims as Hibs pulverised them 8–1 – O'Rourke grabbed yet another hat-trick, as did Alan Gordon, in Stanton and Cropley also chipping in goals. It was whispered, but Hibs were championship contenders and, having beaten Celtic in the League Cup, Jock Stein's side were casting nervous glances towards the east.

Celtic had an early chance to try and put Hibs in their place when the teams met two days before Christmas, but they needed a late Kenny Dalglish goal to salvage a 1–1 draw against the form team in Scotland.

In the build-up to Christmas 1972 Erich was finally able to defy Turnbull and wear a beard . . . albeit it was a fluffy white one, as he played Santa at the children's party organised by the Scottish Football Referees' Association in Inch Community Centre. Fielding a settled team had been the key to Hibs' consistency and forty-eight hours before they were due to face Hearts, they warmed up for the 1973 New Year's Day derby with a 3–2 win at home to Aberdeen. The same evening of the win over Aberdeen, the *Pink News* ran a feature on Erich, calling him "The Iron Man of Easter Road", describing him as one of the most consistent defenders in Scotland and paying tribute to his improvement under Turnbull. Reflecting on a successful year, Erich said, "1972 has been a good year for me, a good year for everybody at Easter Road. I feel my game has improved and I am glad to be part of the Hibs set-up."

The report added, "Schaedler, always fast and hard, has developed in his distribution and positional play and frequently shows there is more than one Easter Road full-back who can go forward. He is regarded as something of an 'iron man' by his colleagues. Schaedler shrugs off injuries and you know it must be fairly serious if any knock demands attention. Few players have made such headway in a fairly short space of time and he deserves credit for working so zealously at the game."

Hibs were already on the crest of a wave when they headed to Tynecastle on New Year's Day. Life couldn't get much better, could it? A ninety-minute masterclass from Turnbull's Tornadoes showed it most definitely could. Hibs scored seven goals without reply against their arch-rivals in what has been immortalised as the club's "greatest game in history". Hearts actually had the better of the opening exchanges, but when Jimmy O'Rourke scored in the ninth minute he opened the floodgates. Alan Gordon added a second in the fifteenth minute, then Arthur Duncan scored two either side of an obligatory Alex Cropley strike against Hearts to make it 5–0 at half-time. Ruthlessly Turnbull implored his team at half-time to show no mercy, to go for the jugular. Hearts put up more resistance in the second half, but Hibs got a sixth in the fifty-sixth minute when O'Rourke cheekily helped himself to a goal-bound Stanton shot. The seventh and final goal is the moment many Hibs supporters remember Erich for best. If you could boil down to one single moment, something that typified the Schaedler spirit, then this was it.

Picking the ball up just inside his own half and careering towards the MacLeod Street end of Tynecastle, Schaedler effortlessly glided past Donald Park. Then as he neared the edge of the box he tried to find his left-wing partner, Arthur Duncan. It was an over-hit pass attempted by a player running at full tilt. But as right-back Dave Clunie attempted to clear, he hadn't banked on Erich coming crashing into him at breakneck pace. Schaedler's crunching tackle – defying odds of around 70/30 against him – saw him do a full somersault practically over the shoulder of the bewildered Clunie. The ball broke kindly to the waiting Duncan, who looked up and lofted a cross to the back post for Alan Gordon to gracefully rise and head home the famous seventh goal.

Pat Stanton says, "The last goal at Tynecastle in the 7–0 game summed Erich up. You've got to remember, it's 6–0, the game is finished. Any player could be forgiven for easing off a little bit. A lot of players would have just let the ball go, but he didn't. If you could sum Erich up in one moment, that was it. He had over-run the ball, and he wasn't really entitled to win it. A lot of guys would have turned away and given it up as a lost cause. Maybe I would have turned away, but not Erich – and it ended up in the Hearts net. In all the years of him playing and what he achieved, that one moment summed it up. If you speak to Davie Clunie right now, he would admire that. Davie was a good competitor too. Davie was no shirker, so you had two guys going for it, and I'm sure Davie even now was glad it was that way – they were two committed guys and they had plenty of respect for each other."

Clunie has nothing but respect for Erich, but he insists he doesn't remember the incident! "I honestly have no recollection," he laughs. "We were 6–0 down at the time, so I didn't really have time to admire it! What I will say is that Erich was a super player. He was one of the strongest and fastest full-backs around. He was a really fit guy and a great professional.

"The Hibs and Hearts players had a lot of respect for each other back then. They had a fantastic team – probably the best they had since the days of Gordon Smith and Lawrie Reilly – and I guess they should have won more Cups than they did. We took a hiding that day, but we did get a bit of revenge the next time we played them, beating them 4–1."

Clunie's teammate in the 7–0 game, Jim Jefferies, who went on to become a Hearts legend as player and manager, would prefer to talk about the 4–1 game than the New Year's Day mauling. But like Clunie, he had nothing but respect and admiration for Schaedler. "They were knocking them in for fun, they were a tremendous side and suffice to say nothing really went for us that day," says Jefferies. "Ian Sneddon had failed a fitness test before the game and Davie Clunie was switched from left-back to right-back, so I got a late call to come in at left-back. The New Year's Day games were great occasions, even if that result was a blow!"

Jefferies adds, "Erich's biggest asset was that he was a tremendous competitor. He was strong in the tackle and very quick."

Hearts striker Donald Ford had come close with a couple of early efforts before the Hibs goal glut began, and he believes Turnbull's side was one of the most complete teams we have seen in Scottish football. Ford, who was Schaedler's Scotland teammate at the 1974 World Cup, said, "That was an excellent Hibs team and it is one of the mysteries that they did not go on and win more trophies than they actually did. They were almost perfect in every position. Erich was an extremely energetic and enthusiastic left-back. Anyone who played against Erich would leave the field after ninety minutes fully aware that they had been in a hard tussle. In football these days there is a lot of cheating behind the referee's back, but players like Erich, Billy McNeill and John Greig were hard and fair – they were never involved in anything untoward. Erich was very quick too – he was a difficult guy to play against. That whole team were difficult to play against, especially that day."

Ted Brack, watching from the Tynecastle terracing that day, says the tackle which led to the seventh goal capped an outstanding performance from Schaedler, albeit there were another ten outstanding performances that day too. "In the 7–0 game, Erich took the early initiative with some driving runs forward. His long throw led to Jimmy O'Rourke's first goal and his crunching tackle on Dave Clunie won the ball for Arthur Duncan to cross for Alan Gordon to score the seventh goal."

Bill Barclay, the Radio Forth DJ, was also there. "The tackle in the 7–0 game sums him up," says Barclay, who would get to know Erich well in his capacity as stadium announcer in the Radio Hibs booth at Easter Road in the Seventies. "He had so much momentum going into a tackle that he would sometimes somersault over. I never actually got into that game until Hibs were 3–0 up. I was late arriving and we were all queuing up waiting to get in. Thankfully, a load of Hearts supporters were coming out and not surprisingly told us to f**k off when we asked what the score was. I did eventually get in and still saw four goals – what a day – and the weird thing was Hearts never played too bad.

"Erich was a great player, and one the fans could identify with. If you're watching the game as a fan, you kick every ball with the players and you would give your all if you could be transported onto that pitch. Erich was like one of us in that respect, he was a 100 per cent man, he didn't want to let anyone down. He played for the jersey and gave his all. He was so fast and he would go in hard."

John Fraser, sitting in the dugout alongside a jubilant Turnbull, watched Schaedler rob Clunie of the ball and expected nothing else from a player as passionate and as fierce as Schaedler. "You see players nowadays, they slide in on their backsides and try and protect themselves in a tackle; Erich didn't go in like that – he went right in with his whole body. You could see it coming too, watching on from the sidelines, about four yards before impact you would wince and think to yourselves, 'Somebody's gonna get hurt here and it's no going to be Erich.'"

Fraser has revealed how a spying mission before the New Year's derby exposed a glaring frailty in Bob Seith's Hearts side: "My role was to go and watch the team we would be playing the next week and then give a full report to Eddie Turnbull," says Fraser. "When we beat the Hearts 7–0, I went to see them the week before. Hearts were at home and they played without a left-winger that day. So I remember compiling my report and saying, 'Under no circumstances will Hearts play without a left-winger against Hibs and give John Brownlie and maybe Alex Edwards the freedom of that side of the park.' You wouldn't believe it, Brownlie and Edwards ran amok down that side of the park and Hearts DID play without a left-winger. They got crucified."

Brownlie excelled in the 7–0 game and he says Schaedler also had one of his best games for Hibs that day. "That 7–0 game he was brilliant, it really sticks in my mind the way he worked up and down that left-hand side. Erich Schaedler became brilliant for Hibs. Obviously Willie MacFarlane spotted what he might be able to become and brought him to Hibs, then Ned moulded him. He was Ned's type of player. He had been a physical player himself, so someone like Erich – who was so wholehearted – was exactly the type of player Ned would respond to and have the patience to work on. It must have been very satisfying for him as a coach to see how far he managed to help Erich progress. He saw a bit of himself in Erich. Eddie had been a forward but they shared that strong will to win. Plus, Erich had tremendous pace. He could get back at people; his powers of recovery were brilliant. He also played really well in the League Cup final too – not as good as Pat, of course – but I remember Erich was excellent too."

Erich was not a drinker, but he craved a celebratory pint when he returned home to Peebles to share the occasion with his brother John. It was just the Schaedlers' luck that the barman was a Hearts fan! "On the night of the 7–0 game, Erich was down in Peebles and was understandably cock-a-hoop," says John. "He said, 'Come on, we'll go into the Cross Keys for a pint and celebrate. We've beat the Hearts.' But when we walked in, the guy behind the bar was a Jambo and he wouldn't serve us. It was the first time I had been barred in my life!"

Beauty had been witnessed at Tynecastle, but the ugly side of the game was lurking days later when East Fife arrived at Easter Road. The Methil side – managed by a former Easter Road favourite Pat Quinn – had no doubt seen what Hibs had done to Hearts and were determined to stop Turnbull's side by any means. Their malice manifested itself when East Fife left-back Ian Printy went in over the top of the ball and broke John Brownlie's leg. As Brownlie left the field on the stretcher, Easter Road fell silent, a last-minute winner from Alan Gordon lifting their spirits, but not enough to mask the realisation that a vital cog in the Hibs wheel had been removed. After such a long run of unbroken team selection, Turnbull would be forced to make changes. Was Hibs' luck running out?

# 11

# SPLIT PERSONALITIES

After John Brownlie's leg break, Des Bremner was pitched in as his replacement, and he would go on to become an exceptional player in his own right. But the equilibrium had been broken. Hibs had swept to League Cup glory, the top of the table and a sensational 7–0 win over Hearts, all with a settled team. Now they had been forced into reshuffling the pack. Perhaps still affected by the mood of Brownlie's plight, Hibs turned in an uncharacteristically bad performance at Tannadice and lost 1–0 in the league to Dundee United – their first defeat in almost two months – then followed that up with a laboured 1–1 draw at home to Dundee. Schaedler did, however, manage to score his first league goal in a Hibs shirt – and with his right foot too – in a 3–1 victory at Muirton Park, the old home of St Johnstone, as Hibs limbered up for a mouth-watering Scottish Cup clash with Rangers at Ibrox.

These were the occasions Erich relished. Several former teammates testify to him coming alive for these matches – where baying Glasgow crowds of 40,000 or 50,000 added to the challenge. Hibs battled back to a 1–1 draw in Govan to force a replay, but in front of an enormous near-50,000 crowd at Easter Road, Rangers edged them out 2–1 to snuff out any hopes of a glorious Cup double.

There was another massive cup tie on the horizon, a European Cup-Winners' Cup quarter-final against Hajduk Split. The Yugoslav side had only just squeezed past Wrexham in the previous round, losing 3–1 at the Racecourse Ground but winning 2–0 on home turf to sneak the tie on the away goals rule. Armed with that knowledge, Eddie Turnbull was confident that his team could march past them to the semi-finals. They seemed destined to do just that, steamrollering their way into a 4–1 lead at Easter Road, but then losing another costly away goal late in the game.

Hibs at their best should have been well capable of defending a 4–2 lead in the second leg, but they were in for a tortuous night in the searing heat of Split. Not that Eddie Turnbull had any intention of playing defensively – the "D" word did not seem to feature in his vocabulary.

As Hibs touched down in a scorching Yugoslavia, Turnbull told the accompanying Scottish press pack, "Hibs will attack. There is no point in building a team that is geared to attack and then asking them to change for one particular game. We have a game on our hands only because of the mistake we made in Edinburgh. I see no reason why we should not be able to score against this team here."

When told that the local media were boldly forecasting a 3–0 win for Hajduk, Turnbull was unperturbed. "Our form was not all that good on Saturday but I make that just one bad game in more than fifty. I am happy with the form of the team and I have no injury worries at all."

There was fantastic news for Erich and four of his teammates on the day they arrived for the return-leg: along with John Blackley, Pat Stanton, Alan Gordon and Arthur Duncan, he had been named in Willie Ormond's Scottish League select squad to play their English counterparts at Hampden the following week. "I can only accept this as a tremendous compliment to the team and the effort the players have put into their game this season," said Turnbull. "I am particularly happy for Erich Schaedler and Alan Gordon, both of whom have improved so much and worked so hard."

Turnbull may have been relaxed when he arrived in what is now the second largest city in Croatia, but mischievous Split fans did all they could to unsettle the Hibs party on the eve of the match, letting off firecrackers outside their hotel and making as much din as possible.

The match was played before a fervent crowd of 25,000, with hundreds more perched on surrounding trees or standing on the buildings that bordered the ground. Fireworks were let off and newspapers set alight as the partisan crowd cranked up the atmosphere to fever pitch. Reporting on the bedlam John Rafferty, covering the game for *The Scotsman,* said, "The atmosphere quickly changed with the start and a deep chanting – or was it baying – had no hint of friendliness."

Although they were used to playing in front of hostile crowds at Celtic Park or Ibrox, Hibs had never played in anything quite so intimidating and it clearly affected their performance. Their usual slick passing style deserted them, and mistakes did not so much creep into their play as swamp it. They were also on the end of some brutal tackles as Split made it clear they were out to win at all costs. The usually unflappable Jim Herriot suffered the most, his nervy mishandling of cross balls effectively giving Split a couple of goals on a plate. Local hero Ivan Hlevnjak tormented Erich and the Hibs defence and he scored one of three goals as Hajduk wiped out then surpassed their visitors' first-leg lead. The other goals came from Ivica Surjak and a Blackley own goal. To compound a night of extreme misery, another over-zealous Hajduk challenge managed to destroy the seemingly indestructible, as Erich dislocated his shoulder and was forced to leave the pitch for the closing stages. Having been favourites to reach a European semi-final for the first time since they had blazed the trail for Britain in the 1955/56 European Cup, Hibs had instead succumbed to an epic failure. Turnbull was livid and accused his team of lacking heart.

The press pulled no punches either at Hibs' awful performance. Rafferty wrote, "A lamentable succession of mistakes sent Hibs out of the European Cup-Winners' Cup. Jim Herriot had a bad time and, as is the way for goalkeepers, his mistakes were vital, and with them went Hibs' lead of two goals. After fifty-two minutes, the dependable John Blackley kicked the ball into his own net when trying to clear a corner. Misery seemed complete for Hibs, but with three minutes to go, Erich Schaedler was tumbled heavily and carried from the field with a dislocated shoulder. It was a harrowing experience for the ambitious Hibs." *The Scotsman*'s sister paper, the *Evening News*, was similarly scathing, saying, "They will be hard pressed to pick up the pieces after the surrender in Split." Their reporter said of Herriot, "I cannot understand why the keeper refuses to wear a cap, for he was blinded by the sun and had to use his hands to shield his eyes when the ball was flashing into the danger zone."

Turnbull had acknowledged before the game that his side had only had "one bad game in fifty", but he overreacted when it all went horribly wrong in Split. The beginning of the end for Turnbull's Tornadoes can be traced back to that defeat. Never one to mince his words, Alex Edwards says now, "Turnbull flipped his lid after the Hajduk Split game. We had hammered them at Easter Road. We were 4–1 up with five minutes to go and lost a sloppy goal, and that came back to haunt us in the second game. Big Jim Herriot was a great keeper for us but he just had a bad day in the away game and we lost 3–0. But Turnbull took it out on the whole team."

Hibs arrived back under a cloud after their nightmare evening at Split, and while the inner fire of resentment and recrimination burned deep within a seething Turnbull, Erich's flight home was particularly painful. His dislocated collarbone had left him in agony on the plane home, and after a sleepless night he was sent to hospital to see a specialist and have X-rays taken. The Edinburgh *Evening News* reported the following day: "It was obvious on the return journey last night that the defender was in severe pain, and Schaedler doesn't complain unless there is something seriously wrong. It's cruel luck on Schaedler, who was in the Scottish League pool to meet the English League at Hampden next Tuesday, and it's bad luck on Hibs, whose two regular full-backs are on the casualty list. The good news from the X-rays was that his season was not over – there was no break and his recovery would not take long."

As well as missing the Scottish League match, Schaedler was out of Hibs' match against Rangers at Ibrox the Saturday after Split, and so too was Jim Herriot, Turnbull's scapegoat-in-chief for the Split debacle. To jettison Herriot, who never played again for Hibs, on the basis of one bad night was unbelievably harsh. The big keeper had been at the spine of the team in his two seasons at Easter Road, playing almost 100 games, and after one uncharacteristically poor performance he was being dropped like a stone. Back living now in his hometown of Chapelhall, the mellow Herriot can forgive Turnbull for his overreaction, insisting that his two years at Hibs were the "happiest of my career".

There was a ten-year age gap between Herriot and Schaedler, but he was very fond of his late teammate. "Erich was a nice boy, but he was very, very quiet. He was still part of the team and a good mixer, but just a quiet laddie," says Herriot, who moved to St Mirren after he left Easter Road. "When I was at Hibs he was still very young though, and he seems to have become more outgoing later in his career at Easter Road. But he was an absolutely terrific guy, on and off the field.

"The camaraderie within that squad was brilliant. We would work hard together on the training ground – under Eddie Turnbull there was no other way – stick together as a team on the pitch, and away from football we would all get together. We would have golfing days and while there was always a bit of leg-pulling and joking, it was all pure, clean fun. We just gelled really well together and the bigger personalities and the quieter guys like Erich complemented each other really well. They all had nicknames: I was Big Bob because they reckoned I looked like the film star Robert Mitchum, Erich was Shades, John Brownlie was Onion, John Blackley was Sloop, Alex Cropley was Sodjer because he came from a military background, Pat was Niddrie because he came from up that way, Arthur was The Flyer, Jim Black was Cilla, and Alex

Edwards . . . well, he was just a cheeky wee so and so! I had been with Alex at Dunfermline when he was only sixteen, and when I saw him at Hibs, I went, 'Aww no! I've got to look after you again!' He still phones me up now and asks if that's the 'world's worst goalie' on the line!

"Alex was one of the obvious talents in the team, but I felt Erich was very underrated. He could tackle, and when he got the ball he would bomb forward. He was great back-up on that side for Arthur Duncan, and those two could shift. All the players appreciated what Erich did for the team; he very seldom made mistakes.

"I remember one game though where I did lose my temper with Erich. Sloop was trying a few fancy things on the ball and when Erich saw him do it, he tried to do a bit of the same. He was being too casual on the ball and I started swearing at him – it was just my luck the ground had fallen silent at that exact moment. My wife was in the stand and when I went into the tearoom after the game she started giving me hell for my language.

"Erich was a nice lad, never any trouble, but a hard guy and very tough in the tackle. He very seldom got booked. You get booked these days if you even look at someone the wrong way. I think Erich would have been off a few times in this day and age."

In the first fixture after Split, against Rangers, Jim McArthur took the banished Herriot's place in a controversial match at Ibrox. It is worth noting that five of the starting XI had not played in the settled run of games in the build-up to the League Cup final and the 7–0 game – Turnbull was being forced to dig deep within his squad to try and keep the season on track. Tommy McLean scored the only goal of the game from what seemed a glaringly offside position, and so strong was the protest from John Blackley that he was given his marching orders. The red card and another defeat meant Hibs' problems were piling up.

Stuttering Hibs followed the defeat to Rangers with a grim 0–0 draw at home to Arbroath, and ahead of an away match at Falkirk there was incredible news from the treatment room: Schaedler declared himself fit and available . . . a little over two weeks after dislocating his collarbone. Reporting Erich's miraculous recovery, the *Evening News* said, "Erich Schaedler, the 'Iron Man of Easter Road', returns to the Hibs side against Falkirk tomorrow at Brockville, having taken what must be record time in shaking off his dislocated collarbone injury. Schaedler, stretchered off five minutes from the end of the Cup-Winners' Cup tie against Hajduk in Split on 21 March, has missed only two games – against Rangers and Arbroath (0–0) – and his return will give a boost to Hibs, who are hoping to end their current goal famine, having failed to find the net in their last three outings."

Alas, even the return of Erich failed to lift the flagging Hibs side, and they slumped to a 1–0 defeat at Falkirk. The lingering bad feeling caused by events in Split was still engulfing what was left of the season, and the remaining four league fixtures failed to yield a single victory.

Despite the incredible highs experienced in that halcyon month that straddled the turn of the year, the end of the 1972/73 season could not come quick enough for a mentally drained squad, and they closed it out by losing 3–0 at Parkhead to a highly motivated Celtic team, who needed the win to keep Rangers at bay and collect their eighth title in a row. As the Hibs players trudged back to the dressing room to leave the stage clear for Celtic to celebrate, they would know deep down that it could have been their title if their luck had held out. In the event, they finished a distant third, twelve points behind Celtic and eleven behind Rangers, although they at least had the consolation of qualifying for the UEFA Cup.

John Fraser says that if Hibs' luck had held out then the sky could have been the limit that season. Brownlie's broken leg and the collapse in Split had cost the club dear. "To me, that was the best Hibs team there has been," says Fraser. "I played with the Famous Five but they weren't a team, they were a forward line. The defence wasn't that clever. They were a Famous Five, but as a complete team, the Seventies team was the best Hibs team. I had played in the Sixties too, in the Jock Stein era, with Peter Cormack, Neily Martin and guys like that. That was a good team, but the Seventies team was a great team – although they didn't achieve what they should have done. They should definitely have won a European trophy; the Hajduk Split game was our big chance, 4–2 up going away from home and we lost 3–0."

Hibs may have limped home in the 1972/73 season, but Turnbull and all of his Tornadoes could be immensely proud of what they had achieved that season, including Erich. Schaedler had featured in fifty-six competitive matches, which would prove to be the highest number of games he managed in one season throughout his career. Erich's wholehearted approach to the game and his ultra-consistent form was not lost on the fans and he was rewarded with a couple of Player of the Year awards from supporters' clubs – no mean feat when you consider some of the achievements of his teammates during that stellar 1972/73 season, the unflappable Stanton and the prolific O'Rourke and Gordon especially.

Thankfully for Hibs, the summer break worked wonders for restoring morale, and the team mirrored their start of the previous year by hitting the ground running and again beating Rangers and Celtic en route to another Drybrough Cup success. The 1973 victory over Celtic at Hampden was nowhere near as thrilling as the epic of twelve months earlier, but a 1–0 win – secured with an Alan Gordon goal in the final minute of extra time – saw jubilant Hibs retain the cup.

Across all competitions, Hibs won nine of their first ten games in the 1973/74 season and perhaps that contributed to a rare outbreak of complacency when they headed back to Tynecastle to face Hearts on 8 September, just over eight months after the 7–0 game. Erich, it would seem, was as guilty as anyone in thinking that Hibs just needed to turn up to beat Hearts, but their arch-rivals were motivated for revenge, and they took it.

Erich's motor mechanic friend, Gordon McDougall, reveals that Schaedler was as guilty as any of the Hibs players of falling into the trap of thinking they had an easy afternoon ahead of them. "It was the first derby after the 7–0 game and the night before the match was the one and only time I can mind that he broke his professionalism," explains McDougall. "He had a wee blue Austin Princess 1100, and the night before that match he decided to bring it in to the garage and change the engine with me. It turned out to be a little more complicated than it should have been, and time marched on. It was about three o'clock in the morning before we got it finished, and Erich must have been tired. Because of the 7–0 game, I suppose it must have been in his mind that the Hearts game would be easy. But Hibs got gubbed that day – they were not at the races. They were well beaten by a Hearts team who were well up for it. I don't think there is any doubt that Hibs underestimated them. Erich scored an own goal to give them the lead. In fact, all of the goals they lost were soft and avoidable."

Jim McArthur had started the season as Turnbull's first-choice goalkeeper, but an injury ruled him out. "I had broken my thumb and was definitely out, so Eddie got Bobby Robertson in a few days before the match and told him he would be playing," McArthur recalls. "He was up to high doe, looking forward to his first derby, and Erich was excited too that his best mate would be playing. But then Ned must have had a last-minute change of heart and he went with Roddy McKenzie instead. That was tough on Bobby, who deserved his chance. Roddy actually missed the cross for the first Hearts goal and Erich headed it in for the own goal."

Jim Jefferies, who had suffered with the rest of his teammates on New Year's Day, believes Hearts could and should have settled the score that day against an out-of-sorts Hibs. "We were obviously well fired up for that one," says Jefferies. "We couldn't wait to play them again and do our best to make amends for the 7–0 game. I think I had a hand in Erich's own goal. I dispossessed the late Bobby Smith on the edge of the box and when I put the ball over, Erich headed it into the net under enormous pressure from Drew Busby.

"We had a chance to wipe the 7–0 game from the record books and played like men possessed. We certainly had a chance to get a high score that day, but we had to settle for 4–1 – which people are obviously not going to remember the same way as the previous game."

Jefferies says derby matches in those days were played in the right spirit and the players from both sides got on well, on and off the pitch: "While Hibs were a fine side, they were a good bunch of lads. In Pat Stanton you could not meet a more modest man, a true gentleman, and Erich was a lovely lad too. Football was different then, when the fans mixed and there was no segregation. In the present-day game, there is way too much gloating, and a 'them and us' mentality.

"When we used to go out in town you would run into Hibs players all the time in certain bars or nightclubs, and there was nothing but friendliness and respect. I'm still very good friends with a lot of that Hibs team."

After shipping four goals against Hearts, goalkeeper McKenzie's stay at Easter Road was a brief one. He only played eleven times for the club, all in the 1972/73 season, and kept one clean sheet – although to be fair to the Northern Irishman, Hibs won eight of those games at a time when they often played with the attitude that attack was the best form of defence.

Stung by their derby defeat, Hibs responded well – winning four in a row and beating the Icelandic side IB Keflavik 3–1 on aggregate in the first round of the UEFA Cup (Bobby Robertson in goals for both matches, and keeping a clean sheet in the home leg) to set up a daunting second-round clash with Don Revie's Leeds United. Before the trip to Elland Road, Erich had the satisfaction of scoring his first competitive goal for Hibs at Easter Road in a 2–0 League Cup win over Raith Rovers. The Leeds v Hibs tie was predictably dubbed the "Battle of Britain", and Turnbull was fizzing at the arrogant noises coming out of Elland Road ahead of the clash. One thing Turnbull loathed was disrespect and it was fair to say Don

Revie's Leeds – the team everybody loved to hate – were casually dismissive of their rivals' chances of eliminating them from the UEFA Cup.

Bobby Robertson, who was in the squad as backup keeper to Jim McArthur, remembers: "Big Jackie Charlton had been on TV saying that we should save ourselves the train fare and not bother turning up. Usually Eddie's team talks were blunt and to the point. I'm not saying he wasn't good at motivating us, because he was, but he would go for the direct approach – and his message usually contained plenty of the language he had picked up in the Navy. I was sitting there with the rest of the lads when Turnbull unravelled a Lion Rampant flag on a table in front of him – and for a man who was not particularly good with words, he then gave this amazing, stirring, eloquent speech that made the hairs on the back of your neck stand up.

"We went out there like men possessed and played them off the park. But they were an excellent side and defensively very strong, and although Tony Higgins had a good chance, he headed just over the bar and we had to settle for a 0–0 draw. As the players were coming off the pitch Turnbull made a beeline for Jack Charlton and caught up with him in the tunnel. Eddie was holding a big wad of notes and he chucked them at Charlton, telling him he could stick his train fare where the sun doesn't shine. I think big Gordon McQueen had to split them up because it was about to get out of hand."

Higgins laughs at that flashpoint. "Eddie went for Charlton and gave him the money for his train fare for Edinburgh," says Higgins. "They were arguably the best team in Europe at that time and the best in England, but we outplayed them that night and we were unlucky we lost on penalties at Easter Road. We could meet the English teams on a level playing field. There was hardly any difference between the top teams in England and the top teams in Scotland in those days."

The second leg was one of the great European nights at Easter

Road – in terms of atmosphere, if not the end result. The tie remained teetering on a knife-edge throughout but again the deadlock could not be broken. The first-leg scoreline of 0–0 was repeated, something of an oddity given that the attack-minded Tornadoes were not exactly known for goalless draws. The game headed into penalty kicks and Pat Stanton was the fall guy – hitting the post as Leeds edged a tension-filled shoot-out 5–4.

In recent years, an elaborate conspiracy theory has attached itself to that Easter Road match, principally fuelled by claims made by former Scotland midfielder Peter Lorimer. He alleges that a group of Leeds players – supposedly wanting out of the competition to redouble their focus on winning the English league title – were in on a betting scam, having a whip-round and putting their money down on a Hibs win at the generous odds of 3–1.

Lorimer has claimed: "Unfortunately young John [Shaw] in goal was wanting to make a name for himself. He was not in on the scam and was flinging himself about left and right, making fabulous saves, until he got injured and had to go off. He was replaced by an even younger lad, a Welsh kid called Glan Letheren. At full time, with the scores level, we had done our money. All bets are settled, of course, on ninety minutes. It went to penalties and Don Revie's view was that having come so far we might as well do our best now to win it. Damned right! We needed to win the match to collect the bonuses to cover the bet! And win it we did."

It's true that Leeds had several big names missing from their side that night, and with regular goalkeeper David Harvey injured they were forced to field nineteen-year-old keeper John Shaw. He in turn had to be replaced by seventeen-year-old sub keeper Glan Letheren when he broke a couple of fingers during the first half. But despite the patched-up nature of the Leeds side, many Hibs supporters who were present that evening insist that Leeds were 100 per cent committed to winning.

Lorimer's betting yarn is undermined further by his own personal intervention. He denied Hibs a goal by making a crucial goal-line clearance from Higgins – hardly the act of a man hoping his team would lose. In particular, Leeds captain Billy Bremner, operating as sweeper, played like a man possessed. He combined unflappable football with a snarling disdain for the home players, and Hibs fans left the ground that night almost hating and grudgingly admiring the little Scots firebrand in equal measure.

It was Bremner who scored the match-winning penalty, and he lapped up every moment of a victory which left their hosts sour. Hibs subsequently accused Revie and his assistant Les Cocker of "coaching" during the shoot-out and UEFA upheld their complaint, fining Leeds and banning Revie from acting in an official capacity against Vitoria Setubal in the next round.

The European adventure was over for Erich and Hibs for another year, and it was back to domestic football and the daunting task of trying to topple the seemingly immoveable Celtic from top spot. Celtic were well on course for a ninth Scottish championship in a row, but Hibs were chasing hard and they managed another New Year's Day triumph over Hearts, Alex Cropley continuing his happy knack of scoring in derbies with a double and Arthur Duncan scoring the other goal in a 3–1 win at Easter Road, watched by another crowd of more than 35,000.

Hibs' league form remained impressive, losing only one First Division fixture between New Year and the end of the season. Crucially though, that solitary defeat was to Celtic, and with very few exceptions every time Hibs won on the run-in, the victory would be mirrored by a Celtic triumph as the gap was maintained. Turnbull's men battled hard all the way but they were unable to make inroads into the lead maintained by Stein's juggernaut. Hibs finished second, a point ahead of Rangers, but four points behind Celtic. It was close, but not close enough to prise the title away from Parkhead. Erich had again broken the half-century mark for appearances that season, playing fifty-two times – and that tally would have been considerably higher if the team had enjoyed longer cup runs.

## 12

# THE MAD KRAUT

Erich Schaedler had proved himself to fans, teammates and managers as a hard, dedicated and highly professional player, but the boy from the Borders had a wild streak. Shades was the nickname he usually went by, but Erich's escapades also earned him the moniker "The Mad Kraut". "They called Erich the 'Mad Kraut' because he was mad, plain and simple, but funny with it," says goalkeeper Jim McArthur, who was usually at the epicentre of any dressing room banter himself. "He used to come in in the morning and he would grab you and give you a bear hug. If it was any normal person, they would let go after a wee while, but if you started screaming he wouldn't let you go. He was laughing as he did it! There was a drying room next to the dressing room at Easter Road for washing your gear and Erich used to pounce on you in there, get a hold of you and hold your head a few inches away from the pipes. You were never in danger because he was so strong; he was just toying with you. He was some boy!"

It seems everyone that Erich played with has similar memories of his playful dressing room shenanigans, pouncing on unsuspecting teammates and getting them in his vice-like grip. "He was one of these guys who understood his body and had done some kind of anatomy training. He could almost send the body to sleep – he knew where people's pressure points were," remembers Tony

Higgins. "Suddenly, he would come up behind you and be pressing the pressure points.

"Craig Paterson's abiding memory is of Erich looking over his shoulder to make sure he wasn't going to sneak up on him. Shades spent his whole time getting people in arm locks. He had a very powerful figure. I remember one incident involving a young guy, Les Thomson. The young boys were getting a bit fed up with Erich's antics, so I told Les, 'Just pretend you're dead and he'll let you go.' Les wasn't convinced and asked me what I meant. 'Just flake out,' I said, 'and we'll kid him on that he's killed you!' So after training Erich came in and, true to form, he got wee Les by the back of the neck. So Les collapses and I ran over pretending to give him mouth-to-mouth. I was saying, 'I think he's gone, Erich. I think he's gone!' Erich was a bit shocked and was screaming, 'Doctor! Doctor!' We laughed about it later but you could see it in his face he was terrified he'd overstepped the mark and hadn't realised his own strength. I think he gave me few meaty tackles at training for a couple of weeks when he realised I was behind the wind-up.

"Erich was occasionally sombre, but he was usually quite high and he was a big presence in the dressing room. He was always bouncing about, full of energy. From time to time you would see him very serious and you kind of left him to it. But generally he was a lively, ebullient character. He had a great relationship with the young players at Hibs; they looked up to him because he was a great professional."

The older, wilier heads saw Erich coming and knew how to stay out of his clutches, but nobody was safe – not even the club doctor. John Fraser recalls, "You could be standing there and he'd creep up behind you and grab you. The club doctor, Jimmy Ledingham, used to come in and Erich would even grab him. He didn't realise his own strength, he would go round doing it to people when they'd least expected it – you had to be on your toes!"

Physio and trainer Tom McNiven says, "In the morning before training I would have to get all the strappings ready for the players, making sure I was protecting and preventing any strains on the joints and muscles. I'd be working away and Erich would just come up and say, 'Morning, Tommy,' and just pick me up, lift me in the air and whirl me round. He put one hand round your back and burl you right round in a oner. You were safe, but if you did that to a stranger they would think they were going to be murdered. When he shook your hand as well, you would grimace at his grip – he was a strong boy!"

Few, if any, were strong enough to beat Erich at his own game, but an acid tongue could occasionally put him in his place. "Aye, some of them could be merciless in the changing room," says Pat Stanton. "He was known as the Mad Kraut, but he just laughed off the nicknames. We all did, it was just part of the fun. I remember one incident when Roy Barry was there. Roy liked the finer things in life. He was a rough player on the park but off it he was well read and very bright and he liked dining out. When you talked to Roy he would tell you where he'd eaten, and described the wine he had chosen and how it had complemented his meal. But then Erich started knocking about with him for a spell, so he would come in and try a bit of the same – trying to act cultured, show what a connoisseur he was, describing the wine he had had. Jimmy O'Rourke cut right through him. He shouted over from the other side of the dressing room. 'What are you talking aboot, Shades?' he asked. 'Listen to you . . . the wine expert fi Peebles!'"

The teammate who ran rings round Schaedler most with his razor-sharp mouth was the cheeky, chirpy midfielder Alex Edwards, or 'Mickey' as he was nicknamed. The pair of them were an unlikely pairing as roommates on European trips, and as Stanton says, "I cannae imagine the conversations he would have had with Alex Edwards – somebody should have recorded those!"

Tony Higgins confirms: "His arguments with Alex Edwards were legendary. Mickey was a wind-up merchant and in some ways they were at complete opposite ends of the spectrum – Erich could be quiet and Mickey never shut up! And although Alex was a very fit guy, he would never admit to it – he would prefer to be known as a bit of a rebel, a bad boy, whereas Erich was the ultimate professional. I always remember we had been away on a European trip where they were rooming together. In those days for European games you would go away on the Sunday to play the game on the Wednesday – you had to be in the city for at least forty-eight hours before the tie. On the Sunday night it was a night out, so some of the guys had a few drinks and, of course, Alex had one or two more than most people. So he came in drunk and Erich was a bit upset. So the next day, Alex woke up with a wardrobe on top of him. It turned out Erich had actually lifted it and put it on top of him for a bit of payback. Wee Mickey woke up and could hardly move for this wardrobe, and he was screaming and shouting for help."

John Brownlie laughs at the constant verbal sparring sessions Schaedler and Edwards used to have. "Tricky Mickey used to take the piss out of him worst. Shades would ruffle wee Mickey up and grab a hold of him, but he would just keep coming back for more, calling him a mad bastard! He'd be shouting, 'Yer mad, yer a Mad Kraut!' We used to keep out of it, saying to Alex, 'That's what you get for winding him up.' If you went too far with Erich he might not get you back right away, but he might wait a couple of days, or a week, and then he'd get you – and he'd tell you what it was for."

The forthright Edwards was not the type of player to back down, but while he had a quirky love-hate relationship with Schaedler, it was essentially good-natured. "We used to bounce off each other a bit," says Edwards. "He was a really nice guy and he would do anything for you, but I would wind him up something terrible. He was crackers. You could wire him to the moon.

"If I bought a new car, he would go out and buy a better one. I remember I bought a fancy Ford Capri, with a two-litre engine, and the next thing I know he's gone out and bought one too – but a three-litre. The wardrobe incident was in Benidorm, I think. Tom

Hart treated us after we had won the League Cup, and he hauled the big wardrobe on top of me. I mind he halved Jim Black's bed out onto the veranda too!"

Jimmy O'Rourke says the European trips – particular the end-of-season get-aways – were excellent for team morale – and distinctly recalls Erich being involved in a few funny moments. "The chairman Tom Hart would take us away every year, and it was great for team bonding," he says. "One time he took us to Benidorm and there were a few of the boys that had birthdays while we were away – Tom Hart found out, gave us a whole load of pesetas, and said, 'Here you go, have a good birthday.' I think that did us for about four days in drink money! We would have a great time but we behaved out of respect to Tom Hart and fear of Eddie Turnbull! Turnbull had a rule that as soon as you come in the hotel after being out you went straight up to the room, no loitering about bars or lobbies. Once you were in you were away to the bed, and the lads abided by that. But that's not to say there weren't a few high jinks too.

"I remember the time in Mallorca that Shades dived off his balcony into the pool. Erich's room overlooked the deep end and he was out sitting there sunning himself on the balcony. It was quite high up, but we were all egging him on from below, shouting, 'C'mon, Erich. Go for it!' None of us thought he would – you'd have to be mad – but he did it! He was fearless. I remember us wincing – it wouldn't have been me!"

You suspect Alex Edwards might have been involved, but he has nothing but admiration for Schaedler, on and off the pitch. "I shared a room with him on European trips and we would have a good laugh. He would look after you on the park as well," says Edwards. "I could look after myself, but I would come in for some treatment because I was wee and some players wanted to try and kick me off the park, but Erich would look out for me and say, 'Just leave him to me.' He was a hardy man. You could take your John Greig, Tam Forsyth, Billy McNeill and all these guys, put them all together and they were nowhere near as hard as Shades. I would get Celtic and Rangers players having a go at me all the time, and I'd be happy to give it right back to them. I would tell them, 'I'm getting fed up of us beating you every week!' Erich's way of dealing with them was a bit more direct – he would just steam into a tackle and they wouldn't come back for seconds.

"He wasn't the best player in the world, but he was still a good player and he brought a lot of energy to the team. You would never see Erich just walking. We would sometimes be coming out of training knackered, sauntering over to our cars, but not Erich – he would be going at 100 miles an hour, jumping over fences, racing into his car. He just couldnae keep still. He had too much energy, which he never seemed to expend; he was hyperactive. He'd always be up to capers in the dressing room too; you'd have to watch your back. You'd be sitting in the bath relaxing and he'd turn the cold hose on you. He wouldn't give any of us a moment's peace. I mind one time John Brownlie tried to do the same. He was messing about and turned the cold hose on Erich and me. So me and Erich went into the changing room and got a hold of his clothes. I had Brownlie's shirt on and Shades was wearing his jacket. When we went back towards the bath, sure enough, Brownlie turned the big power hose on us again. He couldn't work out why we weren't bothered until we said, 'They're your clothes, you daftie!"

Pat Stanton recalls the tussles between Schaedler and Edwards: "The relationship Erich had with wee Alex Edwards was funny. Edwards was always winding Erich up. If Erich had lost his temper, seriously he would kill you, but Alex knew what to say and when to say it. He knew Erich had a sense of humour and liked a laugh most of the time. But Erich could be a bit of a loner at times; he had his deep moments. Some mornings he would come in and grab you and throttle you to within an inch of your life, and other mornings he would walk past you without a word. He maybe had something on his mind. That's where Tam McNiven was a big help. Tam was someone he could go to. But you would hear Erich and Alex talking to each other and you just wondered how far they were going to go with each other – it could be hilarious."

Erich's hard-as-nails approach to football and his obvious physical strength were great attributes, but teammates, opponents and friends are quick to praise his temperament. Schaedler rarely lost his temper and was not the sort to throw his weight about. Nevertheless, he was not a man to be messed with. His friend Frank Dougan remembers how Schaedler jumped in to defend some of his younger teammates in a New Town pub when they were on the end of some threats from other drinkers. "It was in the Wally Dug and there were a whole load of Hibs players just having a quiet night out – Pat, Erich and about half a dozen others. There was a couple of younger Hibs players who had had come along and they were getting hassle from a group of Hearts supporters who were standing at the bar. Erich said, 'C'mon, boys, leave them be. They're just laddies.' He was trying to be reasonable with them, but they kept causing aggro. Erich eventually said, 'Why don't we go outside and settle this?' That was when Pat Stanton, sitting there smoking his wee cigar, said, 'Boys, you really don't want to do that.' They must have seen something in Erich's eyes, because they bottled it. But he was never a violent man or a bully.

"I remember Robin Rae, who used to play in goals for Hibs in the Eighties, took to calling me Mr Dougan at every opportunity. I kept telling him, 'It's Frank,' but no, he kept persisting with MISTER Dougan. I had to pull him aside. 'What's all this Mr Dougan crap?' Robin, who was not exactly a shrinking violet, says, 'Well, Erich's scared of you and if Erich's scared of you then I'm calling you Mr Dougan.' It was just a wind-up by Erich but it worked a treat!"

Pat Stanton also remembers the standoff in the Wally Dug. "That was a lucky escape for those boys. You wouldnae want to bump into Erich in a dark alleyway," says Stanton. "When he was grabbing you it was just playful. I wouldn't have liked to have seen him acting seriously! He would kill you. He was able to keep a lid on it though."

Edwards also praises Schaedler's self-control, but wouldn't go as far as saying that he never dished out some punishment. "Haha, I don't know about that – let's just say no one would get the better of him at training or on the pitch."

Davie Provan, the former Celtic player, would testify to that. "The only times I ever wore shin guards was when facing Hibs defender Erich Schaedler," Provan wrote in 2006. "Every chance he got he'd nail you, but there was always a warm handshake and a smile at time up."

Erich didn't have many enemies on the pitch. Sure, there were a few wingers like Provan that didn't look forward to facing him, but he would never menace somebody for the sake of it. Tony Higgins does remember one worthy adversary though: "Erich used to have some brilliant battles with another player who died early, Johnny Doyle. The confrontation between those two when he played at Ayr United was a sight to behold. I remember playing against Ayr United at Easter Road – Johnnie Doyle was a very aggressive winger, a good winger but very direct – and those two used to kick the shit out of each other. I was sitting on the bench one day and we were all having a good laugh as Doyle cut back from the right wing and ran from right to left across the park – with Erich matching him stride for stride and the two of them getting stuck into each other every inch of the way. I think there was a ball in there somewhere! They were basically fighting each other, punching and kicking each other. It was like a sideshow and everyone just stood back and admired it. It's a vivid memory. Doyle was really quick and aggressive and he was a match for Erich. That day it was humorous to watch – it was like a scene from the cartoon *Roadrunner*."

So was the nickname the Mad Kraut really justified?

"Aye, of course it was," says Alex Edwards, who tells an amazing story to back up his conviction. "He was mad, no doubt about it. I remember one day I had come back to the ground to do a bit of training in the afternoon. I had been injured or suspended and needed a bit of extra work. I was out on the pitch when I saw

Erich Schaedler senior, left, with one of his German Navy colleagues, was first assigned to the infamous *Bismarck* then served on the torpedo fleet before his capture off the coast of France.

Erich as a teenager in Peebles High Street

Erich and his brother John as schoolboys, growing up in Cardrona (both far right, John with glasses) at Lyne School.

Melbourne Thistle show off their impressive trophy haul, which included the Scottish Cup. Top row: (l-r): Charlie Morrison, Tom Cropley, George Young, Gus Henderson, Lenny Young. Middle row: Charlie Murphy, Ninian Cassidy, Jim Thomson, uknown, Billy Blues. Front row: Sandy Brown, Erich Schaedler, Dennis Nelson, Allan Munro, David Ross, Alan Buchanan, Johnny Mochan.

Stirling Albion line-up in 1969: Top row (from left) John Corrigan, Neil Docherty, George Ryden, George Young, Jimmy Logan, Joe Hughes. Front Row: Matt McPhee, Erich Schaedler, Sammy Henderson, Davie Grant, Rab Duffin, Billy Armstrong.

Erich's first ever picture in Hibs colours, taken in the week he signed from Stirling Albion, in November 1969.

Erich's mentor Willie MacFarlane was very much a hands-on manager, and is pictured here delivering instructions to his Hibs players during a training session at Marine Drive, Muirhouse.

© SCOTSMAN PUBLICATIONS

Schaedler on one of his marauding runs up the left wing for Hibs, leaving a trail of bodies in his wake.

© SCOTSMAN PUBLICATIONS

Eddie Turnbull and his Tornadoes, including Erich (far right), raise a toast to the League Cup after bring the silverware back to Edinburgh in 1972 following their 2-1 win over Celtic at Hampden.

© SCOTSMAN PUBLICATIONS

Erich, wearing No.4, and Eddie Turnbull's Hibs team proudly show off the Drybrough Cup, won after an epic 5-3 win over Celtic at Hampden in 1972 and retained the following year when they again beat Jock Stein's team 1-0.

Jeepers keepers. Competition was always fierce for the No.1 jersey at Easter Road during Eddie Turnbull's reign as manager, but there was great camaraderie between the goalies. Erich's best pal Bobby Robertson, left, is pictured with friends and rivals Jim McArthur and Jim Herriot.

Tea for two. Erich has a cuppa with Alan Gordon prior to departing for a European game. Sadly, Schaedler and Gordon are the only two of the famous 'Tornadoes' team no longer with us.

Split the difference. Erich has his arm in a sling after dislocating his collarbone against Hajduk Split. He is joined by Arthur Duncan, Alan Gordon, John Blackley and Pat Stanton after all five Hibs players were selected in Willie Ormond's Scottish League squad to face the English League at Hampden in 1973.

© COLORSPORT

Erich on the run during a match against West Germany in Frankfurt in March 1974 – the pinnacle of his career.

© GETTY IMAGES

The great West Germany side of 1974, World Cup winners in waiting, line up for their March friendly against Scotland, which they won 2-1.

The Scotland starting XI on the night Erich won his only cap. From left: Denis Law, Willie Morgan, Kenny Burns, Tommy Hutchison, Pat Stanton, Martin Buchan, Erich Schaedler, Kenny Dalglish, Sandy Jardine, Thomson Allan, David Hay.

Erich alongside Donald Ford of Hearts belts out 'Easy Easy' – the 1974 World Cup song released by the Scotland squad ahead of the finals in West Germany where they played against Zaire, Brazil and Yugoslavia.

Three's a crowd. Erich pictured at a Scotland gathering with Danny McGrain and Willie Donachie – his international rivals for the No.3 shirt. The trio were all good friends, and McGrain was the first to congratulate Erich by telegram when he was picked to play against West Germany in 1974.

Erich with his father and Peebles Hibs supporter Anne Aitken.

Erich makes a splash with his Hibs team-mates Joe Harper and Iain Munro during a day off at Portobello Baths in 1974. Munro was a good friend of Schaedler's during their two spells together at Easter Road, and gave the eulogy at his funeral in 1986.

Warming up at Dens Park for Dundee.

Signing autographs at Dens Park during his time with Dundee. Hibs may have been Erich's main love, but he always gave 100 per cent for his new club and was a fans' favourite at Dundee, where he played under Tommy Gemmell and Don Mackay.

Five-a-side silverware for Hibs in Schaedler's second spell at Easter Road. Pictured after winning the John White Memorial Fives at Olivebank, Musselburgh, are keeper Robin Rae, Gordon Hunter, Gordon Rae, Erich, and front row: Keith Jardine and Paul Kane.

Erich, at full stretch, tries to prevent Mo Johnston getting a cross in front of 'The Jungle' at Celtic Park during his second spell at Hibs.

Pictured with his beloved Dobermans at the foot of Easter Road, outside Shades Bar at Thorntree Street.

Erich is joined behind his bar Shades in Easter Road by Hearts defender Peter Shields as the two capital teams prepare for the 1983/84 season.

Wearing perm and purple tracksuit, Erich leaves baby Colin Smith looking a little bewildered during Hibs' pre-season tour of the Highlands in 1977.

In action against Dumbarton during the 1984/85 season – the team he helped relegate then joined the following season.

Thirty-two years after Erich played for Scotland against West Germany, his appearance is finally recognised by the SFA with a commemorative international cap. Receiving the honour on Erich's behalf at Easter Road is brother John (second from left), pictured with fellow cap recipients – former Hibs players Alex Cropley, Eddie Turnbull, Jim Scott, Neil Martin and Des Bremner.

someone coming out the tunnel dressed in all the camouflage gear, looking like GI Joe, with the hat on, the lot. It was Schaedler, and he was carrying a shotgun. He had come to shoot the pigeons. I was watching him jumping over the seats and hiding behind the advertising hoardings so he could shoot them. Mental!"

It may sound a fanciful tale, and set against the circumstances of his death a little sad, but Schaedler regularly went shooting. The countryside should have been his usual hunting ground though, not Easter Road!

John Fraser confirms the story. "Erich enjoyed spending a lot of time at the stadium, particularly when he had a flat near the ground. He would often spend his whole day at Easter Road. After training some days he would just appear. We had the old enclosure at the bottom goal, The Cowshed, and a lot of pigeons and seagulls used to fly about there and would drop their droppings all over the wooden bench seats. So one afternoon Erich appeared with a shotgun and he started blasting the pigeons!"

Dougan is another who remembers Schaedler's impromptu shooting expeditions in the heart of Leith. "Yes, he used to go round to Easter Road with his shotgun. I used to go round to Easter Road to collect the lottery tickets that I sold and I would be in the old club shop at the back of the main stand, and all I heard was BANG . . . BANG . . . BANG. I asked one of the lassies in the shop, 'What the hell is that?' And she said, 'Who do you think it is?!' I went out on to the pitch and there was Erich shooting the pigeons with a double-barrelled shotgun. He just loved being around Hibs and Easter Road – he couldn't stay away."

13

# IRON MAN

Athletic, clean-cut, handsome and ripped – Erich Schaedler took enormous pride in his appearance and fitness. Sports science has come on lightyears since Schaedler played in the no-frills Seventies, but back then he was a man way ahead of his time. Blessed with natural athleticism, Schaedler thrived on training rather than seeing it as a chore. His ethos was simple: if it could make him fitter, faster and stronger and better his game in any way, then it was well worth doing. As he moved into his twenties and then thirties, training sessions alone were not enough to satisfy this fitness fanatic's quest for physical perfection. He would train in the morning with his teammates then head to the gym in the afternoon or the Easter Road gym in the evening for an additional workout.

The anatomy and its intricate workings fascinated Schaedler and he would spend many hours soaking up information imparted to him by the Hibs physio Tom McNiven, another man decades ahead of his time in terms of his methods. "To this day, I would say Tam McNiven's methods, his dressings, his advice – they were lightyears ahead of anyone," says John Blackley. "The reason we were so successful was that A) Turnbull came to the club and could guide us all, because guys like me, John Brownlie, Alex Cropley and Erich were all young, so we needed guidance and he gave us it. And B) We had Tam McNiven there to ensure we were fit and relatively injury-free. It was a really good time for Hibs, by a long way the best of my life."

McNiven was one of the unsung heroes of Easter Road, a trusted and respected member of the backroom team with great expertise. The players thought the world of him, and his healing hands were directly responsible for saving and reviving a few careers. He was recruited in 1963 as club trainer, replacing Eddie Turnbull when he left Hibs to take his first manager's job at Queen's Park, and would serve the club into the Eighties, occasionally standing in as caretaker manger, bridging the gap between a couple of the hirings and firings at Easter Road. McNiven was widely regarded as the best in the game and his services were sought by the Scotland team. When Turnbull vetoed his trainer's request to be involved with the international squad on a part-time basis it soured relations between the two men, coming to a head when McNiven walked out on the club, although he later returned when Turnbull's reign as manager ended in 1980. McNiven finally got his wish to accept Scotland's invitation and he was alongside Jock Stein at the 1982 World Cup finals in Spain.

His long service at Easter Road was the happiest time of his career, however, and Erich Schaedler was perhaps his favourite player. The two men had a natural rapport and Schaedler's thirst for knowledge in the treatment room, his honesty and his dedicated approach to training all impressed McNiven. "He was a wonderful fella," says McNiven. "To be quite honest with you, I would have gone anywhere with him. With regard to exercise, there was nobody to beat him. I just had to tell him once and everything he did then was as it should have been, and not ten minutes after it. He picked it up right away, all of the time.

"He was also the strongest fella I've come across. In relation to general fitness and physique he was in a league of his own. He had a lot of electric about him and he was nice to have around the place. I always felt things were better when he was there, because nobody would ever take a loan of him. Not if they realised what they were taking on. And yet he wasn't a violent man. He was quietly confident in his own ability but I don't think he even realised himself what he had.

"I remember when Willie MacFarlane bought him. I first came to the club when Bob Shankly was manager and I'd been there about seven or eight years before Erich arrived. I had seen a lot of good football players between my previous club, Third Lanark, and Hibs and when Erich arrived he was raw. But it was great to see the way he developed. I was very proud when he got picked for Scotland because of his history – his father having been a German prisoner of war."

You might think Schaedler's fearless style of thundering into tackles and immense physicality on the pitch would have made him a regular on the treatment table, but McNiven insists: "He used to go so hard into tackles but I can't remember any particularly bad injuries that he picked up. Any time he was on the treatment table he was itching to get back as quick as he could.

"He was a joy to train and he understood all about fitness. He was my assistant – model if you like – when I used to go and give talks or demonstrations. When I was giving a lecture on phsyio and treatments, I always took Erich to demonstrate. He would lie on the floor or on the table to show what was the right way to do it. You see people now doing press-ups one-handed or with their heels way up in the Highlands. Erich was doing that fifty years ago; he just knew what was good for his body. He knew a lot about anatomy and was very knowledgeable. He understood about muscles – their origins and incessions, where they arrived from – biceps, triceps, which makes it all easier to learn.

"He knew all about kinetics and good movement. These were all integral parts of my training. Nowadays you'll see lots of gyms preaching methods like that – people being taught now how to lie on the power balls and do press-ups to work the different groups of muscles. We may have been taught differently, but we were doing that fifty years ago."

Erich was always a willing student when McNiven had something new to try out and together the two men had the perfect working relationship. "You would lie on your tummy, hands at two o'clock, hands at quarter past nine, things like that – well, no matter what I showed Erich, he understood it and knew what to do. He was completely in tune with his body," says McNiven. "There was nothing I didn't try with him. It was satisfying having a player that could take it all in. He was a physio's athlete, he really was. Although if he had been a boxer, I would never have boxed him – God, the power he had in him! You could feel it crackling off him – raw strength and energy. If I was ever in a battle I'd say, 'Right, I'll have Erich at the front, Erich at the back and Erich either side of me!' That's how much I trusted the fella."

McNiven says the Hibs team of the late 1960s and early 1970s was the best he ever worked with, and believes their camaraderie as well as their ability contributed to their success. "Aye, there were some fantastic players in those days. It was a pleasure working with them," says McNiven. "The likes of Herriot, Brownlie, Schaedler, Blackley, Black, Stanton – and that's just the start of the team! Big Alan Gordon, wee Jimmy O'Rourke, Cropley, Duncan, Edwards, big Neil Martin before that – they were all great players and while we were deadly serious about our football and succeeding as a club, we had our share of laughs too.

"I saw a lot that I had to keep to myself. The players trusted me, and I wasn't the type to go running to the manager to tell tales. When I left football and was working in clinics and hospitals, I really missed the jokes and the company. Erich was a practical joker, but he never took it to extremes and it was never to the detriment of anyone. It was a bloody good laugh."

Pat Stanton says that Schaedler's inside knowledge of the human body could be used as a weapon too when it came to dressing room pranks: "He used to come in and grab you in the morning and hit you on the pressure points. He'd have you close to collapsing. He would put his arms round you and his grip was iron – he was only playing with you, but you couldn't break his grip. He would take a lot of interest in what Tam McNiven was doing – him and Tam were close; they were great pals. Tam was the sort of guy, if you had a wee problem you could go to him and it would not go any further. We've all got things we want to get off our chest sometimes. There would always be some gossip around the treatment table – Tam would hear it all but you knew you could trust him with anything. With other members of the backroom staff, you maybe wanted the manager to know something – something that you didn't want to say to his face, but a message you wanted to be delivered, so you would say to them, 'This is between you and I but . . .' And you knew it would get to the manager. I know a couple of times I was called into the manager's office, and he'd say, 'I hear this,' and you know the message has been delivered. Everyone has their opinions and it doesn't do you any good to bottle them all up. But Tam was a guy you could trust 100 per cent – Erich too for that matter."

Schaedler's selfless attitude was another quality which endeared him to McNiven, who remembers Erich always going out of his way to lend a hand: "Say I was moving some chairs, he was always the first one over to help you. He'd say to the rest of them, 'Wait a minute, Tom's doing all this himself,' and the next minute there would be three of them helping you – and that was only because Erich had spoken up. Mind you, he was so competitive he would even try and turn something like that into an exercise. If you asked him to pick up a normal chair, Erich would have to lift it by one leg to try and build his muscles.

"I remember Erich being a big help on some of the trips too. If we went to an away match or even on tour – we did a lot of that, back and forward to America, Canada, Africa, all over the place – if Erich saw me lifting a hamper by myself, he would say to the rest of the boys, 'Are you going to stand there and let the man do that himself? He's our physio, our trainer, not a labourer.' He would come and lift it and get the others to help. Jimmy O'Rourke was like that as well. They would look out for you."

McNiven's eyes well up at the mention of Erich's death in 1985, a numbing experience he chooses not to talk about, describing it as "one of the worst days of my life". He believes Schaedler had all the attributes to become a trainer or physio himself when his playing days were over. "He was a natural, he would watch and learn. He knew what Petrissage was and how it worked – you wouldn't dig your fingers in, it was lifting and teasing and Erich was good at that. He had good hands.

"I think he would have liked to have been a physio. He was practically my unofficial assistant at times when we were at Hibs. We were playing Celtic and Rangers all the time in big games and I had to keep the team as fit as possible. When they'd come back to training after some of the tougher games, I would say to the lads, 'In and have a sauna or a bath.' And when I brought the table through to give them a massage I'd show Erich what to do – all the different methods. All the lifting and stretching – that's two words I would use a lot during my time as a physio. I brought the plinth right through next to the bath and would shout on whoever was handy to come up for a massage. I would say to Erich, 'You work that side and I'll work that side.' He had the knack and he was always a big help."

Schaedler's fascination with fitness continued throughout his life and career. There were only a fraction of the number of gyms and fitness clubs around in the 1970s and 1980s compared to now, but a focal point for the leotard and latex-clad fitness fanatics in those days was the Edinburgh Club in Hillside Crescent, near London Road. When he wasn't at his day-to-day football training, Erich was practically part of the furniture there. The Edinburgh Club was the brainchild of George Kerr, a world-renowned judo expert. Kerr was a genial, larger-than-life figure and very well known in influential circles in the city and the club, which he ran with his fitness guru wife, Pauline, proved to be a magnet for the city's beautiful people. Kerr has won almost every honour there is to win in judo, famously taking the gold medal at the 1957 European

Championships in Rotterdam, and he has been a legendary figure in the sport since, earning him a richly deserved spot in the Scottish Sport Hall of Fame as one of the original inductees in 2002. He has also coached Olympic gold medallists and in addition to the CBE he received in Britain in the 2011 New Year Honours list, he was decorated with the Japanese equivalent for his services to judo – the Order of the Rising Sun – in the Emperor's 2010 Honours list. That same year he won the highest award in judo, the 10th Dan, only the fifth non-Japanese judoka ever to do so, and even now, at the age of seventy-five, he is running a gym and judo club in West Bowling Green Street, Leith. It is possibly the Edinburgh Club for which Kerr is best known in the city. The club doubled as a fitness and martial arts club, and from the moment Erich walked through the doors he was hooked.

"He was a regular at the Edinburgh Club in Hillside Crescent," says the man nicknamed 'Mr Judo'. "His fitness was phenomenal. He had some pair of legs on him. The only other footballer I could compare him with is Graeme Souness – he had legs like tree trunks. Souness was all legs with a slim waist and no upper body, and to an extent Erich had a similar sort of build. He was so fanatically fit it was unbelievable and he lived like an athlete. He was a very handsome man and stood out from the crowd with his streaky blonde hair. He had a great physique and was like a dynamo. I really don't think there is a bad word to say about him – he was Mr Perfect."

Kerr and Schaedler immediately hit it off – kindred spirits linked by their shared obsession with physical well-being. Erich looked up to the inspirational judo veteran because of his glittering career and the way he had maintained and preserved his supreme fitness, while the admiration was reciprocated, as Kerr was similarly taken with Schaedler's enthusiasm and dedication: "I had been at the top of the tree in my sport and was an Olympic referee at that stage, so there was a mutual respect. I was never a big football fan, but I went along to Easter Road a couple of times to watch him, and he seemed to play like he approached his fitness – fully committed. He did try his hand at judo from time to time, and typically he wouldn't hold back!"

Erich was willing to try his hand at any sport or challenge the Edinburgh Club had to offer, and Kerr remembers he also took an early interest in learning to become a personal trainer: "He was quite keen on squash and judo, and he had the foresight to try and prepare for a life after football. For footballers back then there was no great money, not compared to today, and he was aware that he'd have to explore other avenues when his career was over. I think most of the players back then would get their wages, blow their wages and wait for the next payday to roll around. They get far better advice and wages today, so being a footballer in the Eighties was very different, and Erich knew how to use his time constructively. He wasn't a stereotype footballer, and I admired him for that.

"Erich would be in the gym most days, after training with Hibs. He would have a workout, play squash or just hang about the coffee bar. I think he just enjoyed being in an environment where people were dedicated to their fitness. He showed an interest in studying to become a personal trainer too, and I would help him out in the gym and teach him. He was very fanatical about it. Paddy Stanton was the manager of Hibs at the time, and from time to time Erich would bring him along or a couple of teammates after training too.

"Erich was quite a successful guy, who knew there was a world outside football. During that period he and a business partner opened a pub in Leith Walk, the Victoria Bar. It was a nice, friendly place, and then of course he had his bar Shades at the bottom of Easter Road. He was good with people and would get on with anybody. He was a likeable guy. As a player he would take no prisoners on the pitch, but off the pitch he was affable and easy to get on with. He was a gentleman and we became good friends.

"There were a few complexities to his character, and I only knew him as Erich Schaedler the fitness fanatic rather than getting to know his inner thoughts, although he did become good friends with my wife and I.

"He wasn't a drinker, he didn't smoke and he was a clean-cut kid. He was very bubbly, but maybe underneath all that he lacked a little bit of confidence. I would introduce him to high-fliers in the city – bankers and businessmen – and these guys were thrilled to meet him because Erich was a big name in Edinburgh at the time and he had a reputation for being very fit. They were thrilled to be meeting a famous footballer, and some of them wanted to be seen with Erich Schaedler and to say they had him as their personal trainer. But he could be quite shy. He didn't like too much attention.

"He was a joy to have around though. We had many high-profile sportsmen and women at the club – Alan Anderson of Hearts, Alan Gordon and Pringle Fisher the rugby player – they were a cut above the rest in that they were intelligent, engaging guys."

Kerr, who was on holiday in the Canary Islands when he got the shocking phone call saying Erich had died, believes Schaedler could have gone on to become an excellent coach or used his passion for the gym to carve out a career. Fitness has, after all, become one of the boom industries in modern times. "It was so sad – he had a lot to offer," says Kerr. "He might not have been the right type of character to become a manager, but with his dedication and knowledge I definitely think he would have been able to give something on the training ground."

As he got older, Schaedler never compromised on his regimented training regime, and if anything he paid even more attention to his condition as his career progressed. Football reporter Stewart Brown waxed lyrical about his fitness in a feature in the *Pink News* in April 1977. Under the headline "Fittest Soccer Star in the Country – That's Schaedler!" there was a series of pictures of Erich working out on the parallel bars, lifting weights, doing pull-ups and on the sit-up machine. "Who is the fittest footballer in Scotland? Anyone who has seen Hibs recently will have no doubt that the only choice is left-back Erich Schaedler," wrote Brown. "While other players will be glad to hear the final whistle at the end of the season, Schaedler looks fresh and full of enthusiasm and prepared to run all day. Schaedler was out of favour in the early part of the season but he showed the right determination to fight back and he has been Hibs' outstanding player in the last two months."

Explaining the secret behind his superb condition, Erich told Brown, "I spend a lot of my spare time at the Edinburgh club and the work I put in there, combined with the normal training at Easter Road, keeps me trim. I'm feeling good these days and glad to be established in the team." Teammates reacted to the sight of Erich tearing around the training ground with a mixture of awe and terror – terror that they would be expected to keep up with him!

If Erich was seen as the leader in terms of fitness, goalkeeper Jim McArthur – nicknamed Bimbo – was the butt of many jokes for his constant struggles to stay fit and at a trim enough fighting weight to satisfy gruff disciplinarian Turnbull and his coaching staff. "Eddie Turnbull had signed Jim from Cowdenbeath and it would be safe to say he was a bit on the heavy side," says John Fraser. "At the end of one season, he was taking the Hibs team to Benidorm for a break, but he didn't take Jim McArthur with him. Bertie Auld was the coach at the time and he said to Bertie and me, 'When I come back I want him to have lost two stone. When I come back he better have lost it.' So we got a plastic sweat suit and medicine balls and ran poor Jim up and down the terracing for a whole week. He was actually crying at one stage, but he lost two stone and I admired him for that – that he was willing to do it. I remember after one game, he came up and said, 'Thanks very much, I understand what it was all about now, it's made me a better goalkeeper.' Jim had all the attributes to be a great goalkeeper, the only thing about him was his height – on his line he was brilliant, but it was common knowledge that big strikers would go in hard on him."

Tony Higgins chortles at McArthur's battle against the bulge. "The club were always watching his diet. We had a club chef in the late Seventies, and I remember that when we were all given the full three-courser, Bimbo would be given a wee salad and a baked potato. It should have been torturing him, but he was actually quite cheery. Something did not ring true. So Ally McLeod and I decided to trail him after training. He went straight from training to a fish and chip shop and we caught him in the act with a fish supper in his hands. But we used to get weighed once a week, and Turnbull was always on top of your fitness. The training methods could be deemed modern, given the era that we played in. Eddie would say that you should always be as fit or fitter than any team you play against. You never want to say you lost a game because you were not fit enough. Erich epitomised the fitness we had – he was a beast at training."

Iain Munro remembers trying to take on Erich at training, and enjoyed their jousts. Munro played alongside Schaedler in two spells at Hibs and believes that, if anything, Erich was even more dedicated to his fitness second time round: "He would be the first to admit he was not the most technical player in the world, he was not silky in any way, but he made himself a player through hard work – he would dedicate every ounce of his body to bettering himself," says Munro, now a coach in the United States. "Erich was all about strength. He became an athlete through his strength and determination. He would just work at it and work at it until he was the fittest. He was incredibly driven that way. He wanted to be first in the gym and last out of it. Jim McArthur was at the other end of the scale – he'd be made to wear bin liners and sweat off pounds and pounds, then you'd see him round the back of the stand getting stuck into a fly bag of crisps.

"When I'm coaching kids now I tell them there are four things you need to make it as a footballer: ability, desire, nerve and a bit of luck. Erich had ability, no question, but he built his ability through sheer desire. And nerve? He had that in spades – he was absolutely fearless, nothing fazed him and he was admired and respected for that. Some players need to be motivated, but Erich motivated himself, and coaches and managers liked him wherever he went because of that. They didn't have to motivate him – they had to try and hold him back if anything; his enthusiasm knew no bounds."

McArthur may have been at the opposite end of the scale to Schaedler in terms of natural fitness, but he does remember getting the better of Erich in one sprint – albeit, he used a bit of cunning to claim his victory. "Erich was fit as a flea and he was practically unbeatable when it came to the sprints at training – only Arthur Duncan could live with him for pace," says McArthur. "But there was one pre-season that I had been down at Largs for a coaching course. When you're there, you are basically training full time and when I got back I was as fit as I've ever been. What Turnbull did at training was to use Erich as the hare for us to chase. He would be first to run over a set distance and Erich's time would be used as the mark we had to aim at, making everyone work harder by trying to keep up with him.

"Us goalies, and a couple of other guys who weren't so keen on training, went up to Erich and told him to take it a bit easier, so not to make us look too bad. So he did. He went first and took it a little bit easier. I was second up, and went straight after him and beat his time . . . oh, he was raging about that! I didn't mean to beat his time, it's just that I was fitter than I thought I was. He never made that mistake again – I never even got close to his times after that."

In Erich's second spell at Easter Road, McArthur was reluctantly persuaded to join Schaedler for some extra training at the Edinburgh Club one afternoon – another mistake he didn't make twice! "I had stitches in my knee and had been out of the first team for a few weeks. It was when Pat Stanton was manager and we had a reserve game at Easter Road one night. Before I went to the ground that night I went with Erich to the Edinburgh Club during the day. He was showing me how to lift the weights, but by the time I got out of there my upper body was so sore I couldn't lift my arms! I told them in the dressing room before the game I was in pain. Tam McNiven gave me a massage but I was saying, 'Tam, I cannae play.'

But he said, 'You have to play.' I actually lost a goal because of it. Somebody chipped me from outside the box because I couldn't lift my arms above my head!"

Stanton stresses that Erich's approach to training was measured and responsible. "I found when I was a player, under certain managers, that the training maybe went on too long – to the stage that you weren't getting any benefit from it. Maybe the last half-hour was extending it, simply so you could finish at twelve o'clock," says Stanton. "But the likes of Jock Stein knew how to adapt training to suit the conditions and suit the players. He would treat us as you would treat a racehorse. If it was a warm day, he wouldn't work you up so you'd be lathered in sweat. He would know when to ease off, but other managers would pound you until you were knackered. Erich was like Jock Stein in knowing where the cut-off point should be. He was really in tune with his body and seemed to know exactly how much to put in. If you heard Erich saying at training that we were overdoing it, you would pay attention. Some players, like Alex Edwards, would moan ALL the time, so you just ignored him, but coming from Erich you knew it made sense."

Erich's Iron Man image was not lost on the supporters. They could see week-in, week-out that Schaedler would run from the first whistle to the last. Frank Dougan marvelled at the energetic performances of his friend, and recalls the occasion he discovered just how dedicated Schaedler was. "Erich was very unique," says Dougan. "His fitness was unbelievable. He was a total fitness fanatic. One Sunday morning he asked if I could pick him up. He was running a marathon in Edinburgh and then wanted to go down to his mum's after. So I said no problem and straight from the finish line he jumped in my car and we drove down to Peebles. I left him when he went down so he could go to his mum's, but I later found out that when he'd got down to Peebles, as well as visiting his mum he'd also managed to run another half-marathon down there! That is scary fitness."

## 14

# NATIONAL SERVICE

"Would you play for Scotland or West Germany if both wanted you?" It was a question Erich Schaedler was often asked, and he was unable to give an unequivocal answer. First and foremost, he simply wanted to become good enough to be considered an international-class defender. Although his first allegiance was towards the place of his birth, he would have been proud too to represent his father's country if the call had ever come. Realistically, that was unlikely to happen. Prior to the reunification of Germany in 1990, West Germany were a superpower of world football. They had controversially lost the 1966 World Cup final against England (you may have heard it mentioned from time to time), then finished a creditable third at the 1970 World Cup in Mexico. Schaedler's emergence as a player coincided with the beginning of a golden era for German football, as they won the European Championships in 1972 – beating the Soviet Union 3–0 in the final – and looked forward to staging the 1974 World Cup on home turf. To be blunt, if there was a pecking order at that time for German-qualified left-backs, Schaedler's name would feature a fair way down the list. The established left-back was the marauding Paul Breitner, and there was little chance of anyone dislodging the Bayern Munich man at that time.

Scotland did have a genuinely world-class full-back of their own – Danny McGrain – and while the Celtic defender was seen at his brilliant best on the right flank, he had no difficulty switching to left-back when Sandy Jardine played at No.2. Since Tommy Gemmell's international career had finished, the left-back slot was effectively up for grabs. Other contenders for the No.3 jersey in the early 1970s were Manchester City's Willie Donachie, Manchester United's Alex Forsyth (although he was more often a right-back) and Aberdeen's Jim Hermiston. Willie Ormond took over as Scotland manager from Manchester United-bound Tommy Docherty in early 1973 and after a disastrous debut match in charge – the 5–0 St Valentine's Day massacre against England at Hampden – Ormond set about the task of trying to take Scotland to their first World Cup finals since they qualified for Sweden in 1958.

As a former Hibs player himself, Ormond had watched his old club take the 1972/73 season by storm, and despite the injury to John Brownlie, there were a crop of other Easter Road players worthy of international consideration. In March 1973, Ormond had selected Erich, Arthur Duncan, Pat Stanton, Alan Gordon and Alex Cropley for his squad for the annual Scottish League v English League fixture. That had been just as Hibs were flying out to Split and Erich's dislocated shoulder deprived him of the chance to represent his country. In the event, Stanton and Duncan did play, and it was Arthur's namesake John Duncan of Dundee who scored both the goals in a 2–2 draw. These matches effectively doubled as international trials and Ormond fielded McGrain at left-back and Jardine at right-back in a strong team of home-based players.

Schaedler's shoulder injury had been unfortunately timed, but when he returned to fitness quicker than expected, Ormond kept him in his thoughts and included him in his squad along with club-mate Pat Stanton for the 1973 home internationals against England, Wales and Northern Ireland. The pair got the news just as the Hibs squad were flying out to Benidorm for their end-of-season trip, but Stanton and Schaedler would spend just a few days with their Easter Road mates before cutting short the trip to report for international duty at a training camp at Largs. The rest of the Hibs party stayed out in Spain and flew to London to take in the England v Scotland match in Wembley. "Being picked for Scotland is the greatest thing that has happened to me," said a delighted Erich. "I'll be going all out to earn my place in the team. I don't mind giving up part of my Spanish holiday to do my bit for Scotland. It's a real honour."

Scotland were halfway through their World Cup qualifying campaign when Ormond took the reins from Docherty, and the team were in a strong position to qualify. Under "The Doc", they had beaten Denmark home and away, and in a group of three (nothing like the protracted qualifying pools now), it would all come down to a double-header against rivals Czechoslovakia in the autumn of 1973. The squad for the home internationals hinted at Ormond's plans for those vital matches, and *The Scotsman*'s John Rafferty approved of the national manager's thinking. "When Willie Ormond yesterday announced his pool of twenty-two players for this month's home championship, almost all of the defence which lost five goals to England in the centenary international were missing," said Rafferty. "Out went Aberdeen goalkeeper Bobby Clark, the two centre-backs Martin Buchan and Eddie Colquhoun, and left-back Alex Forsyth. That was the heart of the Tommy Docherty defence and now it can be said with conviction that Willie Ormond is doing it his way. Perhaps he was inspired in the emergence of two talented and inspiring young full-backs, Danny McGrain of Celtic and Erich Schaedler of Hibs. The naming of Schaedler is particularly pleasing, for in Scotland there is no better left-back. The Manchester City man Willie Donachie is listed for the same position, but I would certainly prefer to see the hard-running, strong-tackling Hibs player given his chance. He has earned it. Indeed, one can see a young defence of tremendous skill and talent coming from the pool. Looking forward to the World Cup matches, one would wish earnestly a rear four of McGrain, George Connelly, Derek Johnstone and Schaedler would click."

The twenty-two-man squad was: Peter McCloy (Rangers),

Alastair Hunter (Celtic), Tom McAllister (Sheffield Utd). Full-backs: Sandy Jardine (Rangers), Danny McGrain (Celtic), Willie Donachie (Manchester City), Erich Schaedler (Hibs). Centre-backs: George Connelly (Celtic), Jim Holton (Manchester United), Derek Johnstone (Rangers). Midfield: Billy Bremner (Leeds), Pat Stanton (Hibs), George Graham (Manchester United), Dave Hay (Celtic), Asa Hartford (West Brom), Kenny Dalglish (Celtic). Forwards: Willie Morgan (Manchester United), Colin Stein (Rangers), Lou Macari (Manchester United), Derek Parlane (Rangers), John Connolly (Everton), John Doyle (Ayr United). Schaedler was involved in all of the squad sessions, but he didn't feature in the three matches. The home internationals started brightly, Scotland beating Wales 2–0 in Wrexham thanks to a double from George Graham. But they were poor at Hampden against Northern Ireland in midweek and deservedly lost 2–1, and Martin Peters scored the winner as England inflicted another defeat on them – mercifully just 1–0 this time, after the horrors of February three months earlier. Pat Stanton played against Wales and Northern Ireland but missed out on the Wembley match.

The home internationals had been a crushing disappointment but there was good news on the World Cup front. Denmark had unexpectedly held Czechoslovakia to a draw in Copenhagen, meaning that if Scotland beat the Czechs at Hampden in September they would qualify for the 1974 finals in Germany.

Ormond's side suffered successive 1–0 friendly defeats to Switzerland and Brazil in the summer and that meant the Scots were heading into their clash with Czechoslovakia on the back of an alarming four-match losing run. Schaedler and John Blackley were named in a twenty-two-man squad for the match at Hampden on 26 September. Neither player was picked, but along with a crowd of 90,000 they still witnessed one of the great Hampden nights – not that Scotland did it the easy way, of course. Goalkeeper Ally Hunter made a mess of Zdenek Nehoda's speculative punt and Scotland were a goal down after thirty-three minutes. The legendary Denis Law may have been nearing the end of his Scotland career, but that night he won his fiftieth cap and he marked the occasion by dinking the ball in for big Jim Holton to power home a fantastic header. In the second half Ormond sent Joe Jordan on for Kenny Dalglish and it proved a masterstroke, as the big centre forward bulletted home a winner to send Hampden into rapture.

With Scotland assured of top spot, the final group fixture in Bratislava was rendered meaningless. Leeds United's David Harvey was in goals, as Hunter paid the price for his Hampden clanger and never played for his country again, but Ormond still fielded his strongest side, Jardine and McGrain continuing to hold down the right-back and left-back spots respectively. Scotland's main aim was to avoid injury or needless bookings and in an insipid match they lost 1–0. There was a twist in the tale though: as they came off the pitch they were told the news that England had been knocked out by Poland, and therefore Scotland would be Britain's sole representatives at the finals in Germany the following year.

To prepare for the finals, Scotland had friendlies fixed up against West Germany – home and away. There was no Hibs representation for the first match at Hampden in 1973, a 1–1 draw, but for the second match in March of World Cup year Stanton and Schaedler were both called into Ormond's squad. It was the news Erich had so desperately wanted to hear. He considered his involvement with Scotland to be a privilege and an honour, but to be picked for an international in his father's homeland was a moment to be proud of. It also gave him another chance to play his way into Ormond's final squad for the 1974 finals.

The draw for the World Cup finals had been screened live on TV (still something of a novelty then) on 5 January, and Scotland had come out of the hat against reigning world champions Brazil, Yugoslavia and Zaire. The draw had been made in Frankfurt, and with two of Scotland's Group 2 matches – against Brazil and Yugoslavia – due to take place in that city, it made perfect sense to fix up their friendly with West Germany there too. Schaedler had already been in a few squads, but his opportunity to play had finally arrived – Ormond had selected him at left-back and in Frankfurt he would wear the Scotland jersey for the first time in an international.

"Erich was not big-headed in any way, but when he was picked he did not seem surprised," recalls Stanton. "I think he thought to himself, 'I've earned this.' He got there because he had worked hard, and he would be entitled to say to himself, 'This is down to me and the hard work I've put in.' He also recognised the people who had helped him get there. I remember Tam McNiven, in particular, was delighted for Erich. When you see some guys today that have caps, you sometimes wonder why, but in Erich's case it was an achievement well deserved."

In a wonderful gesture of comradeship, Erich's full-back rival Danny McGrain sent a telegram to Schaedler, congratulating him on his selection. It demonstrated the mutual respect between the pair. Hibs and Celtic had played each other in so many finals at Hampden that McGrain already new Erich well. It takes a great defender to know one, and the Celtic man was a big admirer of Schaedler's all-action style, attitude to the game and personality. "He was a strong person physically, and while it was difficult to get to know someone really well from the Scotland trips, from what I knew I really liked him," says McGrain. "We played against each other a lot, and we had a few tussles down that same side of the pitch.

"Both of us were players who liked to get forward, and were in teams that played that way, so our paths crossed quite often on the football pitch. If I was guilty of a bad tackle against Erich he wouldn't moan about it, but you could be sure at some stage he'd try and get you back. There was nothing dirty about it though, it was a man's game. He was a nice, nice man. I'm a nice man too, but like him, on the park I wasn't.

"Neither of us were dirty, but we made sure we were hard to play against. Erich was the same as me in that respect. He fought for the cause and fought for the team. Physically he was well equipped to play that type of game and he soon got a big reputation that he was a hard man to play against. He wasn't dirty, but exceptionally quick in the tackle. Tam Forsyth (of Rangers and Scotland) was a bit like that too – he was hard, but he always wanted to win the ball. If you were a wee winger, you knew you had to be pretty quick to get past and then get away from Erich."

As he previewed the Frankfurt international in *The Scotsman*, John Rafferty said, "Erich Schaedler, with a wide grin, admitted that he had almost given up hope of getting into a team. He was becoming reconciled to being travelling reserve. Ormond explained, 'He was being kept out by Danny McGrain, whom I consider is the best full-back in Europe.' Schaedler was thick-throated with emotion over a telegram he received from McGrain before the team was announced. He wished him luck. That was nice."

Schaedler's appearance in Germany had generated some interest in the local media and among the Scottish press corps. Although the left-back had visited his father's country as a child and on tour as a Hibs player, arriving in Germany as a Scotland player was the ultimate honour for him. "Erich Schaedler's supporters' club was gathering in Frankfurt last night," wrote Rafferty. "His father was a player with München Gladbach, a team in the German league. He was a member of the Germany Navy during the war, and was a prisoner in Scotland. There, he married a girl from Leadhills, in Lanarkshire. Erich, the Hibs full-back, still keeps in touch with his father's relatives in München; and last night they were making preparations to travel to Frankfurt to support him. He said, 'Two years ago I was in Germany. I met them all, and I am excited that they have all remembered me and are gathering round me to give me what help they can.'"

Around 150 miles away in Erich senior's home city of Mönchengladbach, his brother Wilhelm sat down to watch the match with family friend Robert Inglis. "I watched the Germany v Scotland match with Erich's uncle – he was very proud that his nephew was playing," says Inglis. "I remember when Hibs were here for pre-season and Erich came and visited his family. But they showed the Scotland game live in Germany and it was fantastic to see Erich striding out wearing the Scotland shirt. He did his country proud that night too. Considering he was playing for the first time as an international and the high quality of the West Germany team, it was a very good effort."

Ormond had picked an experimental team for the match in Frankfurt. It was one of the last chances for players to prove to him that they deserved a place in his final squad for the World Cup, and Rafferty explained, "Willie Ormond went as near as possible to the side who beat Czechoslovakia when he announced his team for the match against West Germany. Six of that team were available, so six went in. Then he leaned heavily on experience to fill the other places. Yet there was a pleasant touch of two players, who had been rejected by former clubs, winning places. Thomson Allan, released on a free transfer by Hibs, was in goal and Kenny Burns, once on the Rangers staff, was named among the defenders. Both had the same thought that their success must be encouraging for others who have suffered the bitter disappointment of being discarded. Willie Ormond said of his new goalkeeper: "He is in because of his performances with Dundee. I'm not taking anything away from Jim Stewart, who has been great for me, but Thomson Allan has been so good that he just has to be seen at this level."

The Scotland team that lined up against West Germany in front of a 62,000 crowd in the Waldstadion on Wednesday, 27 March 1974, was: Thomson Allan, Sandy Jardine, Erich Schaedler, Davie Hay, Martin Buchan, Pat Stanton, Willie Morgan, Kenny Dalglish, Denis Law, Tommy Hutchison, Kenny Burns. The West Germany line-up was: Sepp Maier, Berti Vogts, Paul Breitner, Georg Schwarzenbeck, Franz Beckenbauer, Bernhard Cullmann, Jurgen Grabowski, Ulrich Hoeness, Gerd Muller, Herbert Wimmer, Dieter Herzog.

As the teams lined up, several of the Scotland players were notably nonplussed when "God Save the Queen" was passed off as the Scottish national anthem. West Germany were trying to put on a show for a capacity crowd and underline their position as World Cup favourites. The pressure was on. They were hosts and the nation fully expected them to deliver in the 1974 finals. Nothing less than a comfortable victory against Scotland would do.

Rafferty reported: "Ormond dreaded a nervous start and Schaedler soon relieved his anxiety with a cool interception." The Germans were powerful and fast in every department, and in the early stages of the game Grabowski and Hoeness were giving Scotland a torrid time. There was a scare when Wimmer got on the end of one of the many balls being fizzed into the Scotland penalty area and hit the crossbar with an acrobatic header. The Scots could not stem the flow, however, and unfortunately Pat Stanton was to shoulder the blame for two rapid-fire West Germany goals. "In three minutes from the thirty-second, Germany scored twice, and each time Pat Stanton – who had played so much above his recent form – had to hang his head, blaming himself," said Rafferty. "Wimmer was streaking through and was clear of the defence when Stanton tripped him. Breitner scored from the penalty spot with a kick no goalkeeper would have stopped. The capacity crowd in this reconstructed stadium was ecstatic with that goal, and even more with the next one, for it was such a goal as it would thrill any crowd. Stanton was dispossessed away out on a touchline, and Hoeness and Grabowski broke together. No Scot could get near them and the final slick shot from Grabowski was the perfect ending to such an exciting burst. We trembled then, lest there should be an avalanche of goals. But half-time arrived with the score still 2–0."

Stanton admits it was not one of his finer performances in a Scotland shirt. YouTube footage from the match shows him caught flat-footed for the penalty, and it is indeed most "un-Stantonlike" the way he scythes Wimmer to the ground. "I've played against some very good teams," says Stanton, "but that West Germany team were exceptional. It was no surprise to go see them go on and win the World Cup. They were a handful."

Scotland were staring at a painful defeat and there was an air of anticipation that West Germany could go on and score a few more – friendly or not. However, some tactical tinkering from Ormond and a couple of considered substitutions – Bobby Robinson of Dundee and Donald Ford of Hearts, coming on for Kenny Burns and the great but fading force of Denis Law – saw Scotland finish the game as a far more cohesive unit.

"The Germans seemed to be playing well within themselves and set on giving the crowd a treat to go with the beautiful night," said Rafferty. "But, as has happened so often before, once a team are allowed to get into the game it is very difficult to push them out. And this the Germans found to their sorrow.

"In the seventy-eighth minute, Scotland scored – and what a neat goal it was. And what a shock to the opposition, who had become near enough arrogant. From Hutchison, the ball went to Robinson; Dalglish ran intelligently and invited the pass. When the ball did arrive, the Germans waited for offside, but Dalglish took the ball past the advancing goalkeeper and scored cleverly." In his summary of the game, Rafferty gave Ormond credit for the way Scotland had regrouped at the interval and emerged in the second half as a team transformed: "Scottish supporters trekked to Frankfurt, apprehensive about the chances of this crippled Scotland," he said in his match report. "In the first half, apprehension became embarrassment as West Germany played as a team which could win the World Cup, while Scotland trailed in their shadow, having us wonder how they had ever got into this company. And then, in the second half, Willie Ormond substituted Bobby Robinson for Kenny Burns, who had hardly been noticed by the Germans in the midfield, and took off Denis Law, who was a caricature of the once great player we used to thrill to, and sent on Donald Ford in his place. In the second half the game was completely turned round.

Almost certainly, this started when the Germans, with what was almost arrogance, began to put on a show, and Scotland seized the chance of working out a pattern and almost snatched a draw to the astonishment of those who remembered the pathetic first half."

Rafferty also picked Schaedler out as one of Scotland's most impressive men on the night, while recognising that the Germans had every right to be considered strong contenders for the World Cup later in the year: "Willie Ormond, of course, was delighted with the result. He had worried in case his inexperienced players would be taken apart and humiliated, but although it looked at one time as if that would be the case, they came out of it well in the end, and with a result which will impress the other countries in Scotland's World Cup section.

"The goalkeeper, Thomson Allan, has almost certainly played himself into the pool. He could be faulted at times for punching instead of clutching, but it has to be remembered that it was his first big occasion. A pleasant surprise was the form of Erich Schaedler, who played above his club best, but the outstanding success was Martin Buchan, playing at centre-half and controlling the local hero Muller until he had him complaining bitterly about the lack of space he was being allowed. Yet one had to admire this German team when they were going flat out. They have such great players. Full-backs Vogts and Breitner, who are fast and tough and aggressive and have powerful shots, and there is uncompromising strength in Schwarzenbeek and elegance in Beckenbauer; but above all, they have what we must continue to envy, the dash of Hoeness and Grabowski, and the cunning and power of Muller."

After the game, Ormond declared himself satisfied with the performance in West Germany, which would stand Scotland in great stead for their World Cup group matches in the country against Zaire, Brazil and Yugoslavia. "Helmut Schoen [the Germany coach] told me at the end he thought his team got worse in the second half, but I disagreed. We got better," reflected Ormond. "In the first half, too many men were coming back and cluttering up the middle of the field. When Bobby Robinson went on, he was finding space and they all spread out to make a good pattern. That aspect of the match was most encouraging."

Davie Hay says, "It was a top-quality German team. I was captain for the night, and while Willie had tinkered with the team a little to allow him to finalise his plans for the World Cup finals, we were still decent enough and we put up a good fight. It was a good experience and it was a good way to prepare for the finals."

Sandy Jardine, on the opposite side of the pitch from Erich at right-back, says, "We played very well in that match. Willie experimented a little, and we were not at our strongest, but we acquitted ourselves well against a world-class team. I think their level of experimentation wasn't quite the same, because they were trying to find the right mix for the finals, but Willie was still looking to give one or two players a chance to play themselves into the pool for the finals, guys like Erich and Thomson Allan. We only lost 2–1, and when you consider that was against the team who would soon become world champions, it shows the strength we had in the squad. Who knows how we might have done if we had been at full strength that night."

Sadly, Erich Schaedler never received a cap in the game against West Germany. Prior to 1974, the Scottish Football Association would only issue caps for home internationals – an injustice highlighted in the award-winning book *My Father and Other Working-Class Football Heroes*, written by Gary Imlach, whose father, Stewart, had played for Scotland at the 1958 World Cup finals but because he hadn't played against England, Wales or Northern Ireland never received a cap. Imlach's book led to a concerted campaign against this absurd bureaucratic anomaly, and the SFA finally relented in 2006, agreeing to issue retrospective caps to more than ninety players – including Imlach, Eddie Turnbull and Erich Schaedler. David Taylor, the then SFA chief executive, said, "We will award a commemorative Scotland cap to any pre-1975 internationals who did not receive one under the previous system.

This is an entirely new initiative by the SFA board of directors that will give a tangible souvenir for those who did not appear in the British Championship.

"Times have changed, and although the British Championship was once seen as the highlight of the season, playing for Scotland in any match is a great honour. That is why we have taken this step, and I hope that it will be welcomed by the players and their families."

This was indeed wonderful news for the Schaedler family, and on 30 April 2006, at a ceremony at Easter Road, Erich's brother John proudly received Erich's Scotland cap. He was in good company – former Hibs players Alex Cropley, Des Bremner and Neil Martin, Jim Scott and, of course, Eddie Turnbull were there to receive the richly deserved Scotland caps that they had long been denied. It is a shame Erich never lived to hold the cap in his hands, but it now takes pride of place in John's home.

Schaedler did return with one keepsake from the match in Frankfurt: the No.8 shirt worn by Herbert Wimmer. Fittingly, Wimmer is a Borussia Mönchengladbach legend, winning five national championships and two UEFA Cups with the club. He also won the 1974 World Cup and the 1972 European Championship with West Germany. It would have been nice to discover that the Mönchengladbach connection had prompted Schaedler and Wimmer to swap shirts at the end of the match, but no such luck. On my behalf, Robert Inglis kindly tracked down Wimmer – still living in the city and involved with the club – but the former midfielder said he had no distinct recollection of his exchange with Erich at the end of the match. The shirt adorned the wall of the Victoria Bar in Leith Walk for many years, but after his death it has passed through several pairs of hands and is now in the ownership of a private collector. The strip actually went under the hammer at a football memorabilia auction Royal Highland Showground in Ingliston in November 2011. It appeared in the catalogue as follows:

*A WHITE WEST GERMANY INTERNATIONAL SHIRT*

*No.8, with crew-neck collar and embroidered cloth badge, inscribed Deutscher Fussball Bund, some slight staining and small tears on front. The shirt was worn by Herbert Wimmer and gained by Erich Schaedler as a swap after the International match against West Germany played on 27 March 1974 in Frankfurt.*

The shirt was sold for £500 to an anonymous bidder. Explaining the shirt's history, auctioneer David Convery told me, "The shirt was bought directly from the player by an Edinburgh-based football memorabilia dealer, who then put it through my auction. It was bought by a private English buyer."

An interesting footnote from the same game is that Erich's Hibs' teammate Alex Cropley bagged the best shirt of all from that match. Cropley, an unused substitute in Frankfurt, swapped with the great Franz Beckenbauer, and he has been kind enough in recent years to allow the Hibernian Historical Trust to exhibit the striking white shirt in the display cabinets within the new West Stand.

## 15

# THE BIGGEST STAGE

After the friendly in Frankfurt, the hype behind the World Cup finals ratcheted up a few notches – particularly as Scotland would be Britain's sole representatives on the biggest stage in football. Unlike his flamboyant predecessor Tommy Docherty, the Scotland manager Willie Ormond was not one for hyperbole. He preferred a low profile, and he was shrewd enough to engage with the nation's press over a drink or two and keep them onside. Ormond had gained a lot of respect for his tactical nous in the friendly defeat against West Germany and hopes were high that the British Championship in May would provide Scotland with a strong springboard for the World Cup finals. It was a golden chance to prove that Scotland were worthy of their place in Germany, and the chips were stacked in their favour given that all three of their matches would take place on their Hampden home turf.

Ormond gathered his squad – including Schaedler – at Largs to prepare for the three matches in three days. First up were Northern Ireland, and Scotland fell flat, losing 1–0 to a goal from Tommy Cassidy of Newcastle United. Willie Donachie was given the nod at left-back but was replaced at half-time by Cassidy's club-mate Jimmy Smith, more of a winger than a full-back. Ormond was philosophical about the defeat and took it on the chin. A win against Wales on the Tuesday night would keep Scotland in contention, and they delivered. Goals from Kenny Dalglish and Sandy Jardine sealed a 2–0 win and set up a winner-takes-all battle with England on the Saturday.

After some hard work on the training ground, the laid-back Ormond allowed his players off the leash to unwind with a drink or two in the Ayrshire seaside town. It was when they sauntered back to their hotel that the trouble started. Jimmy "Jinky" Johnstone spotted a rowing boat and decided it would be a bit of fun to take it for a spin in the Firth of Clyde. There was one small problem – it had no oars. Schaedler and Davie Hay were two of the first to realise that Jimmy the Sailor Man was drifting away fast and they decided to form an impromptu rescue party.

"Who can forget the boating escapade," laughs Hay. "What happened was that we had been for a couple of pints in Largs. When we saw wee Jimmy starting to disappear, Erich and I jumped in another boat, but it started to take in water. Jimmy didn't have oars and neither did we, but we had two bits of wood to get us going. I remember Erich saying to me, 'It's all right for you. Willie won't give you any grief. You'll always get a game no matter what you've done – I've got nae chance!' "

Jardine says, "Everyone mixed very well together. We'd just played Wales and we had the next day off before preparations began for the England match on the Saturday at Hampden. Willie had given us his blessing to go for a few pints, and we went to a hotel in Largs. And it *was* just a few pints. People nowadays might think of footballers going out for a drink and taking it to excess, but we just had a few pints – with full permission – because we knew we had to get ready for the England game. It was about 11pm when Jimmy decided to get in the boat, and when he started drifting out, Erich and Davie Hay jumped in another boat to try and rescue him. But there was a hole in their boat, and when they'd only got about twenty-five yards out it started taking on water. So as they were both bailing out water to stop sinking, Jimmy was getting further and further away, and we had no option but to call the coastguard. It hadn't been at the end of some riotous night, as it had been reported at the time, it was just a funny escapade that got a little out of hand."

As the rest of his teammates stood on the shore laughing, their mirth turned to concern when they realised Johnstone was fast becoming a speck on the horizon as he drifted and drifted further out to sea and HM Coastguard had to be scrambled to save him. The media had a field day. Johnstone was pilloried and Ormond got it in the neck for the apparent lack of discipline within his squad.

There was only one way for Johnstone and the rest of the team to answer the critics and repay their manager – beat England. They did just that. Joe Jordan's goal and an OG from Colin Todd not only gave Scotland a welcome win over the Auld Enemy, it also clinched the British Home Championship trophy and sent them on their way to Germany on a high. As Scotland's players celebrated on the Hampden pitch, Johnstone – drowned by Peter Shilton's over-sized yellow goalkeeper's shirt that he had claimed in a swap – danced in front of the press box and shot them a two-fingered salute. Well, it did finish 2–0!

Ormond now had to get down to the business of selecting his final squad for Germany. From a preliminary squad of forty he had to slash the group to just twenty-two players. Listed at No.22 in the Scotland squad list submitted to FIFA was the name Erich Peter Schaedler – he had made it! The other twenty-one players joining Erich on the plane to Germany, in order of squad number, were: David Harvey (Leeds), Sandy Jardine (Rangers), Danny McGrain (Celtic), Billy Bremner (Leeds), Jim Holton (Manchester United), John Blackley (Hibs), Jimmy Johnstone (Celtic), Kenny Dalglish (Celtic), Joe Jordan (Leeds), David Hay (Celtic), Peter Lorimer (Leeds), Thomson Allan (Dundee), Jim Stewart (Kilmarnock), Martin Buchan (Manchester United), Peter Cormack (Liverpool), Willie Donachie (Manchester City), Donald Ford (Hearts), Tommy Hutchinson (Coventry City), Denis Law (Manchester City), Willie Morgan (Manchester United), Gordon McQueen (Leeds). Bursting with pride, Schaedler said, "To play for your country is the dream of every professional footballer and it was a real magical moment for me to gain selection to the final squad for West Germany. Just to be picked was a fantastic honour."

The news that Erich had made the squad was met with congratulations from his club-mates too. "Erich was made up when he got named in the World Cup squad and we were delighted for him too," says Jim McArthur. "He got the blazer and all the gear and just loved it all – being part of the Scotland set-up. He was in the squad for around three years, off and on, and it was quite an honour to be part of that squad in Germany."

Blackley agrees: "The '74 squad was something else. I thought I had come from a great squad at Hibs, but this was a cut above even that. I remember seeing Willie Morgan of Manchester United come in, and I wisnae sure if I liked him. He would hang about Bremner and Law, and I thought he had an air of arrogance about him. There was a balls-up with the room and Willie ended up the odd man out and came into our room – best decision I ever made because he was brilliant, he was a great lad, and my first impression could not have been more wrong. All the Scotland players liked Shades too, because he did have a great way about him.

"It was great to have Erich alongside me in the '74 squad – it was great for Erich too, to have come so far in quite a short space of time. And to get his cap against West Germany was a real bonus for him too. He was funny on these trips to Germany – he would come over all proud about his roots. I remember the pre-season trip to Germany with Hibs, when he had been to see all his cousins over there in Mönchengladbach. He had picked up the pronunciation and was saying it a different way to the way we would, so we were taking the piss out of him . . . and then we ran!"

From the original forty-man squad for the 1974 finals, those that didn't make the cut were: Jim Brown, Kenny Burns, George Connelly, Jackie Copland, John Duncan, Archie Gemmill, Jim Hermiston, Derek Johnstone, Bobby Lennox, Lou Macari, Frank

Munro, Derek Parlane, Bobby Robinson, Jocky Scott, Jimmy Smith, Graeme Souness, Pat Stanton and Colin Stein. To a man, the 1974 squad members I have spoken to in the course of writing this book believe Schaedler's inclusion was thoroughly merited, but Erich's selection did not go down well with one of the men Ormond discarded before West Germany – Jim Hermiston, the Aberdeen captain, who quit football to join the police in 1975 and later emigrated to Australia. "I was at the peak of my career and was angry I wasn't picked to go to West Germany for the finals," said Hermiston in an interview in 2005. "Willie Ormond named me in his first squad but when he then cut that to twenty-two, he picked Erich Schaedler of Hibs instead. No disrespect to Erich, but I was a better player than him and was captain of one of the best sides in the country. I felt cheated."

Other players like Pat Stanton accepted Ormond's decision with dignity. The former Hibs captain is disappointed that he never played at a World Cup, but he has never harboured any grudges. "It was one of these things," says Stanton, "but it was good to see Erich and John Blackley in the squad. I know Erich only won one cap, but with so many top-class guys playing in that era even getting one cap was some achievement. I ended up with sixteen and I'm proud of that. There were so many good players around. It was the same then as it is now though – there are certain players who get capped easier than others, purely because of the club they are at. People would say that's not the case, but it is the case. Players can be at clubs like Hibs, Hearts, Dundee United and Aberdeen and be overlooked, then as soon as they go to a bigger club they get capped straight away."

Martin Buchan won caps at Aberdeen and Manchester United and he believes Erich Schaedler was a class act on and off the pitch: "Erich was nicknamed the 'Mad Kraut' and, like everyone, I was shocked when I heard what happened to him later in life. I would not have thought he was the type of guy who had demons or problems, at least that's the impression he gave. He appeared to be confident and content. Our paths only briefly crossed at club level because I left Aberdeen for Manchester United in 1972.

"Tommy Docherty did a lot of the spadework in putting together the 1974 World Cup squad. He started the campaign off and provided the framework for the squad and Willie carried on the good work. It was a good group of players and characters but it wasn't all sweetness and light – there was a mixture of experienced and younger lads, and while we might have given the impression of one big happy family, there was the odd problem along the way. It didn't affect the way we went out and played though. There had been problems during a trip to Norway leading up to the finals, but for the majority of the time it was a happy camp.

"Shades was full of character and he got on very well with Donald Ford, the Hearts player, as the two of them knew each other from the Edinburgh rivalry. He was a very capable player though. He may have been the twenty-second man on the squad list, but that meant nothing. He deserved to be there and he looked completely at ease amongst the rest of us."

Before flying out to the finals, the Scotland squad had a duty to take care of . . . recording their World Cup song. Some of Scotland's World Cup songs are fondly remembered, such as "Ally's Tartan Army" (1978) and "We Have a Dream" (1982), but it's fair to say the 1974 offering "Easy, Easy" split opinion. Released by Polydor, the idea was to tap into The Bay City Rollers sound. The song was penned by Bill Martin and Phil Coulter, the esteemed songwriters behind Bay City Rollers' No.1 "Shang-A-Lang", but the tartan-clad pin-up boys were unavailable, so the squad had to sing it themselves. A picture of the 1974 squad belting out the song wonderfully captures the image of a beaming Erich at the front alongside a sheepish-looking Donald Ford, lustily belting out classic lyrics such as, "Yabadabadoo we support the boys in blue / Yes it's easy, easy" and "Ring a ding a ding / there goes Willie on the wing. Ring a ding a dong / Now we know we can't go wrong!" "Easy, Easy", which also featured on a Scotland World Cup album, made it to

No.20 in the UK charts before heading for the record store bargain buckets.

A fortnight before the finals Scotland played two warm-up matches. The first, away to Belgium, they lost 2–1; the second, in Norway, they won 2–1, but the trip to Oslo saw the wayward Johnstone blot his copybook even further by breaking a curfew and having a few too many pints. Billy Bremner got in on the act too to leave Ormond embarrassed and the press, who witnessed the pair's session first-hand when they walked into the same bar, grumbling about indiscipline. At the end of his tether, Ormond toyed with the idea of sending the errant pair home, but the SFA decided they should remain part of the World Cup squad.

Danny McGrain denies that a drinking culture affected the squad in any way, however. "I'm not saying one or two of the boys didn't have a drink, but we all knew the importance of being at a World Cup," he says. "It was the first time as a country we had made it to the World Cup in sixteen years, and for guys like Denis Law and Billy Bremner, who knew it would be their last World Cup, they knew it was a chance of a lifetime. They were not there to mess about and do anything stupid. It was a top-class squad though. Willie Ormond could have fielded two teams; he had cover for all eleven positions."

Scotland were based at Erbismuhle, near Frankfurt, and as the only British team there, they found that security was especially tight. The 1972 Munich Olympics had been blighted by terrorism and tragedy, and the Germans were taking every precaution to prevent a repeat. The IRA had also allegedly made a threat towards the Scots, supposedly because they had a Rangers player within the squad – Sandy Jardine. A heavy security detail was assigned to shadow Scotland wherever they went, but the squad saw this as reassurance rather than an inconvenience, and morale remained high within the squad.

"It was a happy camp," says the former Manchester United defender Martin Buchan. "There was a great atmosphere surrounding the finals, although there was heavy security. There had been word of a threat made by the IRA that there might be an incident. We were the only team from the British Isles who had made it to Germany for the finals, so there was an edge to security. We had a squad of German anti-terrorism lads who looked after us very well. They told us exactly what to do if we came under attack, and I remember when we were on the bus going to the games or leaving the base, we were shadowed by a helicopter. If you looked up from the bus, you could see the security guards with their feet on the rails of the helicopter and guns in their laps, ready to respond if they had to. But fortunately nothing happened to mar the football."

Danny McGrain remembers Erich was completely unfazed by the high security alert and actually struck up a rapport with the specialist team of soldiers who followed the Scotland squad's every move. "Erich was a madman, but a very likeable madman," laughs McGrain. "When we were over at the World Cup there had been an IRA threat made against Sandy Jardine, so we had security guards with the squad at all times and Erich would hang about with them. He was fascinated by all their defence techniques. I remember him asking them if they could do a death grip like Doctor Spock from *Star Trek* – God knows what he would have done to the rest of us if he'd managed to learn the Spock grip!"

Tommy Hutchison, the former Coventry player, said Jimmy Johnstone was the opposite of the fearless Schaedler – he had a bout of nerves every time he clapped eyes on a machine gun. Speaking in the excellent BBC series *That Was the Team That Was,* Hutchison said: "Everywhere we went, even the hotel, we had to have police with us and they all had guns. Wee Jimmy was frightened to death, which gave the rest of us a laugh. He kept saying there could be snipers. He used to walk out the hotel with his Celtic bag up at his face. He'd say, 'Look, I play for Celtic,' as if that was going to save him."

Sandy Jardine also recalls the strong spirit within the Scotland squad, and recalls Schaedler soaking up the experience. "I already knew Erich well because although I played for Rangers I was an Edinburgh lad with plenty of pals in the city, and quite a few at Hibs – guys like Nello [Peter Marinello] and John Murphy. Some of my pals would tell me how hard Erich would go in at training. There are some tackles you wouldn't go into full-throttle at training, but Erich treated training like it was a Saturday. He would never hold back with his tackles; it was just the way he played and trained," says Jardine.

"As a person he was a little bit different to your average footballer. He had a deep side to him, but he was still a good mixer and was popular with the rest of the Scotland team. As a player, he was as wholehearted as anyone could be. He really got wired in, and anyone that played against him knew they had been in a game.

"One of wee Willie Ormond's strengths was that he knew how important team spirit was. There were a lot of exceptional players in that Scotland team, and the crop of younger players – which included Erich and myself – were delighted to be in the company of players like Billy Bremner and Denis Law. Nobody acted like a superstar though and we all mixed very well.

"He was such a wholehearted player, who always gave 100 per cent. He would have been truthful enough to admit there were classier players, but Erich is a classic example of how hard work and sheer determination can help a player maximise the abilities he had. If a lot of players had Erich's attitude, they would not go far wrong."

Scotland's Group 2 rivals Brazil and Yugoslavia raised the curtain on the 1974 World Cup on 13 June, fighting out a disappointing 0–0 draw at the Waldstadion in Frankfurt – the same venue Scotland had visited for their March friendly with West Germany. The next day in the Westfalenstadion in Dortmund, it was Scotland's turn. They would play Zaire, the first "black" African nation ever to make it to the finals. Ormond selected McGrain at left-back, with Jardine at right-back and Schaedler had to be content with watching the match from the sidelines. Goals from Peter Lorimer and Joe Jordan saw the Scots race into a 2–0 lead after thirty-four minutes against their tactically inexperienced opponents, but there was a noticeable relaxation in Scotland's play thereafter – some of the players keener to conserve energy for their upcoming match with Brazil rather than go for the jugular and get a few goals. It was to prove a fatal error in terms of their qualification chances.

The same full-backs kept their places as Scotland could – and should – have beaten Brazil in the Waldstadion. The South Americans were not of the vintage of their peerless 1970 team, and were guilty of some cynical tackling against the Scots. When Billy Bremner squeezed a rebound past the post from a couple of yards, a golden chance had been blown. Dressing room despondency deepened when the news came through from the Parkstadion in Gelsenkirchen that Yugoslavia had put nine goals past Zaire, showing the ruthless streak which had deserted Scotland in their opening match.

There was a pleasant surprise for Schaedler and Blackley when they received a visit from some familiar faces. "I was there with Bertie Auld, Eddie Turnbull and Tom Hart," says coach John Fraser. "Hibs had flown us over there and we watched two of the games. We went to see John and Erich at training and Willie Ormond was very accommodating. It looked like they were both savouring every moment of being at the World Cup finals."

Erich stayed on the bench for Scotland's third and, sadly, final game at the 1974 World Cup against Yugoslavia. Needing a win to progress, Scotland – in all white – battled bravely in a tense contest, but fell behind nine minutes from time when Stanislav Karasi scored. Joe Jordan equalised in the eighty-eighth minute, but it was too little too late. It was a glorious failure from Scotland, a phrase they would become well used to in future World Cups.

Schaedler's chance of playing at a World Cup had been and gone, but in fairness to Ormond it would have been difficult to drop McGrain or Jardine. McGrain says, "There was a lot of competition for the full-back places at the World Cup. Willie Donachie was competing for the No.3 shirt as well, but they switched me to left-back and played Sandy at right-back. If it had been me and I had gone to the World Cup and not played, I would have found that hard, but Erich was the kind of guy that didn't let it get him down. I had to work hard to keep him out of the Scotland team. I always knew I had guys like Willie Donachie and him breathing down my neck and wanting my jersey, so I had to work that bit harder and make sure I stayed in the team.

"But Erich was an important part of the squad and was always jovial. In Germany, Erich always had a smile on his face – he was full of beans. He was just immensely proud to be there, for him, his family and his club. For me, he encompassed what football was all about. He worked as hard as he could and got into that Scotland squad thanks to his own dedication and commitment to the game."

Broadcaster Arthur Montford covered the tournament for Scottish Television, and he feels Erich was a shade unlucky not to have featured: "I interviewed him several times in the build-up to the World Cup and I found him extra helpful and a nice man. Erich was under the spotlight with the scribes of the day because of his background, being of German extraction, and he had to cope with some extra media attention. He was also a terrific full-back and I really feel he was a player who was a bit unlucky not to at least get one game at the 1974 World Cup," says Montford. "I feel he should have perhaps been given a chance, because I think he would have added something to the team with his attacking style of play, getting forward the way he did for Hibs. Willie Ormond switched Danny McGrain from right-back to left-back, but I don't think he looked completely comfortable on what was not his favoured side.

"Scotland deserve a lot of praise for the way they performed at the World Cup though. They would regret not getting more goals against Zaire, but not to lose to Brazil was outstanding.

"I think Erich Schaedler was certainly worthy of international recognition. I found him A) very co-operative, B) very courteous, and C) an excellent full-back who can consider himself unlucky to get only one Scotland cap."

Davie Hay, who played in all three of Scotland's matches in West Germany, agrees that Schaedler was unfortunate to miss out, but he says it is testament to his character that he never grumbled. "Because of the quality of players in the squad, he never got the opportunity to play at the finals. He was a good lad though; I enjoyed his company. I always remember how much he put in at training," says Hay.

"The '74 squad really gelled as a group. There were one or two who preferred to keep themselves to themselves but when it came to training there were absolute no issues or complaints – everyone was completely committed and that made us strong as a group. In that era there was no spitting the dummy out. The manager picked the team, and even if you weren't in, you may have been disappointed but you always respected his decision. Erich came into that category – he never made the team at the World Cup finals, but you never heard a murmur of discontent from him. He was just proud to be there. We all were. It was a privilege to be part of that squad. I think Eddie Turnbull would have had a lot to do with that – in the shaping of Erich as a footballer and a person. He would have instilled discipline and respect. A lot of the credit for the Scotland team spirit was down to Willie Ormond.

"Willie was first class as a manager. I really enjoyed playing under him. I think a lot of his philosophy was down to his own career as a player. He had been in a Hibs team geared to attacking football, and played his part in the Famous Five, one of the best forward lines Scotland has ever seen. That positive attitude came through in his management style – as a player it was great to be set out to attack, it made it far more enjoyable to take that positive attitude out on to the pitch.

"There was a lot of pressure on us to win the Zaire game, and we didn't know it at the time, but our decision to take our foot off the gas after we went a couple of goals ahead had a massive bearing on whether or not we made it through."

Buchan also rues the lack of killer instinct shown in the Zaire game and says Scotland's failure to make it past the group stage haunts him to this day. "I couldn't play in the game against Zaire and John Blackley played in my position," he says. "Against Brazil and Yugoslavia we gave as good as we got. I can count myself fortunate, because I played thirty-four times for Scotland – and three of these games were against Brazil, in Rio in 1972, the 1974 World Cup and in 1977 in a friendly at Hampden. That in itself is an education in the game. What ultimately stopped us qualifying, of course, was that we never scored enough goals against Zaire. I watched the game recently on TV and I couldn't believe it, but it was there in front of my eyes: Billy Bremner was playing keepy-up with the ball instead of driving us forward. We should have shown far more urgency and tried to score more goals – exactly what Yugoslavia did when they played Zaire and beat them 9–0. In fairness to Zaire, though, they played out of their skin. It was their first ever game at a World Cup and perhaps they only had one good game in them. Unfortunately, it happened to be against us. The Brazil game is remembered for Billy Bremner's miss, when he was a toenail away from poking the ball into the net. So near yet so far, but that is the Scotland motto, isn't it?"

It was scant consolation, but Scotland hold the distinction of being the only unbeaten participants in the 1974 World Cup. Even West Germany, who beat the Netherlands 2–1 in the final, lost to East Germany in the first group stage. Schaedler, unfortunately, never got the opportunity to play for Scotland again.

"To be honest, I don't think Erich ever got the recognition he deserved," says former Scotland international Tommy Gemmell, who later signed Schaedler for Dundee. "He won only one Scottish cap – ironically, against West Germany in 1974 – and it was just his bad luck he was up against someone such as Danny McGrain at that time. Danny, of course, was more at home at right-back, but he could fit in very well on the left with Rangers' Sandy Jardine on the other flank. It was a world-class partnership at the time and, alas, it meant Erich was overlooked on many occasions.

"Scotland had an abundance of excellent left-backs at the time and there were others such as Manchester City's Willie Donachie and Manchester United double act of Alex Forsyth and Stewart Houston. Arthur Albiston was coming along as one for the future. I have absolutely no doubt Erich would have added massively to his international tally if these guys hadn't been around at the same time."

16

# MR CHARISMA

The Tartan Army mustered a healthy contingent of supporters for the friendly match against West Germany in March 1974, and the legions grew in size for the World Cup finals three months later. In the crowd in Frankfurt watching Erich Schaedler make his debut as a Scotland player was radio DJ-in-the-making Jay Crawford, en route to the World Cup. Within a year, the two men – local celebrities in Edinburgh within their respective professions – would become firm friends. Bizarre tales of intrepid, madcap travel plans are common among the fanatical Tartan Army, many who have gone to great lengths to see Scotland play all over the world, and Crawford reveals he took a roundabout route to the Waldstadion. "The first time I really became aware of Erich Schaedler was that match in Germany," says Crawford. "I was in Rhodesia as it was then – Zimbabwe now – and was there up until around October/November 1973, when a guy I had been working with in London wrote to me and sent me a clipping of Billy Bremner being carried off the pitch shoulder high at Hampden Park after Scotland had beaten Czechoslovakia, which meant, of course, we had qualified for the 1974 World Cup.

"So this pal of mine said, 'Let's go to Germany for the World Cup.' So we both arrived in Germany as the advanced Tartan Army at the end of January 1974 and of course it didn't kick off until the end of June. But there was a friendly against West Germany in

Frankfurt and me and my mate Brian went along. I still have the ticket. Because Erich's dad was Grman and the way his name was spelt attracted attention, his presence caused a bit of a stir amongst the Germans. And when his name flashed up on the scoreboard, the Germans were up on their feet cheering. To them it was like the equivalent of Angus McTavish coming up on the screen – it was a very German name. Because I had been out of the country for so long, Erich wasn't on my radar as a player because I hadn't really seen any Scottish football, so I was oblivious to the players in the great Hibs side of the early Seventies. He was picked for the Scotland squad fifteen times I think, so the West Germany game was the moment he actually got his chance [to play]."

Schaedler's name had registered with Crawford, and after watching the full-back put in a hard shift against the World Champions-in-waiting, he was greatly impressed with the Hibs defender as a footballer. Little did he know that fate would soon pitch them together as housemates and pals.

"After the World Cup I went to the Greek Islands for the summer and then came back and then got the job for Radio Forth in the October of 1974. The station wasn't launching until January of '75 so I was looking for a flat in Edinburgh. Me and another one of my flatmates got a place in Lixmount Gardens in Trinity, and before long Erich was taking the other bedroom in this flat.

"When he moved into the flat, he and I immediately hit it off. We became good friends. I think it was partly down to what I was doing – he liked that, I think; he found that quite glamorous. He was divorced by then and we were single guys out and about in Edinburgh. We had a good laugh, these were great times. It was a golden era for the city, especially for radio, and it was exciting when Radio Forth launched.

"When we were in the flat at Lixmount Gardens, Erich still had his green 1974 World Cup Capri – I think the whole Scotland squad had been given Capris as part of a sponsorship deal. I had a Mini and we would jump into the cars and race each other into town.

"He absolutely loved the Edinburgh life. Everything about Erich was immaculate – his car was immaculate, he was immaculate. The way he kept his room and kept his shit together; he was very well organised. Because he wasn't a drinker he was always up. He was bright and he never had that hungover attitude that affects most people after they've had a drink. I never saw him like that. He was Mr Charisma.

"We used to go to the Burnt Post in Lothian Road, which was owned by a friend of his, and sometimes if they had been playing on a Wednesday night I'd meet him there, and a couple of other players. In those days the pubs were meant to shut at ten, but we'd go there and get a bit of a lock-in. But Erich would only ever be drinking a half-pint. I don't think I ever saw him with a pint. He'd only have a half and he would only have two or three. He enjoyed socialising and proved that you don't always have to have a drink to be like that.

"Erich was a guy who just couldn't sit still. He was super fit, and we were both members of the Edinburgh Club run by George Kerr. When we were at the Edinburgh Club, if we were in the steam room he would be doing press-ups. It was like he didn't want to waste a single second if he could fill it doing something useful. His fitness levels were just fantastic."

Crawford was a Scotland fan first and foremost, who, like Schaedler in his younger days, had a leaning towards Rangers, but Erich's association with Hibs and the fact that he was mixing socially with a few of the other Easter Road players, soon drew him towards the green half of the city, and he would pop down from time to time to watch Turnbull's team in action. "It was a strange thing for me because I was actually brought up a Rangers supporter, but it changed when Erich and I shared a flat," says Crawford. "I remember coming home one Saturday night and putting on the highlights. It was a Hibs v Rangers game and while I was watching it I suddenly thought to myself, 'I don't know any of the Rangers players, apart from Sandy Jardine. . . I'm sharing a flat with Erich

Schaedler and know all the Hibs players – what am I doing?' All the sectarianism used to piss me off, so I ended up becoming more of a Hibs fan because of Erich – plus it was the closest team geographically to my hometown of North Berwick!

"I have met a lot of footballers over the years, and some of them have a big ego. Others have come from a hard upbringing and maybe come across as being a bit guarded or socially awkward. But Erich wasn't like that at all, which I suppose was all part of his upbringing – growing up in a place like Peebles rather than growing up in a housing estate in a tough area. He was always warm and engaging and drew people towards him."

Schaedler's passion for Hibs may have quickly rubbed off on Crawford, but the disc jockey's on-the-pulse musical taste didn't influence his friend. "Erich had very strange musical taste," laughs Crawford. "It didn't matter what genre it was, it had to be instrumental. He didn't like anyone singing. He liked some classicial music and some jazz or film soundtracks, so he had this really quite bizarre taste in music where he didn't actually like songs. That was his thing."

Schaedler stayed in a few houses during his time at Hibs, in Newhaven, in Musselburgh and in a flat near the ground in Easter Road to name a few, and although he and Crawford eventually went their separate ways after Lixmount Gardens, they remained friends. "I'd bought a flat by the end of 1975 in Gorgie Road and I moved out, but we kept in touch," says Crawford, who had a long and prosperous broadcasting career. "As time went on and he bought the Victoria Bar in Leith Walk and over the years, I would just pop in and catch up with him. We did a few charity things too. Radio Forth had a charity football team and we used to have some ex-pros who would turn out for us. Graeme Souness's brother Gordon was a regular for us too. I was always on at Erich to come along, but he'd always say, 'I'll referee, but I cannae play.' That went on for years, but I finally managed to twist his arm and got him to play in a charity game in Penicuik."

In the weeks before Schaedler moved into his new pad in Trinity, he was getting back to his day job after the buzz of being at the World Cup finals with Scotland. He would have been frustrated at missing out on an appearance, but was determined to go back and prove himself worthy of further opportunities on the international stage by playing to the best of his ability at club level. With no summer holiday to speak of, no sooner had Schaedler returned from Germany than he was whisked away on more travels with Hibs on their pre-season tour of Norway. He must have been frustrated at failing to get a single minute of action during Scotland's three group matches in Frankfurt and Dortmund, and it would be a relief to get back to playing with his club. Schaedler played ninety minutes in each of three games in July against OPE Östersund (1–1), Rosenborg (3–1) and Nessegutten (4–0). Hibs returned to Scotland for their Drybrough Cup defence, winning their quarter-final 2–1 against Kilmarnock, but missing out on the chance of a third trophy in a row by losing 3–2 at home to Rangers in the semi-finals. Hibs did, however, take revenge on Rangers in the League Cup, beating them home and away to qualify from a tough section.

The UEFA Cup also got off to the perfect start. By a quirk of fate, Hibs had been drawn against their pre-season opponents Rosenborg, and they returned to Norway to again win, this time by the more slender scoreline of 3–2. The second leg was an altogether different story, as Rosenborg were annihilated by the Tornadoes, back to their brilliant best. Goals rained past the bewildered part-timers as Pat Stanton, Alex Cropley, Joe Harper and Iain Munro all scored doubles, with Alan Gordon also chipping in as Hibs came within a goal of double figures, 9–1, a European record victory for the club.

More good news followed in the first derby of the season, as an own goal from Dave Clunie and a goal from Arthur Duncan secured a 2–1 win against Hearts. Then Hibs continued their slick progress through the League Cup by beating Kilmarnock in the quarter-finals and Falkirk in the semi-final at neutral Tynecastle. Hibs had made it to Hampden again. Another major final loomed, and inevitably it was Celtic who were standing in their way.

A league fixture one month before the final proved a disturbing dress rehearsal for Hibs. Dixie Deans helped himself to his now customary hat-trick in a 5–0 cakewalk for Stein's side at Parkhead, and four days later defensive frailties were exposed again – this time in the UEFA Cup, as the mighty Juventus stormed back from 2–1 down to win 4–2 to leave Hibs facing an impossible task for the return leg in Turin. A bad week for Erich got even worse when he picked up an injury and was forced to sit out the Cup final. Watching from the sidelines must have been painful as Dixie Deans did his usual demolition job on Hibs, scoring yet another hat-trick in a 6–3 win. Des Bremner wore No.3 in Erich's absence, while Deans' opposite No.9, Joe Harper, also scored a Hampden Cup final hat-trick and still finished on the losing side.

Former Aberdeen striker Harper had arrived from Everton towards the end of the previous season, and his arrival was viewed by many as upsetting the applecart, particularly as he was seen as the man who displaced and eventually replaced fans' favourite Jimmy O'Rourke, who was sold to St Johnstone at the end of the 1973/74 campaign. Harper, an intelligent, outspoken character, didn't hit it off immediately with all of the Hibs players, but he says Schaedler was a definite exception and made him feel very welcome. "We roomed quite a lot together on trips away, and although he could be a serious lad, I found him a really nice guy," says Harper. "He loved his football and was completely dedicated to Hibs. I had some trouble settling in at Hibs. Some of the boys saw my arrival as unsettling what had been a close-knit squad. But when I signed, I had no idea that they were going to get rid of Alan Gordon, or getting rid of Jimmy O'Rourke. But Erich was one of my pals there. He saw me as an asset and not as a hindrance, and I really respected him for being willing to give me a chance. We had a lot of good times together."

After the League Cup final defeat to Celtic, Erich was back a week later as Hibs beat Morton 5–0 but then endured a woeful seven days. In reality, Hibs had very little chance of wiping out the deficit from their first leg against Juventus, even in the eyes of the eternal optimist Eddie Turnbull, but no one could have predicted just how comprehensively the Edinburgh team would be outplayed in Turin. Juve, with a certain Fabio Capello wearing No.10, simply tore Hibs to shreds, José Altafini rounding off the 4–0 rout, adding to the brace he had scored at Easter Road.

On a lighter note, forward Tony Higgins remembers an amusing anecdote from the trip to Italy. "These European trips were great for team-building," he says. "We went away on the Sunday because you had to be there forty-eight hours before the game and Eddie would occasionally let you have a beer on the first night. He wanted to keep the squad together and morale high, so on the Monday it had been arranged for us that we would all go to the pictures together. When we went into the cinema it was a Clint Eastwood film, which sounded okay, but when it came on it was dubbed in Italian! Everyone was mumping and moaning and the only time there was any interest was when there were sex scenes – wee Micky [Edwards] would be shouting and bawling! But Eddie made us sit through the whole film in Italian."

Hibs had been given the runaround in Italy in more ways than one, and Schaedler rounded off a miserable week by picking up the only red card of his Hibs career in a downbeat draw against Dunfermline. Reports of the match made little mention of the incident which led to Erich being sent-off, choosing instead to praise the physical dimension he gave Turnbull's defence!

Erich was suspended when Hibs ended league leaders Rangers' record as the only unbeaten team in Britain that season, and Des Bremner's impressive form at left-back kept Schaedler on the bench until he returned to the starting XI for a 2–0 win against Dumbarton in mid-December. Hibs headed back to Tynecastle for the 1975 New Year's Day derby, but fanciful talk of trying to repeat the 7–0 game of two years earlier evaporated as the visitors found the home defence as determined as their own, and the game petered out into an unremarkable 0–0 draw. Turnbull's team were again mounting a title challenge of sorts, but a few careless points were allowing Rangers to pull away at the top as they sought to end Celtic's run of nine championships in a row in what was the final year of the old eighteen-team First Division. Celtic were having a disappointing season by their own immaculate standards under Stein, but that didn't stop them doing a Cup double over Hibs, winning 2–0 at Easter Road. It was a painful exit for Hibs, who had harboured high hopes of winning the Scottish Cup in this their centenary year. But from the moment inexperienced goalkeeper Hugh Whyte, making only his third start, spilled the ball for the first goal, the supporters' optimism, like every other Scottish Cup dream they have harboured since 1902, fell flat.

Turnbull didn't tolerate a team that felt sorry for itself, and although Rangers rather than usual suspects Celtic were going to deny them the title, it was testament to Hibs' professionalism that they finished the season so strongly, remaining unbeaten for their final eight games. They did have to suffer watching Rangers winning the title at Easter Road, however, securing the point they needed with a 1–1 draw – Colin Stein again scoring against his old club. In the end, they finished seven points clear of Hibs, with a further four points back to Celtic and Dundee United.

## 17

# SHADES OF GREEN AND BLUE

Scottish football was given a dramatic makeover for the 1975/76 season, a 10-14-14 team league replacing the 18-18 two-tier model, but one drawback of the newly launched Premier Division was that teams would play each other four times in the league campaign. Hibs headed to Ireland to prepare for this groundbreaking season, which would begin with the formal recognition of the club's centenary – a midweek match against Derby County, in which Bruce Rioch scored the only goal for the English champions. The complexion of the team had dramatically changed as Turnbull searched in vain for a new winning formula, and although the core of Erich, Pat Stanton, Alex Edwards, John Blackley, John Brownlie and Arthur Duncan remained, the team never looked like matching the dizzy heights of the 1972/73 season.

The pre-season Irish trip almost never got off the ground for one player, Joe Harper, when he was involved in an amazing standoff before the team had even boarded their flight at Edinburgh Airport. "When we went to Ireland for a pre-season tour, the chairman Tom Hart had been on at me to shave my beard off," says Harper. "I thought he had been joking at first, but it soon became clear he was serious, and it escalated to the point that he warned me that if I didn't get rid of the beard I wasn't going to Ireland. I was livid because Erich, Tony Higgins and one or two others had moustaches at that time, and I felt I was being victimised. I was stubborn, and my view was that if they had facial hair then so could I, and I turned up at Edinburgh Airport still sporting the beard. Tom Hart and Eddie weren't to be messed with, and I could see them at the airport deep in conversation, looking stern, and nodding over at me. I was due to be sharing a room with Erich in Ireland, so he had my bag with my shaving gear in it. Eventually I backed down and went to the toilet to shave it off."

Jim McArthur laughs, "Aye, Eddie and Tom had a thing about you looking as clean-cut as possible, and beards were frowned upon. When I arrived at Hibs from Cowdenbeath, I had been a student and had a big moustache like Fu Manchu. They were quick to make me tidy it up!"

With shaving disputes behind them, Hibs began the campaign fit and spring-heeled, racing through their League Cup section with five wins from six, then opening the new Premier Division season with the perfect result – a 1–0 win over Hearts – in which the beardless Harper scored with a tremendous strike from outside the box.

The UEFA Cup draw had handed Hibs another glamour tie, at home to Liverpool, and given Erich's own admission that he had played one of his worst games in a Hibs shirt the last time the clubs met in Europe five years earlier, he was pumped up for this chance to exorcise that ghost from his past. Erich, along with Brownlie, Blackley and Roy Barry, was outstanding in a famous 1–0 win. Harper scored the winner in front of the old Cowshed, but Brownlie missed a penalty and, in truth, a massive opportunity to seize a strong upper hand had been squandered. A 1–0 win against Liverpool was not to be sniffed at, but it was a precarious lead to go and defend at Anfield.

Before the Merseyside return, Turnbull suffered one of his most humbling defeats – and he was quick to point the finger. Despite holding a 1–0 lead over Division One Montrose from the first leg of their League Cup tie, Hibs contrived to lose 3–1 after extra time at Links Park, and Turnbull blamed Stanton and Higgins for the chastening defeat, axing them from the team. It led to a transfer request from Stanton, and sadly the captain and manager were careering towards an irretrievable breakdown in their working relationship.

With both of the scapegoats absent at Anfield, Hibs lost 3–1. Stanton was made to play in the reserves before he was summoned back into the first team almost a month later, while Higgins had to wait a little longer to regain favour.

Stanton's return coincided with an upturn in Hibs' form and he scored a memorable goal at Tynecastle in November, equalising with a header so deep into injury time the clock had almost struck five o'clock. "I think that was the same game Erich enjoyed a little retribution on one of the Hearts players, Kenny Aird. I'm sure it was," says goalkeeper Jim McArthur. "There wasn't much happening and the ball was nowhere when Erich put this winger right into touch – he needed treatment on the track. As the game went on, they got a corner and Erich sauntered over to the near post. I shouted to him, 'Hey Erich! What happened there, what was all that about?' and he just turned to me and said, 'He kicked me a couple of years ago!" So he had stored it in his mind for years and picked his moment to get revenge."

Schaedler then got on the scoresheet in incredible fashion in a league game against Celtic at Parkhead on 10 December 1975. The game was a rearranged fixture, and a controversial one at that. The original match was played in October, and a Stanton and Harper-inspired Hibs turned on the style, building a well deserved 2–0 lead. Fog started to envelope Celtic Park as the game headed into its dying minutes, with Hibs looking certain to complete a fine victory. But with the Celtic fans in The Jungle singing "We Cannae See!" referee Iain Foote fell for their protests hook, line and sinker and abandoned the match – with a mere seven minutes on the clock! The Hibs players were justifiably livid, and Alex Edwards left the pitch flicking V-signs towards the celebrating Celtic fans. Against that background, the replayed match had an added edge, and in an attempt to defuse tensions, referee R.H. Davidson was in charge rather than Foote. Fog again hung ominously in the air, but this time the match was allowed to run its course. *The Scotsman*'s John Rafferty said, "The 33,000 crowd that turned out cannot expect to see a better game of football this season."

In a ding-dong battle, Harry Hood gave Celtic the lead on the hour mark, but then as Raffety explained, "In the seventy-second minute, Celtic lost a goal from an atrocious blunder in defence. Schaedler took a free-kick at least forty yards out. He flighted the ball high into the goalmouth, but it seeemed too far. Edvaldson rose to head, but was short. He blinded the goalkeeper [Latchford], who allowed the ball to bounce under his body and into the net. A forty-yard scorer never seemed on in this great game."

After their ignominious exit to Montrose from the League Cup, Hibs sought redemption in the ever elusive Scottish Cup. In the third round, Hibs battled past Dunfermline 3–2, thanks to a late Bobby Smith winner, and in the fourth round goals from Derek Spalding and Alex Edwards gave Hibs a hard-fought win at Tannadice in a replay after the teams had finished deadlocked 1–1 at Easter Road. The omens were good and when the quarter-final draw pitted Hibs against Motherwell, the fans started to dream of another run to Hampden. An entertaining 2–2 draw at Fir Park meant the sides had to do it again at Easter Road, but again they finished all square, the Hibs goal coming from the intelligent head of Pat Stanton – what turned out to be his last goal for the club.

Ibrox was selected as the venue for the second replay, but Motherwell, who Hibs had beaten three times out of four in the Premier League, gained the upper hand, winning 2–1 and booking their place in the semi-finals. Another big Cup opportunity had passed Hibs by.

Turnbull and Stanton's crumbling relationship had come to a head, and to the dismay of the Hibs supporters, their talisman would soon be abruptly shown the door at Easter Road. The mercurial midfielder was still at the peak of his powers, and

Turnbull's haste at getting rid of the best player at the club was pounced on by Jock Stein, who took him to Celtic in a heartbeat. In a straight swap, Jackie McNamara came to Hibs. He too would become a Hibs legend, but the loss of Stanton left a dark cloud hanging over the Easter Road club. "It was disappointing, the way it finished for me at Hibs, but Eddie and I didn't see eye to eye," says Stanton. "After the defeat against Hajduk Split, things were not the same. It wasn't just me that saw the change – there were a few others as well, and maybe some of the others weren't as vocal as me. But nobody can stay at a football club forever. I was lucky myself, playing so long for the team I supported, then going to another great club. I also got to keep playing in green and white, but it wasnae as nice a strip as the Hibs!"

With Stanton out in the cold before his controversial departure in the early weeks of the 1976/77 season, Hibs did at least manage to keep their eyes on the prize of a European spot and finished the 1975/76 campaign in third spot behind champions Rangers and runners-up Celtic. The void left by Stanton was partly filled by McNamara, a strong character and a fantastic footballer, and another big influence in the dressing room arrived in the shape of central defender George Stewart, signed by Turnbull from Dundee. Stewart, who had grown up in Edinburgh south side alongside his mate Jimmy O'Rourke, was a lifelong Hibs supporter, and after a long career with Dundee he was honoured to finally get his chance to wear the green and white shirt.

"I soon got to know Erich very well and we became good pals at Hibs," says Stewart. "Erich's work-rate was terrific, but he was a hard player. To give you an example, when Eddie Turnbull was the manager we used to have a practice match on a Wednesday, and one week I could see before the game that wee Willie Murray was down in the dumps. I asked him what was up, and says, 'Aw, Ah'm no looking forward to this, George.' I said, 'What's up with you? Were you out drinking or something?' and Willie said, 'I couldn't sleep last night because I knew I'd be playing against Erich.' I started laughing and told him not to worry, but he said, 'Would YOU want to play against Erich?' He had a point, because Erich didn't do friendlies. If it was training or a testimonial it didn't matter, he would get wired in. At training, you couldn't keep up with him – he would leave you trailing in his wake.

"My personal memory of Erich as a player was that he was undaunted by any team or anyone. When I was at Dundee we would go to Ibrox, Parkhead or even Pittodrie, and there was an element of fear among one or two of the players. Some of them were petrified of going to these places. But Erich didn't give a damn who it was. It could be Real Madrid, and he'd just say, 'Bring it on.' It was just eleven men in his eyes. His attitude was, 'You've always got a chance, what's there to be worried about?' He was an incredible guy and he was always fun. He used to go along to the fitness club that George Kerr ran, and was in to keeping himself in tip-top condition. George used to organise charity runs, but even in those, Erich wasn't for hanging about. It would leave from Princes Street, and Erich would just say, 'Right, see you in Musselburgh,' and he was off. They wouldn't see him for dust. He always wanted to be first, and they'd all be toiling behind him. He was so competitive. If you wanted to take Erich on then you were an idiot."

Schaedler was absent through injury for the beginning of Stewart's first season at Easter Road – the 1976/77 campaign – and in his absence Hibs' start to the season was a mixed bag. For the first time in Turnbull's reign they failed to qualify from their League Cup section. Rangers pipped Hibs to top spot, despite a brief throwback to the Tornadoes days – a thumping 9–2 victory over St Johnstone in which John Brownlie tucked away two penalties. Little did the Hibs fans know they had just seen the last of their hero Pat Stanton in a Hibs jersey. He came on as a sub for Stewart, but it was to be his final game for the club he had served with such distinction.

Stewart was sad to see Pat Stanton go, so soon after arriving at

Easter Road, but he was delighted to be rubbing shoulders with some of the survivors of the Tornadoes era. "When I went to Easter Road my first defence was Brownlie, Blackley, me and Erich," says Stewart. "There weren't many John Brownlies about. Defending wasn't his strong suit – he had to work on that – but going forward he was one of the best in the game. Erich was the opposite in some ways, and there was a great balance when the two of them were at their best.

"I remember at half-time in a game against Rangers I said to Eddie Turnbull, 'Boss, I'm not wanting to speak out of turn here, but what did Erich do in that half? I hardly saw him touch the ball.' Eddie didn't disagree, but he pointed out, 'Aye, but do you see where Tommy McLean is playing?' And he was absolutely right. Tommy McLean had been out the game, practically standing at right-back next to Sandy Jardine, because he didn't want to go anywhere near Erich. That's the effect Erich had on opposition players. I always felt you'd win the war if you had Erich in the team. Because they were all feared of him. Even Tam Forsyth of the Rangers didn't fancy tangling with Erich."

Bobby Smith deputised for Erich at the beginning of the 1976/77 season and was one of the brighter prospects at Easter Road, but a lot of experience had been lost and Hibs were struggling to live up to their exploits of recent seasons. Schaedler finally made his belated seasonal debut in the UEFA Cup first-round tie at home to Sochaux, acquitting himself well in a 1–0 win. The Hibs back four defended stoutly in the away leg too on a snowy night in France, a 0–0 draw which can be seen in black and white on YouTube. It earned Hibs a second-round tie against little-known Swedes Östers Vaxjo. Buoyed by a routine 2–0 win in the first leg, Hibs headed to Scandinavia, where they were expected to ease through. But their run of bad luck in Europe continued following an abject display. In front of fewer than 2,000, the Swedes upped their game considerably from the first leg and tore an unsuspecting Hibs side to pieces, racing into a 4–0 lead before Bobby Smith scored to give Turnbull a glimmer of hope that his side could score again and squeeze through on away goals. They didn't, and Turnbull and his squad were left with another uncomfortable flight home.

The European exit seemed to affect morale, and left Hibs struggling to string together a winning run in the league – too many draws blighting their attempts to haul themselves up the table.

The Scottish Cup campaign started promisingly enough with a solid 3–0 win over Partick Thistle, but there were horrors in store in the next round. A 1–1 draw at Arbroath, in which Erich set up John Blackley for a Hibs equaliser, was an embarrrasment. But far worse was to follow in the replay. Ally McLeod gave Hibs the lead as a storm lashed Easter Road, but Arbroath kept plugging away and dumped Turnbull's team unceremoniously out of the Cup with two goals in as many minutes. The season was in freefall but Hibs did succeed in maintaining their handsome record in Edinburgh derbies. McLeod scored the winner in a January clash at Tynecastle and got among the goals again when Hibs won 3–1 at Easter Road in March. Those two wins were book-ended by a 0–0 draw and 2–2 draw, so in a season of disappointments, at least Hibs had managed to go through the campaign without losing a derby. It couldn't cover up obvious signs of decline in Turnbull's new-look Hibs team though, and crowds were dwindling too. Hearts finished ninth and were relegated, but Hibs hadn't fared much better, finishing only seven points clear of their city rivals in sixth. It was the lowest position Hibs had occupied during Turnbull's time at Easter Road and they had managed a pitiful tally of only eight wins and thirty-four league goals in thirty-six games.They had also missed out on a place in Europe. The magic was fading. Schaedler, hampered by an Achilles injury, had mustered only thirty-one starts in the 1976/77 season – his lowest since his first full season at Easter Road in 1970/71, and the new campaign was to prove a turning point in his career.

With no European campaign to look forward to, Hibs instead found themelves pitched into what was effectively a consolation competition, the Anglo-Scottish Cup. To add insult to injury, Hibs had to come through a preliminary round, played over two legs against Ayr United. The first leg at Easter Road is notable for heralding the first competitive airing of the famous Hibs "Bukta" strip. During the pre-season photo-shoot, Erich is pictured proudly wearing the new trailblazing "sponsored" kit – but your eye is not drawn to the strip but the Medusa-like perm swirling around his head. There was no shame in it back then though. Perhaps in thirty years' time, we will look back at the sleeve tattoos which are *de rigueur* with footballers now and similarly cringe. But in 1977 and 1978, the dreaded perm was all the rage for any dedicated follower of fashion. The Bukta kit got off to a winning start, Hibs edging Ayr 2–1 and drawing the replay 2–2 to progress without fanfare to the first round proper. After some of the memorable European encounters it must have been difficult for players like Erich, John Blackley and Arthur Duncan – among the precious few survivors of the early-1970s side – to motivate themselves for the Anglo-Scottish Cup.

Hibs' recent habit of proving a soft touch in domestic Cup competitions continued in the streamlined knock-out version of the League Cup. This time it was Queen of the South who seized upon Hibs' vulnerability, winning the first leg at Easter Road 2–1 and holding on for a goalless draw in the return. Another exit to lower-division opposition and a far cry from their titanic tussles with Celtic at the start of the decade.

Having negotiated the preliminary round, Hibs reached the quarter-finals of the insipid Anglo-Scottish Cup and they beat Blackburn Rovers home and away to set up a semi-final with Bristol City. Erich's place was no longer guaranteed by this stage, and he floated in and out of the team as Turnbull's team selections fluctuated wildly.

Sensing a vastly different club from the one he had loved at the start of his Hibs career, Schaedler tabled a transfer request in October 1977 and was punished with a spell in the reserves. Another

Tornado departed when John Blackley was sold to Newcastle (later to be joined there by John Brownlie) days after a 3–1 defeat to Celtic, in which Danny McGrain broke his leg and was ruled out of the 1978 World Cup. Erich's own days at Easter Road under Turnbull were numbered too. He played in the Anglo-Scottish Cup semi-final at Bristol City, which Hibs lost 5–3, then in the grim surroundings of Clydebank's Kilbowie in a 1–0 loss on Bonfire Night, before he was told he was to be transferred to Dundee in a swap deal for Bobby Hutchison. Britain was in turmoil in 1977, crippled by industrial action and national strikes, and no newspapers were printed at North Bridge in Edinburgh during the week Schaedler moved from Hibs to Dundee. His transfer had gone under the radar.

George Stewart was sad to see Schaedler depart but accepts that once a certain line had been crossed with the manager, there was little point in sticking around. "Eddie Turnbull was by far the best manager Hibs will ever have, but that didn't mean that he didn't fall out with people – just ask Pat Stanton," says Stewart. "Erich wouldn't bow down to anyone, and maybe he was just a bit strong-willed for Eddie Turnbull in the end. I knew Bobby Hutchison, who was coming as part of the swap deal from my time at Dundee and, with no disrespect to Bobby, I would have kept Erich at Hibs. But that's what Eddie did. He was much like Alex Ferguson that way – if he felt a player's time was up or there had been any kind of problem, then he was out the door pronto. Erich was never a problem, but for some reason Eddie got rid of him."

Alex Edwards, one of the longest-serving members of the Tornadoes team, agreed: "I was surprised when Turnbull got rid of him. I was the last one to go, but I thought Shades could have still done a good job for Hibs. That's what football clubs are like though – once they felt you had done your stint they would just get rid of you."

Turnbull's decision to go for a straight swap of Hutchison for Schaedler did not go down well with the fans. Any time a Tornado left it was accompanied by a feeling of gloom among fans, who could see the side they were now watching was a pale imitation of the team who had dazzled so brightly in the early years of the decade. It was unfair on Hutchison too. If he had arrived at Easter Road on a straightforward transfer then he would have been judged on merit and the fee alone. But because it was Schaedler who had to make way for his arrival, Hutchison was always on a hiding to nothing with the supporters. They had lost one of their favourite players, and Hutchison was a convenient scapegoat if the going got tough.

Turnbull's decision to let Erich leave was questionable, but the manager had shown that if his relationship with a player had deteriorated to a certain level, then there was no point prolonging the situation. If Erich had stayed, it is almost certain he would have been spending most of his time rotting away in the reserves and barely speaking to the man who, by his own admission, had been the biggest influence on his career. Eddie had made Erich the player he was, and it was better all round for Schaedler to seek a fresh start and put the spark back into his football. The same went for Hutchison, as he too was out of favour with his club.

The forward had started the season well enough for Dundee, scoring against Airdrie in the league, then again against Montrose in the League Cup. But Ian Redford then Billy Williamson leapfrogged him in the pecking order at Dens Park and left him making sporadic appearances from the subs' bench. It was a good time for Hutchison to move on to pastures new, and Turnbull must have believed the change of scenery would work the oracle. Whether it was worth sacrificing Schaedler though was questionable to say the least.

18

# VOYAGE OF DISCOVERY

Erich Schaedler's move from Hibernian to the City of *Discovery* in November 1977 was a coup as far as Dundee manager Tommy Gemmell was concerned. Gemmell was a household name as one of the famed Lisbon Lions, playing (and scoring) in Celtic's famous 1967 European Cup win over Inter Milan. Jock Stein's illustrious side had become the first team in Britain to lift the trophy, and Gemmell had ensured his place in history. A goalscoring left-back with a thunderous shot, he had served Scotland with great distinction too, playing in the 3–2 win against then world champions England at Wembley in 1967. After leaving Celtic for a spell at Nottingham Forest, Gemmell spent his final five years as a Dundee player, peaking with a sweet League Cup victory over his former club Celtic in 1973, a game in which he was captain, with Erich's three-time teammate Thomson Allan in goals for the Dark Blues.

Gemmell hung up his boots in 1977 to take the reins from former Rangers manager David Smith. Smith had steered Dundee to the League Cup triumph – but had been unable to keep them in the Premier Division, and when he failed to get them promoted at the first attempt he stepped aside.

Gemmell's appointment as manager was unconventional. The Dundee chairman had asked him, as a senior player, if he could recommend anyone to succeed White, and Gemmell had initially suggested Bertie Auld – then in charge of Partick Thistle. However,

Auld did not want to uproot from the west of Scotland, and as the two Lisbon Lions had a chat, Auld asked Gemmell out of the blue, "What about you? You'd be perfect for the job."

Gemmell put his hat in the ring and had an on-the-spot interview with the Dens Park board of directors. They bought into his ideas to revive the club and gave him the job. Gemmell was an exciting recruit and hopes were high he would be the man to lead them back into the top flight. Finding a settled left-back was one of his early challenges, and during that 1977/78 season he used six different players – including Erich – in that position. The other five who wore the No.3 shirt for Dundee that season were Dave Johnston, Alec Caldwell, Iain Phillip, Dave McKinnon and Billy Williamson, who ended up scoring forty-four goals during the campaign when moved forward.

Gemmell, already familiar with Schaedler and his qualities, was delighted to get his man, and looking back now on their time together, he says, "Erich was a player I know I could always depend upon. He was a fabulous team player who was an automatic first-team choice, as far as I was concerned. Obviously, I knew a little bit about playing at left-back, so I was aware of what I was looking for in a player in that position. Erich never let me down, not once. He performed with a great verve and gusto. His enthusiasm was infectious and it got through to his colleagues in the dressing room on match day.

"I was always impressed by his dedication to being fully fit. He would give everything in training with the lads and then go and work out in a gym in Edinburgh later on. Now that's what I call dedication, because you better believe I put the Dundee boys through it during our routines.

"When I was at Celtic, big Jock Stein emphasised how important it was to be completely fit. Any slackers were quickly found out and that would mean a few games sitting in the stand. No one ever attempted to pull the wool over Big Jock's eyes. He got us up to such a speed that we always believed we would score at least one goal in the last fifteen minutes or so in any game. We were aware we had superior fitness to most of our opponents and that's why we scored so many goals late in a game. It was no fluke. I took that belief into management and I worked the lads hard every day. Erich was a more than willing participant in all our routines. However, I have to say I was more than a little surprised when he confided in me that he thought he could still add to his fitness levels, and that's why he worked out on his own later in the day at a gym near his home."

Schaedler was Gemmell's type of player, the ultimate professional, but there were many others who failed to fit in with the new manager's philosophy. Dens Park ought to have been fitted with a revolving door during the Gemmell years at Dundee, as more than thirty players came and went. Two notable departures in the weeks before Erich's arrival were Gordon Strachan and legendary winger Jimmy Johnstone. The former was deemed a little too lightweight to deal with the blood and thunder of the First Division and was allowed to depart for Aberdeen, where he went on to become one of Scotland's finest midfielders in modern times. The world-class Johnstone, meanwhile, was still capable of dazzling on the pitch, but while his arrival had been heralded as a major transfer coup, he was still prone to mischief. Gemmell had, a tad naively, been confident he would be able to keep his former Celtic teammate on the straight and narrow, but the little redhead would give his manager constant disciplinary headaches. Gemmell swiftly recognised he could not curtail the extra-curricular activities of Jinky, and after starting only two games in the No.7 shirt, the flawed genius had packed his bags, finishing his playing career with cameos on the books of Shelbourne in Ireland and Elgin City in the Highland League.

Strachan and Johnstone had departed by the time Erich arrived at Dundee, and with their swap deal complete, Schaedler and Bobby Hutchison made their debuts for their respective new clubs on the same day, 19 November 1977. For Bobby, it was a bad start to his Hibs career, playing in a 3–2 loss at home to Partick. He would only get on the scoresheet for Hibs at the thirteenth attempt and that barren spell must have made it even harder for him to shake off the tag as the man who was brought to the club instead of Shades. For Erich, it was low-key debut, a goalless draw at Dumbarton where at least he had the satisfaction of contributing towards a clean sheet. Thomson Allan, Erich's old teammate from Hibs and Scotland, was in goals, but soon left the club to be replaced by Ally Donaldson, back for his second spell at Dens. The paltry Boghead crowd of 1,700 was the lowest Erich played in front of that season, and would have been a quick reminder to him that he had dropped down a division. On the plus side, he got to wear Dundee's classic Admiral kit, resplendent with red and white "braces", although the "Bukta" version he had left behind at Easter Road wasn't too shabby either!

Erich would have been determined to get back to the Premier Division as soon as possible, and Dundee were in a handy position to challenge for the two promotion spots in Division One. As the season unfolded, Morton, Hearts – then managed by Erich's 1974 World Cup manager Willie Ormond – and Dundee started to break away from the pack, and you can imagine Schaedler being pumped up for his first match against Hearts as a Dundee player, more so because the game was at Tynecastle and he would be sure to attract some extra interest from the home supporters. These were the type of matches Erich loved and a rousing 2–2 draw kept his team firmly in the promotion race.

Prior to Erich's arrival at Dens, Dundee had suffered a humiliating 6–0 League Cup exit to Queen of the South, who were one of the struggling sides in their own division. A trip to Celtic in the Scottish Cup in February 1978 represented a chance to salvage some pride against illustrious opponents, but the trip to Parkhead quickly developed into another Cup nightmare, particularly for manager Gemmell, who was left embarrassed in the ground he had enjoyed so many wonderful memories. Celtic produced their best performance of the season to thrash a dazed Dundee 7–1 – the scoreline eclipsing the fact that Schaedler happened to score his first goal for Dundee. It seems that Dundee did not even play too badly; they just happened to be against the wrong team in the wrong place at the wrong time.

"Celtic scared the life out of Dundee with a second-half performance which even the hyperbolic superlatives which come cap in hand with the football writers' book of jargon would struggle to accord an appropriate phrase," wrote *The Scotsman*'s Mike Aitken. "Celtic were brilliant, wonderful and just too marvellous for words."

Describing Erich's goal, an early equaliser before Celtic got back to the job of dismantling Dundee, Aitken said, "In the ninth minute Munro had conceded a free-kick for a foul on Sinclair. While Celtic regrouped in force through the middle, Jock Scott struck a sharp ball into the left side of the box, where full-back Erich Schaedler zipped in and beat Latchford with a low drive to the near post. It was a cleverly constructed, neatly taken goal."

It often follows in football that a team who have just come off the back of a thrashing then redouble their concentration levels and turn in a far more solid display in their next match. Dundee, to their credit, did just that, managing back-to-back clean sheets in league wins against East Fife and Montrose. The Dark Blues were still bang in contention for promotion, but unfortunately Morton and Hearts were showing no sign of slowing down ahead of them. With four league games remaining, a hefty blow to Dundee's hopes was delivered by Dumbarton, who beat Gemmell's side 2–1 at Boghead.

The Division One promotion race had developed into a cliffhanger. Morton would definitely be promoted to the Premier League and had more or less clinched the championship heading into the final game, at home to third-placed Dundee, with second-placed Hearts needing a nine-goal swing to win the title. The table after thirty-eight league games read as follows:

| | Pld | W | D | L | F | A | Pts | GD |
|---|---|---|---|---|---|---|---|---|
| Morton | 38 | 25 | 8 | 5 | 83 | 39 | 58 | +44 |
| Hearts | 38 | 23 | 10 | 5 | 76 | 41 | 56 | +35 |
| Dundee | 38 | 24 | 7 | 7 | 88 | 42 | 55 | +46 |

Dundee therefore headed to Cappielow, needing to win and with a superior goal difference, hoping that Hearts would drop at least a point at Arbroath. Schaedler, like all of his teammates, must have been relishing the challenge, especially as it was Hearts that stood between him and a swift return to Premier Division football. In a thrilling encounter in Greenock, Dundee did all they could, winning 3–2 thanks to goals from Ian Redford, Bobby Glennie and Billy Pirie's forty-sixth strike of the season. But bad news filtered through from Gayfield. Hearts, who had led since the eighteenth minute through Eamonn Bannon, had held on and had edged the second promotion spot. As Morton celebrated winning the championship, the disconsolate Dundee players trudged off to the dressing room to reflect on an agonisingly close call. It was no consolation to Dundee that they had been the most entertaining attacking side in the division – their three goals against Morton taking them beyond the ninety-goal mark.

Erich must have had mixed feelings as he watched Scotland play at the 1978 World Cup finals in Argentina with the rest of the nation that summer. On the one hand, he must have been reflecting on his involvement in the previous finals in Germany four years earlier. On the other, he was probably glad he wasn't involved in this particular expedition, as Ally MacLeod's wildly optimistic pre-tournament boasts imploded against Peru and Iran before a famous yet fruitless 3–2 win over eventual runners-up, Holland.

Erich was absent for the first five games of the 1978/79 season, including home and away League Cup defeats to Celtic, but was back in his familiar No.3 shirt for a home game against Montrose in early September. Schaedler's return to the side helped shore up the defence, and in the period between mid-September and mid-November, an efficient back four which also included centre-half Bobby Glennie and right-back Les Barr racked up seven clean sheets in ten games. Dundee were not as free-scoring as they had been the previous season, but points win prizes and they were keeping it tight at the back, getting results and shaping up as genuine promotion favourites.

It was a turbulent time for the club as Gemmell struggled to keep everyone happy, and shortly before Christmas 1978 Erich asked to be put on the transfer list. He was the sixth player to have asked for a move from Dens Park that season, joining Thomson Allan, Iain Philip, Jocky Scott, Billy Pirie and John McPhail.

January 1979 was a particularly harsh winter, and Dundee never played a single competitive match for the best part of two months. The players were forced to train in some horrendous conditions, but the Arctic chill never fazed Erich.

"Shades was a really decent guy to be alongside on the pitch and at training, but he was one of a kind – not like the other guys when it came to his fitness regime," says Bobby Glennie. "He thought he was invincible and the tougher the challenge, the happier he seemed. It really sticks in the mind, the memory of him training bare-chested, stripped down to his shorts, regardless of the weather. We would sometimes train down at the beach in Monifeith, and it could be absolutely Baltic down there. We'd all be wrapped up and complaining about the icy blasts, but it didn't worry Shades. I think he saw it as a challenge and would be slagging the rest of us, asking, 'What's the matter with you all?'

"He was a chirpy presence to have around, was a dependable player, very consistent, and you knew that he would give everything he could in every match. He was super fit and there wasn't an ounce of fat on him. He always seemed to be the first in at the ground to report for training at 9am, and you have to bear in mind that he was travelling through from Edinburgh every day. He put some of the others to shame with his dedication, I have to admit, but it could be inspirational too. If you were subconsciously thinking about taking it a little easier than normal at training, a quick glance over at Erich could be all you needed to give yourself a shake and work a bit harder."

Eric Sinclair winces at the memory of Erich's fearless approach to a winter on the east coast of Scotland. "He was mental," says Sinclair with a chuckle. "Everyone else would be wrapped up in woolly hats and gloves, but not him. He'd be strutting about in a T-shirt, or even with nae top on at all. We called him the Mad German – he was some boy!"

The fans too lapped up Schaedler's hardman image. Dundee supporter Scott Glenday remembers seeing pictures in the local newspapers of Erich, stripped to the waist, braving the elements at training. "A photograph I'll always remember seeing of him was of Erich stripped to the waist running with the rest of the squad during a winter training session," he says. "It really epitomised the flamboyancy and toughness of someone we all adored, a happy, good-looking kind of lad who always appeared to be very fit, seemed to love his football and appreciate the rapport he had with the fans."

It was the end of February before Dundee were able to resume their season and Gemmell's tough training regime throughout the unexpected shutdown was rewarded as his side returned with a crucial 2–1 victory at home to fellow promotion chasers Clydebank, both goals coming from Ian Redford.

The Scottish Cup was behind schedule, but Dundee showed their appetite for the competition by first beating Falkirk 1–0 at home in the third round and then returning to Dens a week later to thump Premier Division St Mirren 4–1 in the fourth round. Gemmell's side were in the quarter-finals, and again the draw had handed them the toughest of ties in Glasgow, a meeting with Rangers at Ibrox.

Gemmell put his heart and soul into his preparations for the match, and Erich too was chomping at the bit. Eric Sinclair recalls, "Tam Gemmell arranged a shadow game on the Wednesday to prepare for the match. He organised the team with a back four to play against the formation Rangers were likely to play, and he was keen that we paid particular attention to what he saw as their main threat to us, Davie Cooper. So, he asked Jim Shirra to play the part of Davie Cooper and imitate him.

"Tam stuck him on the right wing, where he would be up against Erich at left-back. So as soon as the game kicked off, Erich went charging over to Jim and sent him flying into the air. Tam blew his whistle for a foul and restarted the game . . . only for Erich to do it again. It happened a third time, again Erich absolutely clattering poor Jim. Tam asked, 'Settle down. What's going on here?' Only for Erich to say, 'That's what I was going to do to Davie Cooper, so I thought I might as well get some practice in.' Poor Jim Shirra had had enough. He said, 'Can someone else be Davie Cooper?' It didn't do us much good either. I'm sure we got beat at Ibrox."

Dundee did indeed lose, in what was an incredible Cup tie. Rangers smashed in five goals by half-time and Gemmell – with the 7–1 defeat at Celtic twelve months earlier still haunting him – must have been fearing an even more painful lesson from the other half of the Old Firm as goals rained down on Dundee in the first half. It was Erich who unwittingly started the deluge as he was penalised for handball as the ball struck his arm from a Tommy McLean free-kick. Sandy Jardine slammed home the penalty to put Rangers one up. Dundee showed an admirable desire to fight for pride throughout though, and the game finished 6–3. Incredibly, there were eight separate scorers, only Dundee's Stewart MacLaren scoring a double alongside Jim Shirra's goal, while for Rangers the scorers were Jardine, Alex MacDonald, Gordon Smith, Tom Forsyth, Bobby Russell and Davie Cooper.

Rangers would go on to deny Hibs' Scottish Cup glory in the final, winning 3–2 in the second replay after two 0–0 draws. That would have hurt Erich, even though he was no longer at the club, especially as his old left-wing partner Arthur Duncan was the unfortunate player who gifted Rangers the cup with a headed own goal in extra time. Just as Dundee had done after the 7–1 rout at

Celtic Park the year before, they responded to shipping six goals by plugging the gaps and gave their manager a lift with five consecutive wins – four of them with clean sheets – to keep the promotion push on course.

Bogey ground Boghead again tripped Dundee up in a 3–2 defeat on Grand National Day, but with ten Division One matches remaining in a season congested with fixtures after the harsh winter, Gemmell's side could sense this might be their year. Four more straight wins against Raith, Hamilton, Clyde and Airdrie had Dundee in pole position not only to be promoted but to win the championship, but a 2–1 defeat against their nearest challengers Kilmarnock led to an outbreak of nerves on the run-in – sharply illustrated by two defeats in four days to St Johnstone and Arbroath.

Gemmell needed to get his side focused for the final two league games inside three days, both at Dens Park, against Raith Rovers on Tuesday, 8 May, and Ayr United on Thursday, 10 May. Dundee were also under enormous financial pressure to deliver top-flight football, and if they failed the cash-strapped club could be staring at ruin. They were still playing catch-up with their fixture backlog, and Kilmarnock had already completed their league schedule and sat top of the league by two points and with a superior goal difference. Clydebank were alongside Kilmarnock on fifty-four points, having also played all thirty-nine league matches, but with a similar goal difference. So, Dundee sat third, needing two points from two games to be promoted and three points to go up as champions. At least their fate was in their own hands. They all but took part of the promotion part of the equation at the first time of asking, Ian Redford and Stewart MacLaren scoring the goals at Dens Park as Dundee beat Raith Rovers 2–0.

Dundee fan Charlie Taylor remembers, "An almost unique memory that I have of Erich was that Tuesday night game against Raith in May 1979, where a win would all but clinch us promotion, with one game to play. It was 0–0 at half-time, and when the teams came out for the second half, Shades was on the Dundee fans' side of the ground. He looked over, then put his hands together in prayer! It was a nice wee touch, I thought, to show the rapport he had with the fans."

Scott Glenday, a lifelong supporter who became a leading figure in the Dundee Supporters Society, also remembers the special relationship Schaedler enjoyed with the fans. "Shades was hugely popular during his time at Dundee and he is fondly remembered for his long throws, ability to strike a ball and most of all his determination to win a tackle," says Glenday. "He always looked the part and never failed to acknowledge the acclaim he received from the fans when taking up his position at left-back and heading towards the South Enclosure."

With promotion more or less assured, heading into that final game against Ayr the table still looked incredibly tight:

| | Pld | W | D | L | F | A | Pts | GD |
|---|---|---|---|---|---|---|---|---|
| Kilmarnock | 39 | 22 | 10 | 7 | 72 | 36 | 54 | +36 |
| Dundee | 38 | 24 | 6 | 8 | 67 | 34 | 54 | +33 |
| Clydebank | 39 | 24 | 6 | 9 | 78 | 50 | 54 | +28 |

Only an unlikely 5–0 defeat against Ayr United would undo their promotion, while a draw would be enough to clinch the title. Lose to Ayr, Kilmarnock's arch-rivals, and the title would be heading to the west coast.

In a tense match at Dens, Ian Redford, showing maturity beyond his years, led from the front and scored both goals in a 2–2 draw to ensure Dundee were going up as champions. This time, Gemmell's side had shown resilience and character right until the end and atoned for the disappointment of twelve months earlier. In the changing room afterwards, it would have hit them that they were back in the big time – in the Premier Division. As if to emphasise the point, they had one final assignment to take care of, a Sunday Forfarshire Cup semi-final against Dundee United. The Forfarshire Cup was a bit hit and miss in those days, and some seasons it would not even be played to a conclusion. But bragging rights were there to be won, and after a 2–2 draw in front of 12,170 fans in their rivals' back yard across Tannadice Street, Dundee nudged ahead in extra time to win 3–2. The final wasn't played until the beginning of the following season, and the apathy for the competition was evident, as only 2,000 fans turned up at Station Park to see Forfar win the Cup 3–1.

As he had done the previous season, Erich missed the start of the 1979/80 season through injury and made a belated return to Premier Division football in mid-September, playing in a 4–3 win at home to Morton. Though, his absence had spared him from a 5–2 mauling from Hibs at Easter Road. With the Eddie Turnbull era nearing its end and Hibs still reeling from their Scottish Cup near-miss against Rangers in the epic 1979 final, that 5–2 scoreline against Dundee was to be the exception to the rule for Schaedler's former club as they spent the rest of the season lurching from one bad result to another.

Dundee were generally finding life in the Premier difficult too. They had been soundly beaten 3–0 in the first league derby of the season at Tannadice – another match Erich missed – but in the reverse fixture at Dens in front of 16,300 – the biggest crowd the ground had boasted in years – Eric Sinclair scored the only goal of the game to revive spirits.

By November, and with Schaedler again the owner of the No.3 shirt, Dundee were showing some good form, and recorded wins against Hibs, Partick and Rangers, although they exited the League Cup on aggregate to Hamilton. The rivalry with United continued to intensify, and another league trip to Tannadice three days before Christmas resulted in defeat, this time 2–0, a game which saw Schaedler red-carded for only the second time in his career. Worse was to follow in the Scottish Cup at the hands of United – very much the emerging force in Scottish football under Jim McLean. The city was buzzing when the rivals were pitted against each other in the third round, but the excitement felt by Dundee supporters was replaced by horror as they were thrashed 5–1, Willie Pettigrew scoring four goals. In a violent match which was quickly dubbed the "Battle of Tannadice", referee Ian Foote struggled to keep control and Stewart MacLaren and Eric Sinclair were both given their marching orders. This was one of star man Ian Redford's final games in a Dundee shirt, and it was a hammer blow to the fans when their most valued asset was sold to Rangers for a bargain £200,000.

Dundee's league form was struggling to pick up, and despite a creditable 2–2 draw at Celtic Park secured thanks to a Roy Aitken own goal, Gemmell's side looked destined for the drop. Celtic and Aberdeen were duelling for the championship and when Billy McNeill's side arrived at Dens on 19 April 1980, two points and a victory looked a formality for the challengers, especially as Dundee had only won one league match since the turn of the year. The game, played at a sun-kissed Dens, followed the script early on, Celtic taking the lead through Roy Aitken, but then the game was turned on its head in astonishing fashion. Erich had one of his finest games in a Dundee shirt. Taking a few steps back to the terracing wall, he launched one of his trademark thunderbolt throw-ins to set up seventeen-year-old Iain Ferguson for his team's first goal at the back post. For the third goal he then showed his pace to full effect, racing up the left wing and playing a neat 1–2 with Peter Mackie, to set up Ian Fleming. With Celtic stunned, Erich then thundered through from the back to win the ball in the air to pave the way for the fifth goal.

*The Scotsman*'s W. H. Kemp got a little carried away when he said, "It was a victory on par with that of Berwick Rangers over big Rangers in the Scottish Cup thirteen years ago."

A beaming Erich told Kemp, "All the bad breaks we have had this season were suddenly on the other end. It was wonderful."

A proud Gemmell gave an interview on the pitch with *Scotsport*'s Arthur Montford afterwards, in which he described the match as "a wonderful advert for attacking football". However, the Dundee manager must have known deep down the victory would be in vain. Relegation was still staring his team in the face, although at least it had given the Dundee fans something to cheer in what had been a trying season. "Last week they were screaming for my blood and this week I'm the greatest guy in the world and that's how this game goes," Gemmell told Montford.

The 5–1 win over Celtic was indeed too little too late, and Kilmarnock scrambled clear of the drop, adding insult to injury by beating them 2–0 at Dens. With Dundee already doomed, they headed to Celtic Park for the final fixture of the 1979/80 season, and lost 2–0. There was a funereal atmosphere at the end of the match, as Celtic's win was not enough to prevent Alex Ferguson's Aberdeen winning the championship by a point – the first team outwith the Old Firm to have won the league flag since Kilmarnock in 1965. These were exciting, changing times for Scottish football, but Dundee would be on the outside looking in during the 1980/81 season, condemned to a return to the First Division, and joined by Hibs, who finished bottom of the league in a chaotic season for the Easter Road club which included the arrival of George Best and the end of Eddie Turnbull's reign as manager. Willie Ormond was the man initially tasked with filling the big shoes left by Turnbull.

There was a changing of the guard at Dundee too, and Gemmell's failure to keep Dundee up cost him his job. He is grateful for Erich's contribution during his spell at Dens. "Erich didn't score a lot of goals, but goodness knows how many he set up with his raiding down the flank. And could that boy shift," says Gemmell, still full of admiration for his former charge. "His pace was awesome and, once again, I don't think people realised just how quick he was because of his running style. It looked effortless when he got into his stride, but take my word for it, he could scorch across that turf. Just ask any opponent who was up against him back then. If Erich got away from a rival player, they knew there was no catching him.

"He was a model pro too, never any trouble on or off the park. He was a guy you could trust. All he wanted to do was play football to the utmost of his ability, and I know he was appreciated by all of his teammates. No one ever complained about the effort we got every match day from Erich. Certainly, I was a fan. I've just completed a book where I talk about all the great players I've faced, such as George Best, Johan Cruyff, Eusebio, Franz Beckenbauer and so on. I've compiled my list of the best I've ever come up against and I've also named the very best of my Celtic teammates, such as Jimmy Johnstone, Bertie Auld, Bobby Murdoch, etc. I was also asked to put together my top Dundee team. Erich Schaedler was a shoo-in. I didn't have to hesitate for a moment when I had to name my left-back. There was only one man for that position in my Dundee dream team – Erich Schaedler."

## 19

# DON AND DUSTED AT DENS

After Tommy Gemmell's four-year reign as manager of Dundee ended, in came Donald, or "Don", Mackay, an up-and-coming young coach. Mackay had been a goalkeeper for Fofar, Dundee United and Southend in his playing days, before using a coaching job with Bristol City as a stepping stone to his first managerial role with Danish club Norresundby, winning them promotion at the first attempt. Schaedler would only play one full season under Mackay, but he enjoyed his most consistent run of games at the club and the 1980/81 season was a campaign to remember, even if it got off to a stuttering start. Dundee failed to score a goal in their first three First Division fixtures as the new manager took time to ensure his team gelled.

The young manager was instantly taken by Erich's conscientious approach and recalls, "At training he always worked his socks off. I can remember that when training was finished he would go back out there and do a bit of work on his own. Often, it was just a warm-down, but nobody had even heard of warms-downs then – which are now a big part of the modern game – so in many ways he was a man before his time with his fitness regime."

The League Cup would provide Mackay with his first victory at the helm, and it would also prove to be the start of an exciting adventure which started at Dens Park in front of 3,000 fans and finished in the same stadium in front of a raucous crowd eight times that size.

Dundee's first-round opponents in the League Cup were Arbroath, and Erich and his fellow defenders had an uneventful evening as two goals from John Fletcher ensured a 2–0 victory. The second leg was even more comfortable, as Dundee again won, this time 3–0. Kilmarnock were next up and after two hard-fought 0–0 draws, even extra time after the second leg in Rugby Park failed to yield a goal. When the tie was finally settled on penalties, Dundee held their nerve and won 5–4 in the shoot-out to reach the quarter-finals. It had been a while since Dundee had enjoyed a Cup run of any note, but if they wanted to go any further in the competition, they had the most daunting obstacle blocking their path – Alex Ferguson's Aberdeen, the tournament favourites and reigning Premier champions.

Mackay had his defence working like a well-oiled machine. The regular back four of Erich, Les Barr, Cammy Fraser and Bobby Glennie were an experienced, physically strong and well-organised unit and to them Aberdeen represented a challenge to be relished rather than feared. The backline held firm in the first leg at Dens Park, although Aberdeen remained overwhelming favourites to win the return match at Pittodrie three weeks later. Before heading north, Dundee's defence continued to perform at the top of their game, and arrived at Pittodrie on the back of five consecutive clean sheets.

Among Aberdeen's many strengths was their formidable home record, but Dundee belied their First Division status with a wonderful peformance. Cammy Fraser scored the only goal of the game as the Dons were unceremoniously dumped out of the Cup by their lower-league visitors. Ferguson, as you might expect, was livid. "I don't think Fergie spoke to me for about six months after," laughs Mackay.

Dundee had made it into the semi-finals and their chances of reaching the final soared when they avoided Celtic and Cup holders

Dundee United, and instead came out of the hat against Ayr United, a tough nut to crack, but like Dundee, a First Division side. The first leg at Somerset Park ended in a 1–1 draw, but Dundee edged the second leg 3–2 to book their place in the final.

Bobby Glennie remembers what a tough competitior Erich was in that match against Ayr. "He was a hard player on the pitch, and wingers knew they would be in for a tough game when they came up against him," says Glennie. "I remember the League Cup semi-final against Ayr United when he and his teammate Stewart MacLaren were involved in a clash of heads. I think MacLaren cracked his cheekbone and had to go off. Shades's head was in pretty bad nick too, but he didn't want to go off. He insisted on playing on, even though he didn't know what day of the week it was. He did come off in the end, for Les Barr, but only because the rest of us were worried about him and had got word over to the bench that it might make sense to make the change."

They had made it to a glamour final at Hampden . . . or so they thought.

United had beaten Celtic 4–1 on aggregate to reach the final, and rather than have thousands of people migrating from Dundee to Glasgow for the day, the Scottish Football League controversially decided to keep the match in the city. Erich was one of the few Dundee players with Cup final experience, as a winner and a loser, and while he hailed the 1972 triumph as the "sweetest moment of my career" in an interview ahead of the Dens final, it was clear the 1974 defeat to Dixie Deans-inspired Celtic was an experience he dearly wished to expunge. "I've never felt so low in my entire career," said Erich. "All the hard work in reaching the final counted for nothing. Of course, there always has to be a loser, but in my second League Cup final appearance it was an utter humiliation. It took me a long time to get over that defeat and I still have vivid recollections of Celtic's Dixie Deans doing somersaults all over Hampden as he celebrated the completion of his hat-trick that dreaded afternoon." Typically, though, Erich stayed positive ahead of the match against United, and he added, "There's nothing more rewarding than a Cup winner's medal. Every footballer wants to be a winner and there's no bigger prize than emerging from a Cup final victorious."

Schaedler admitted he would be disappointed not to run out at Hampden with his teammates, but said in the Cup final programme, "This afternoon's final is another historic moment, with Dundee staging a final on their own ground against our city rivals Dundee United just down the road. It's a great thing for Scottish football to have the final staged in Dundee, and there's no doubt in my mind that a full house at Dens Park with 24,700 in the stadium will create a really superb atmosphere, equal in many ways to a big Hampden attendance.

"In a final there are no clear favourites. United might be in the Premier Division while we are striving to win promotion to the top ten elite, but I am positive it will be a very close final. United have toppled Celtic on the way and we have knocked out Premier League champions Aberdeen in the quarter-finals. That game alone showed that Dundee are a club on the move and we go into this Bell's League Cup final with great confidence.

"The spirit at Dens Park is the best I have known in my three years with the club. Our new management team are leading by example. Everyone is working so hard at the game and we have shown tremendous improvement this season. That's why we are in the final – and ready to give our all to succeed."

A bumper crowd of 24,456 shoehorned themselves into Dens Park for the final, and while Dundee went out hoping to give their all, there was no stopping the juggernaut from across the road. Despite Dundee's home advantage, United had gone into the Cup final as strong favourites in a Premier Division v First Division battle, and the gulf in class showed. "Maybe Dundee were too determined to be determined," wrote *The Scotsman*'s Mike Aitken. "United, without touching their best form, won very comfortably against a Dundee side who hardly did themselves justice." Graeme

Payne pulled the strings for United as they dominated the game and was the provider for Davie Dodds' opening goal on the stroke of half-time. Two goals from Paul Sturrock in the second half rubbed salt into the wounds for disjointed Dundee.

Aitken added: "Dundee manager Donald Mackay pondered why his side should choose this day of all days to have such a 'nightmare'. Of course, Mackay must have suspected that it was asking too much of his inexperienced men to repeat the feat of beating Aberdeen. Dundee are short of Premier Division standard at the moment. In a sense, the League Cup run was a diversion from Dundee's main aim of promotion. However, their success in the competition has probably brought added confidence to their play in the league. I expect them to come up with Hibs next season. Heaven knows Scottish football needs both of them to succeed."

Looking back on the final now, Mackay feels that the occasion was devalued by playing the game at Dens and insists Hampden might have inspired his players. He says, "The League in their wisdsom decided that the final should be played in Dundee, to avoid the fans having to travel to Glasgow, and the venue was decided on the toss of a coin. We won and the final took place at Dens Park. But it never felt like a Cup final – it seemed more like a local derby – and we just never rose to the occasion. It was a sore one for our supporters to take, losing a final on home ground against our greatest rivals."

It was indeed a sickening experience for Dundee to lose the Cup final to their greatest rivals on their own turf, but they showed admirable character to dust themselves down and switch their focus back to winning promotion.

Schaedler's old club Hibs were the pace-setters in the First Division under new manager Bertie Auld, and Dundee were tucked behind them in a tight chasing pack which included St Johnstone, Raith Rovers, Motherwell and Ayr United. March was to prove the pivotal month in Dundee's promotion quest, as they won five straight league matches. A goalless draw against bottom-of-the-table Berwick was a mere blip, as Mackay's side marched on. Sadly for Erich, injury ruled him out of the run-in, with a young full-back Stewart McKimmie handed his chance. By the final game of the season, Dundee's fate was in their own hands. A win at Firs Park, the home of East Stirling, would secure a return to the top flight behind champions Hibs. Eric Sinclair scored the only goal of the game and Dundee had done it at the first time of asking under Mackay.

Like his predecessor Gemmell, Mackay is full of admiration for the role Erich played in getting his team promoted and helping to bring a crop of young players through. "I only had Erich for one year, but he made a big impression in that time," says Mackay. "When I came to Dundee in 1980 the club had just been relegated from the Premier Division to the First Division, and he was one of the senior players. He was fantastic to have around the dressing room – he was great fun and an excellent left-back.

"The 1980/81 season was one of real ups and downs. That might sound strange, given that we won the championship and got to a Cup final, but it was the manner in which we lost the Cup final which makes me look back with a little sadness on that year. Apart from that though, there is no denying it was a good season. We went on a long unbeaten run and I remember us winning promotion by beating East Stirling in the final game. I had watched them play in midweek and was taken aback by the poor state of their pitch, so on the Thursday and Friday before the game I made the players train in a public park in Dundee. There was a lot of mumping and moaning, but when they got to Firs Park and saw what they would be playing on, they saw the thinking behind it. It was a bit bumpy, but we adapted and got the result – we won 1–0 and we were up."

Young prospect McKimmie, who would go on to become a star performer for Aberdeen and an established Scotland international, had impressed at left-back at the end of the promotion-winning campaign, and when the 1981/82 season started with Dundee back in the Premier Division he retained possession of the No.3 shirt. Chic McLelland, a Scotland Under-23 international signed by Mackay from Motherwell, and Danny Cameron – recruited from Preston North End – were other rivals for the jersey. Schadler knew that with Mackay keen to keep costs down and blood young players, his days at Dens Park might well be numbered.

The League Cup had received yet another makeover, and with sections restored, Schaedler was given a run-out in a meaningless 3–2 defeat at Morton. He retained his place for the first match of the Premier Division season, against Hibs at Easter Road on 29 August 1981. Dundee lost 2–0, but Erich was just weeks away from making a quick return to Easter Road – this time as a Hibs player.

Mackay had the difficult job of balancing the books and one of the difficult decisions he took was to let Schaedler leave Dens Park on a free transfer. "Because Erich was one of the senior players who had been in the Premier League, he was also on one of the better salaries," he explains. "We were in a tough position financially and I had some difficult decisions to make in terms of getting the squad and costs down to a manageable size. It was one of these tough calls managers have to make, and I had to let Erich go. It was no reflection at all on Erich and, as I recall, he took it well – I couldn't say that about a few of the other senior players because some of them fell out with me big time.

"I didn't have a choice though. We were heading back to the Premier Division and I had a lot of bright young kids coming through the ranks. There were nine or ten of them who were pushing for a place in the Scotland Under-21 or Under-23 team, and financially it made sense to allow them to play their way into the team and allow me to balance the books. It was something that was very important to the club at that time and important to me too. It was my first real managerial job, even though I had worked in Denmark, and I went into it with my eyes open. There were always going to be difficult decisions to make, and that can lead to your popularity taking a hammering with certain players. There were a few senior players I crossed swords with from time to time, but Erich wasn't one of them.

"Back then you had to be so much more than a manager to keep your head above the water and get the best out of the players and do your best for the club. You were virtually a manager, a coach, a chief executive, a mother and father – all rolled into one! That was part and parcel of management in the Eighties.

"I had Stewart McKimmie and Tosh McKinlay both coming through and I couldn't hold them back any longer. Both went on to become full Scotland internationals, and Stewart played his part in Aberdeen's great success under Alex Ferguson. It's never easy letting anyone go, but Erich got himself fixed up in no time – a good player like that was never going to be short on offers.

"Hibs had just come up with us from the First Division and as fate had it, they offered him the chance to go back – which he grabbed with both hands. So even though it wasn't with us, he was back in the Premier League."

Mackay added, "The Dundee job could be tough at times for me because I think some people never forgave me for coming from over the road from Dundee United. Any time things started to go a little bit wrong, they would be quick to remind me of the club I had played for! I was a young manager and of course I made mistakes – you have to make them if you are ever going to succeed in the long run. We won the First Division in my first season, managed to stay up in our first year in the Premier League, then managed to finish sixth after that."

The Dundee fans were sad to see Schaedler go. In his four years at the club he had proved himself 100 per cent dedicated to the cause, and although Hibs were closest to his heart, Dundee had come a close second. "He still is and always will be one of my all-time favourite Dundee players and I know that is a view shared by many fellow fans of a similar age," says Scott Glenday. "He was a tough, committed and wholehearted player who gave his all for Dundee. I've no doubt fans from every club he played for feel exactly the same. Shades could only play the game one way and it was the way supporters of any club love – from the heart with passion, pride, guts and determination, doing the jersey proud and that's how we will always remember him."

Likewise, his teammates were sorry to see him go, and they still have some colourful memories of him in the dressing room. He tried to teach them a thing or two about style too – even if his wasn't to everyone's taste! "Male grooming is all the rage now, but Erich was the first guy I saw in the dressing room with a bag full of creams, gels and shampoos," says Eric Sinclair. "He always took plenty time over his appearance. He paid a lot of attention to his hair and was always dressed immaculately. He didn't get any stick at all for it – we were all feared of him! It was just accepted – he was a wee bit different, a little eccentric, but he was just a guy who liked to look the part. He looked after himself. His wee bag of creams and products was always by his side, and none of us were brave enough to go near it. We didn't fancy being on the wrong end of one of his headlocks!"

Bobby Glennie also says Erich cut some dash at team social occasions too. "He was some boy at the nights out," says Glennie. "If we were going out for a few drinks, Shades would turn up with a pint of milk.

"We would ask him, 'Erich, what's with the pint of milk?' He explained that most pubs didn't have milk behind the bar, so he would bring his own so he could have it with a Malibu!"

Sinclair points out that Erich's cool, calm and collected demeanour was at odds with the way he drove. "He was into his fast cars. He would drive through from Edinburgh some of the time, but quite often I would pick him and Cammy Fraser up from the train station in Dundee and drive them to the ground or to training. I remember we'd been training up at St Andrews one winter, and because all the pitches were frozen the only place we could fix up a friendly was at Pittenweem. So, he picked me up in his Alfa Romeo, and I swear he was absolutely fleeing down the road. I got out and said,

'Never again!' He was a total madman behind the wheel, but he just thought that was the norm."

Turning to his football attitude and ability, Sinclair adds, "Erich always did his best. He was never hiding, and would always give his all. You could rely on him and he was good about the dressing room, a really popular lad. And don't forget, he was a very good footballer too. All right, he was a hard man, but that was just part of his game – he was also an excellent player, and it's to his credit that he never played dirty. He played the game hard but fair. He would always put a shift in and he would tackle a lion, no problem. That made him one of the most popular players with the fans."

Ian Redford, who played with Schaedler during the Gemmell years, found him a fascinating – if occasionally introspective – character. "I broke into the first team at a very early age and I remember Tommy Gemmell signing Erich from Hibs. He was a very wholehearted player – the type of guy who would run right through a brick wall. He was very brave and a fearless player who others looked up to," says Redford, who won a string of honours with Rangers and Dundee United and even made the breakthrough into professional golf. "Off the field though, I found him a quiet guy.

"I remember we went on a tour to Australia, in 1978 I think it was. I had originally been due to go with the Scottish Youth squad to the European championships, but I picked up an injury and big Tom decided that I should come on the tour. Erich was the kind of guy who was happy to go off on his own and do his own thing; he was a bit of a loner in that respect. There were times you felt he didn't want company. I'm happy to go and do my own thing sometimes, but if somebody suggested coming along with me I would say, 'No problem', whereas with Erich you got the feeling on one or two occasions that he just wanted to be alone. There were a few demons I think, although I have no idea where they came from.

"He could be the life and soul one moment and a bit deep the next. He fancied himself as a bit of a kung-fu expert and would flaunt that a bit – he had a bit of banter going on with the young lads in the team, trying out some of his moves on them. I liked him a lot. I was very sad and sorry to hear that he had taken his own life, but looking back, he was quite an intense guy. He was slightly manic in so much that he was the life and soul some of the time, then other times you could almost see the dark clouds circling around him.

"That tour of Australia would have left anyone needing time to themselves, mind you – we played all over and were away for ages! We started off in Melbourne and went to Adelaide, Newcastle, Brisbane, Perth and ended up going to New Zealand. We were away for a whole month, and coming on the back of a long hard season, it was quite exhausting. We couldn't wait to get back."

Redford, who often played against Erich after they both left Dens, adds, "As a footballer, you couldn't fault Erich. He brought a lot of experience with him to Dundee – and we knew from what he had done at Hibs, and the fact he had played for Scotland, that he was capable of playing football at the very top. After he had left Dundee, I remember the game Hibs played against Manchester United at Easter Road. Bryan Robson had a reputation as being one of the hardest in the game, but it would seem that Erich was ready to prove that he was even harder and sorted him out. He was a strong player. You would just bounce off him.

"Although I played against him when he went back to Hibs, because I was left-sided – the same as him – I was never directly up against him, and I would be playing on the other side of the pitch. But I remember even at the small-sided games in training he wouldn't hold back.

"He looked after himself. You can see now that he was way ahead of his time. Nowadays players – nearly ALL players – tend to try and look after themselves, but Erich was doing that back then in a way which was different to most of the professionals. There was a bit of a drink culture at Dundee, and a lot of the boys in that Dundee squad enjoyed being out on the booze, but Shades was all about self-preservation, he really looked after himself and was dedicated to staying as fit as he could be. A lot of people looked up to him, and with good reason."

# 20

# HOST WITH THE MOST

Bertie Auld is first and foremost a Celtic legend, as one of the heroes of the Lisbon Lions. But the chirpy Glaswegian undoubtedly served Hibs well too, as a player then trainer under Eddie Turnbull, and as a manager. Having been at Easter Road during the early 1970s, he knew only too well that standards had slipped when he returned as manager in 1980. He guided Hibs to the First Division title and promotion back to the Premier League, but with experienced players thin on the ground he braced himself for a grim battle against relegation.

When the opportunity to sign Erich Schaedler presented itself at the beginning of the 1981/82 season, Auld didn't hesitate to recruit his former teammate. "Erich was a manager's dream," says Auld, who had been taken with Schaedler's application during their first spell together. "Even when he arrived at Easter Road as a young boy he was eager, willing to learn, strong, adaptable and, above all, focused. It did not matter what you asked him to do, he was willing to do it. He was a fitness fanatic, looked after himself, looked after his boots and appearance and was the perfect professional footballer. He had tremendous inner strength.

"When he arrived from Stirling Albion and I saw what he was made of, I was surprised that I hadn't heard of him before; he was a breath of fresh air. And that's the reason why I signed him when I became manager.

"I had a lot of good players, but I was missing someone like Erich and all the pluses that came with him. I went to the chairman Tom Hart and said, 'I don't know what happened when he was here the first time and how he was allowed to leave, but I would love to have him back.'

"We had a lot of talented individuals, guys like Jackie McNamara and Alastair McLeod, and big Gordon Rae and Craig Paterson were shaping up to be excellent young players, but Erich made a big difference to that dressing room. He was the type of character who immediately lit the place up – when he walked in to that dressing room, it was like somebody had turned the fluorescent lights on. You need someone like that to give the place a lift, and he was a very honest person who people could relate to and trust.

"We had just won the First Division and got back into the Premier League, and he was exactly the type of player I was looking for to make sure that we stayed there. He was very physical, but never dirty. In all the times I saw him play, I can't remember him once going over the ball. Everything went into the game, he would be willing to run non-stop for ninety minutes and more, and he had a tremendous willingness to win."

With the deal to take Erich Schaedler back to Easter Road done, Erich made his "second debut" as a sub in a 1–0 defeat at Pittodrie on 19 September, and again came off the bench – to a rousing reception from the Hibs fans – in a draw against Dundee United a fortnight later. Bobby Flavell started the season as Hibs' left-back, but he could play a number of positions, and was soon switched to accommodate Erich's arrival. He was back in his cherished green and white No.3 shirt again, and wasn't ready to give it up without a fight.

Erich had witnessed a period of decline towards the end of his first spell with Hibs, and although they had bounced back from their relegation, there was still an air of gloom about the place. For all his positivity as a person, Auld often erred on the side of caution and Hibs could be a fairly unattractive side to watch as a result. The 1981/82 season was a largely mediocre affair, and dwindling gates reflected that. While never in serious danger of another catastrophic relegation, Hibs plodded along in mid-table and a 6–0 thrashing from champions-elect Celtic in the penultimate league game of the season demonstrated how ordinary they were as a team.

A couple of highlights in a largely forgettable season actually came in friendlies. The first game in October 1981 saw George Best back at Easter Road – this time with his new club San Jose Earthquakes. Schaedler had missed the whole George Best circus at Hibs, as it coincided with his time at Dundee, but he had played against the flawed genius a couple of times in the 1980/81 season – in which Hibs and Dundee were both promoted. The American side, coached by former Scotland and Dundee player Jim Gabriel, put on a show at Easter Road, and in what was in truth an exhibition match, Schaedler grabbed a rare spectacular goal in a 3–3 draw.

Goals weren't Schaedler's speciality but robust challenges were, and his physical style of play was among the talking points after a last-minute friendly Hibs arranged with Manchester United on Boxing Day 1981. Hibs were one of the few clubs in Britain with undersoil heating, and as an Arctic blast decimated the festive fixture list north and south of the border, Ron Atkinson accepted an invitation to bring his team of stars to the perfectly playable Easter Road. The match piqued the imagination and a healthy crowd braved the cold. It may have been a friendly, but Bryan Robson never saw it that way – and nor did Atkinson, when a bone-crushing challenge from Schaedler took him out of the game. Robson had the reputation of a hard man, but Erich showed that there were harder players around. A furious Atkinson, wearing his trademark sheepskin, went charging down to pitch-side to voice his fury, while Bertie Auld, even more outrageously attired than Big Ron in an oversized bunnet and puffing on a fat cigar, chuckled quietly on the Hibs bench.

Fashion disasters were the order of the day, because YouTube footage shows Jim "Bimbo" McArthur wearing a pair of figure-hugging shiny green tracksuit bottoms, which would not have looked out of place in New York's Studio 54 nightclub, to protect himself from the rutted ground. McArthur says he could almost feel the shuddering force of Schaedler's challenge on Robson from his goalmouth. "Most people remember that Man U game for Erich's challenge on Robson," says McArthur. "It was the first time Bryan Robson broke his collarbone when Erich cemented him. Ron Atkinson came down from the stand with his fur coat. He was on the pitch going mental at Erich. He absolutely cemented him and we were going, 'Oh no.'"

Amid the sideshows, Hibs and United traded goals, Willie Jamieson opening the scoring before Frank Stapleton equalised to keep Atkinson from completely exploding. "This was one of those rare footballing occasions when just about everyone went away with something to feel pleased about," reported *The Scotsman*'s Mike Aitken. "All round, it was a fixture worthy of the season of goodwill. Even Bertie Auld's bunnet found a Christmas companion in Ron Atkinson's fur coat. Both managers looked as if they would have felt at home in the Crazy Gang, which, when you consider their profession, perhaps isn't so daft. I found United's expensive galaxy of stars just a shade disappointing. Bryan Robson, who went off before half-time after hurting his ribs in a clash with Erich Schaedler – at full throttle as usual – was industrious, made himself available for colleagues and moved eagerly between front and back. What was less obvious was why United had paid £1.8 million for the plain virtues of Robson. For that kind of cash I'd be looking for more of a Diego Maradona than a Des Bremner!"

The Manchester United match was one of few highlights in a season immersed in mediocrity, and Bertie Auld may have saved Hibs from a second financially catastrophic relegation, but that didn't keep him his job for long. The board still had ambitions of waking up the sleeping giant – despite the stark lack of resources

– and they listened to complaints that Auld's style of football was driving fans away. They gave him a chance at the start of the 1982/83 season, but when the League Cup section yielded just one win out of six, Bertie was sacked after a final humbling 3–1 defeat at Airdrie.

Auld is one of life's most enthusiastic characters and despite the way it ended for him at Easter Road, he has nothing but warm words to say about Hibs and Erich Schaedler. "I am delighted and honoured that I knew Erich though – to meet him, to play alongside him, to coach him and to be his manager," he says. "Looking back, I am glad I was able to bring him back to Hibs. It gave me a real lift and the faith I had in him was quickly repaid. I had no doubts he would fit in right away, and I was right. He wasn't the captain – Jackie McNamara was my captain – but he was a leader on the park and a leader in the dressing room. The young players looked up to him and the older pros really enjoyed having him around. I honestly can't remember one single player ever having a bad word to say about him. He was the life and soul at times, and he was humorous too. One of his party tricks was to pick people up with one hand while they were sitting in a chair.

"You've heard that saying about someone having an infectious laugh? Well, Erich's style of play was infectious – as soon as he was on the park he would give 100 per cent, and off it he was similarly dedicated. Like every other professional he had mediocre moments during a game, but if he had a bad touch on the ball, he would be determined to make up for it as soon as he could. Erich wasn't the classiest player, but I'll tell you this much – he couldn't be more wholehearted. It was a physical game in those days and he excelled at it. He had that tremendous long throw, which was a great weapon to use, better than a corner, and we scored a lot of goals from using that intelligently.

"The supporters loved him because his game was all about passion and enthusiasm. He was like one of them. Whenever he pulled on that Hibbie strip you could see it getting tighter and tighter because his chest was puffed out with pride. He just wanted to get out on that park and do his best for the team and for the fans. Sure, some players have more ability than Erich did, but most of them don't have what he did – Erich Schaedler gave you everything he possibly he could and more."

Auld's replacement had to be a name big enough to pacify the fans, and the board delivered, appointing club legend Pat Stanton to the post. Pat was quick to surround himself with similarly Hibs-minded people, and appointed Jimmy O'Rourke and George Stewart as his assistants. But while Hibs had the dream team in the dugout, they still had a nightmare team on the park! There was a smattering of good players and an emerging crop of talented but raw youngsters, but with money too tight to mention, many of the squad were not up to the job, and Stanton and Co. just had to soldier on with what they had at their disposal.

The management trio had all played alongside Schaedler, and they were delighted to discover that his professionalism had never wavered. He was the type of role model they needed to pull their young squad through some arduous times. "He was never ever any bother to anyone – the perfect professional," says Stanton. "If you were making up your team lines on a Friday, or maybe a Saturday morning, you would put Joe Bloggs down, and you'd wonder about his attitude and how he would cope against the player he would be directly up against, but Erich, you could put his name down and you would know exactly what you were getting. It was the same with players like Jackie McNamara and Ralphie Callachan. If you have four or five of these guys you've got a chance."

George Stewart agrees: "It was great to have Erich back. His experience and his knowledge of the place was so important. We had signed young guys like Gordon Hunter, Paul Kane, Callum Milne, Kevin McKee, John Collins and Mickey Weir – a lot of young Hibs folk – and Erich was there to take them under his wing. He was an inspiration to these guys."

The 1982/83 season was largely a write-off for Erich, however. Having started the season strongly and rarely played in a losing team, he was injured at Celtic Park a month into the season and spent the next five months out – the longest spell on the sidelines he ever endured in his career. After an Achilles operation, Erich returned to the team at the end of January for a daunting Scottish Cup trip to Easter Road, and it was a comeback to forget as a rampant Aberdeen won 4–1. Erich was clearly not back to full fitness and managed only three more matches that season. As Hibs literally limped to the end of the season, they were thrashed 5–0 by Aberdeen in the final game of the season.

Erich missed the start of the 1983/84 season as he worked on ensuring he was fully fit, and he eventually returned in a League Cup win at Dumbarton. While there were other old heads such as John Blackley and Jackie McNamara and Arthur Duncan around, he was a big influence on the young players coming through – Kevin McKee, Paul Kane, Brian Rice and Graham Harvey.

"Erich used to take a lot of kids under his wing – he had a lot of time for the young players. He mixed more with the younger players than the older players," says Stanton. "He was full of advice and having people like that about the place and having players like that exposed to that is a massive plus in their development. Guys like Johnny Collins, Paul Kane, Gordon Hunter – it wasn't an accident that all these young guys made the grade. It was having guys like Erich around that made it possible. I had people like Tommy Preston when I was a player, and guys like that will impart pieces of good advice that stand you in good stead the rest of your career. Erich was a great help in the dressing room and a great help with the laddies. It was a tough season, but during that period Hibs were on a low."

Jimmy O'Rourke agrees: "George Stewart and I were Pat's assistants and we needed a left-back so we were happy to have Erich. We knew what we were getting and we knew that we could depend on him. He didn't disappoint us. He was a strong, strong man. You always got a 100 per cent of him – the same commitment."

Commitment alone wasn't enough to lift Hibs during a difficult season, however. Schaedler received a lot of plaudits for the manner in which he was able to channel his aggression. If he had a temper, then it rarely bubbled to the surface, and he displayed admirable self-control. His teammate Bobby Thomson was another physical player, but the big centre forward had a little more difficulty in keeping a lid on his emotions. In a remarkable game against St Johnstone in November 1983, Thomson went berserk and was sent off for attacking a linesman in front of the old South Stand, an act of violence which saw him carpeted by the SFA and banned for six months. The irony was that Hibs were cruising towards a 4–1 victory at the time he lost his rag. Who knows what he might have done if they had been losing!

The low point of the season arrived in the Scottish Cup. After being held to a 0–0 draw by East Fife, Hibs headed to Methil for the replay three days later and were embarrassingly beaten 2–0, with goalkeeper Alan Rough breaking his ankle. For the first time since 1978/79, Hibs and Hearts were back in the same division, but the derbies were not going well either. Erich missed the first clash of the season, a 3–2 defeat at Tynecastle, but played in the three draws that followed. Having dominated the fixture in the Seventies, Hibs' habitual failure to win Edinburgh derbies was to prove a thorn in their side throughout the 1980s and the early 1990s.

Money was getting tighter at Easter Road and Stanton was in a difficult position as he worked with a threadbare squad. On the plus side he had a talented crop of young players emerging. He had no option but to pitch some of them straight into first-team football, ready or not, although time has proved that the tough baptism was the making of many of them, including John Collins, Paul Kane, Gordon Hunter and Mickey Weir.

The season actually started promisingly enough, with a 0–0 draw at home to Celtic, followed by a 1–0 win at Dundee, but any early optimism vanished after a particularly ugly Edinburgh derby at Easter Road. Paul Kane had given Hibs the lead on the stroke of half-time before Craig Levein equalised. Crowd trouble was rife and when Hearts supporters came on to the pitch and confronted the Hibs players, the flashpoint interrupted the flow of the game. As fans headed towards the exits on a dark day for football in the capital, Hearts' sub Derek O'Connor scored an injury-time winner. This sent Hibs into a tailspin. The fans were disillusioned and in front of a paltry crowd of just 3,642, a 3–2 defeat at Easter Road to Dumbarton was the final straw for Pat Stanton. He tendered his resignation after the game and it was accepted. Another Tornadoes legend, John Blackley, would step up from the playing staff to take the reins.

By this time, Erich was juggling his football career with a new vocation as a publican. He had bought a share of the Victoria Bar on Leith Walk, and also opened his own pub, Shades, at the foot of Easter Road, which sat on the corner of its junction with Thorntree Street. Erich's former Hibs coach John Fraser said, "I was partly responsible for him getting his pub. I was the first one among them to get a pub – I had Tipplers in Bread Street and the Learig in Restalrig Road. A guy in charge of Drybrough's Brewery would always come to me first to ask me about the players who wanted to open pubs, asking if they were the right type of guys and whether I could vouch for them. He was the man who said yes or no. He would come to me for a character reference and I would say they were all good, reliable guys who were capable of running a pub and could be trusted. Alex Cropley, Erich, Pat Stanton, Jackie McNamara, Ralph Callachan, Jimmy O'Rourke, Eric Stevenson, George Stewart and a few more all had pubs. We kept in touch when we were both running pubs – I would pop in to Shades and the Victoria Bar and Erich would pop in to Tipplers and the Learig. He was a jack-the-lad, but he was never a drinker."

Regulars at both pubs also speak warmly about the host with the most, and though he wasn't much of a drinker himself, Schaedler seemed a natural working behind a bar and chewing the fat with the regulars. In a recent tribute thread to Schaedler on the fans forum on Hibs.net, Keith Addy said, "I worked for Erich in Shades Bar as an under-manager. You will never meet such a nice, generous guy. I can remember a time when Hibs played Aberdeen in the League Cup final (1985). Hibs got beat 3–0 that day and he was gutted for all of the supporters.

"In the dining area of Shades, all the Hibs supporters were dancing and shouting as if they won. Erich, who was not working that night, told me to get the Hibbies in order and stop dancing on top of the tables. So I shouted and got the situation under control. It was nice and quiet and the jukebox was off. Next thing while I'm down the stairs changing a barrel, the rumpus started again. All I could hear was singing, dancing and the jukebox going even louder. As I walked up the stairs, worrying what Erich was going to think, lo and behold there was Erich with a Hibs flag, dancing and singing on top of the table. I just looked at him and he gave me a wink. Some man!

"Alex Edwards was the boss of the brewery at the time – Alloa Ltd – but Shades would be getting all types of beer into his pub. We had just bought Carlsberg, and Shades had a tenancy – we thought he'd be buying regular supplies from us. It would show up on his computer that he hadn't been buying any Carlsberg, and when somebody popped in he had Tennent's on tap instead! He was buying kegs of beer from all over the place."

Serving behind the bar in November 1983, Schaedler was involved in an alarming incident, when an armed man burst into his pub with a loaded double-barrel shotgun. Schaedler, together with two off-duty detectives who were in the bar, overpowered and disarmed the assailant, and after a High Court trial after which the gunman escaped with a fine, they later received awards in recognition of their bravery.

The *Evening News* reported: "Hibs star Erich Schaedler and two police officers received letters of commendation from the Secretary of State for Scotland and also meritorious awards from Lothian and Borders Police. Constables Stewart Leslie and William Adair were talking to Mr Schaedler in his Easter Road public house when a man who had been banned from the premises burst in carrying a loaded shotgun. He pointed it at the footballer, but PC Leslie grabbed the barrels and forced them towards the ceiling. The two others joined in the struggle and the man was disarmed. Two live cartridges were found in the shotgun and the man was fined £400 in court earlier this year [1984].

Erich said, "When the man walked in, we just made a grab for the gun. I didn't have time to think about it then but afterwards I started to shake a bit at the thought of what might have happened."

Erich's friend Frank Dougan also remembers the incident: "There were always people coming in and out of the pub offering to sell stuff, and this guy had been in earlier in the night and had been sent away with a flea in his ear. He reappeared an hour later with a double-barrelled shotgun. Erich jumped over the bar and said, 'Son, I've worked too hard for you to take this off me!'"

It wasn't only Hibs fans who were regulars at Schaedler's bars. A thriving Edinburgh branch of Dundee supporters – the Capital Dark Blues – got off the ground thanks to Erich's generosity in allowing them to use a room in his pub to hold their regular meetings. Scott Glenday also recalls popping in with a group of Dundee fans before a match against Hibs and getting the warmest of welcomes: "We ventured down Leith Walk to find his pub before a game at Easter Road. He was back at Hibs but wasn't playing that day, and when he came in he got a rousing reception from supporters of both teams. I remember he had a 'tougher than Tannadice pies' caricature with him in his classic Seventies Admiral Dundee top behind the bar. He spent time with us, made everyone feel welcome and walked down the road with us to the game. We were proud as punch giving it, 'One Erich Schaedler,' as we made our way through the streets of Leith to the ground in the presence of the man himself.

He wasn't at Dundee any more, but to those present that didn't matter; he was one of our heroes and he loved it."

While Schaedler was clearly a popular publican, one or two of his friends and teammates were surprised to see him enter the licensed trade. There were not a lot of options available to footballers at that time, and it was the "in" thing to do, but to some of his closest friends it didn't seem like an obvious route he would ever go down. "There was something about Erich having the pubs that didn't fit," says Jim McArthur. "Don't me wrong – he loved being behind the bar and the punters loved having him there, but to me it was out of character." Jay Crawford agrees: "At that time, to have a pub was something ex-players did. I never thought it really suited Erich. I think he did it because he was thinking of what he was going to do at the end of his career. There must have been a worry." Bertie Auld also found it an unusual business venture for Schaedler: "It was the last thing I would have seen him doing, to go into a pub. It was right out of character, I thought. I don't know what sort of publican he was, but I do know that he would have put everything into it and been very engaging and good company for the punters. He was a great mixer and was full of conversation."

Erich was thirty-five when John Blackley got the Hibs job, and the pair of them were involved in an intense relegation battle. Blackley was unable to stop the rot that had set in in the last throes of the Stanton era, losing three of his first four games in charge, but Hibs picked up some important points as they fought to steer themselves away from the drop zone. A six-game losing streak between December 1984 and January 1985 was snapped in style with a memorable 2–1 win against Rangers at Ibrox. Brian Rice and Colin Harris got the goals, while Erich and the back four played out of their skins in front of an inspired Alan Rough to secure an unlikely win, and more importantly for the club, a survival lifeline.

The win over Rangers instilled some belief and galvanised Hibs into a battling effort to beat the drop. Young Gordon Durie, signed from East Fife, was proving to be a shrewd buy and his dynamic style – combined with a long throw-in to rival Erich's – had helped breathe life into the team, along with the trickery of winger Joe McBride, the son of namesake Joe who had been Erich's teammate when he first arrived at Easter Road from Stirling in 1969. Hibs were refusing to go down without a fight, and in a midweek derby against Hearts at Tynecastle they salvaged a remarkable point. Unbeknown to Schaedler and the supporters in the Gorgie Road end that night, it would be the last time they ever saw Erich Schaedler play for Hibs.

The game started terribly for Hibs when they lost a goal within a minute, inevitably scored by their chief derby tormentor John Robertson. Sandy Clark made it 2–0 after twenty minutes and Hibs were not only staring at a derby hiding but a mortal blow to their hopes of avoiding relegation. To add to their woes, Schaedler picked up an injury and made way for McBride. It was to prove a game-changing substitution. McBride put Hibs back in the game with a goal in the eighty-fourth minute then scored an equaliser three minutes later to send the Hibs fans huddled in the Gorgie Road end into a state of delirium.

It was the end of the season for Erich but not the end of the road for Hibs, who travelled to Dumbarton on the Saturday, backed by a huge travelling support after the club laid on a fleet of free buses, and won 2–0. Erich's old pal Iain Munro – back for his second spell at Hibs, having rejoined from St Mirren – had taken over at left-back. Hibs had somehow scrambled to safety, although the fact that it had been a season to forget was illustrated by the meagre crowd of 7,000, who watched them beat Rangers at Easter Road on the final day of the season. It was the same day as the Valley Parade disaster at Bradford – football was well and truly put in perspective.

John Blackley had kept Hibs up, but as he spent the summer scratching his head how he could improve the team with meagre resources, he had some tough decisions to make. Looking at his squad, he had to be ruthless and one of the hardest decisions he ever had to make was telling Erich Schaedler that he was being freed. "It's a cruel thing to say, but when you're the manager in that situation and money is as tight as it was then, there was no room for sentiment," says Blackley. "Iain Munro was there too, and he was in his thirties too, so I couldn't afford to have two left-backs of that age. Shades was starting to get one or two injuries at that time and a tough decision had to be made. There was absolutely nothing personal to it – how could there be; I thought he was a brilliant guy – but the decision that I thought was right had to be made for the football club.

"He took it on the chin but I can imagine Erich taking that really badly and being really down after that. Even after he signed for Dumbarton he used to come in and see us. We had a good relationship because he was someone you could rely on and you knew he would never create a problem for you. He was as good as gold, very professional. There was never any chance of him becoming a problem. He just wanted to do well for Hibs. So letting him go was as tough as it gets."

Iain Munro, who stayed on at the club as club captain as Erich departed for Dumbarton, admits the exit hit Schaedler hard. "The first time he left Hibs and went to Dundee you could see that he didn't want to leave, but that happens at clubs, sometimes a change of manager or circumstances takes it out of your hands, and you just have to accept it. The second time he left Hibs he went to Dumbarton, and I think that hurt him. He would have stayed at Hibs all of his life if he could. I'm just surmising, but maybe if he had been at Hibs, surrounded by people he knew and at the club he obviously loved, he might not have felt as low as he must have done."

21

# SON OF THE ROCK

It was ironic that Erich, having played a pivotal role in helping to relegate Dumbarton during his final season with Hibs, should then end up at the club he helped condemn to the drop. As the name of the ground Boghead suggests, Dumbarton was not awash with glamour, and they were a club that had been punching way above their weight.

The arrival of the wealthy Sir Hugh Fraser as chairman had lifted any of the gloom still lingering from the relegation. Fraser used a one-third stake he held in sportswear manufacturer Bukta, the company behind the classic Hibs strip of the Seventies, to finance his shareholding in Dumbarton, and picked up his controlling interest in the ailing club for a bargain fee of around £80,000 in May 1985. The new man in the boardroom wanted to get Dumbarton back into the top flight at the first time of asking, and he said in his pre-season message, "I am hopeful that we will have learned many valuable lessons from last season's campaign and will therefore be well equipped to mount a major challenge for the First Division championship. Defeat is a word which I dislike, and Davie Wilson and his team have assured me that they will go all out to make season 1985/86 a memorable one for all Sons fans." Sir Hugh had been chairman of House of Fraser, Harrods and Whyte and Mackay – and this heavy-hitter brought a presence to the club. Sadly, he died of cancer at the age of fifty – two years after Erich's death.

Dumbarton had an excellent blend of youth and experience, with Schaedler recruited by manager Davie Wilson, the former Rangers and Scotland winger, to bolster the latter category as the oldest member of the squad. Alongside him were other older heads, such as goalkeeper Gordon Arthur, captain and central defender Mark Clougherty, centre forward John Bourke, and Joe and Tommy Coyle – the elder brothers of Owen Coyle, also on the books at his first professional club.

Coyle, who has become one of the brightest managers in English football, remembers Schaedler as a shining example of professionalism. "I had been at Dumbarton from the age of thirteen as a schoolboy signing," he says. "The great thing about the club was that they would allow the youth players to train with the first team, and the older professionals that were there were all welcoming and eager to bring on the younger players – there were no egos. It was the best education you could get in football, training with the senior players. We looked up to the older guys and listened to what they had to say, and Erich came into that category.

"I was only a kid, but I had no problems settling in at Dumbarton as my brothers Joe and Tommy were both there too. I was still only 5ft 4in when I was seventeen and built like a jockey's whip, but the manager recognised that I had something, and told me to stick at it. He said I would grow, and the encouragement was non-stop.

"Erich was a fantastic man – people always said that. As a young kid, learning the ropes, he was one of the first to take time out to talk to the young players and he would always be helping out with little pieces of advice on the training ground too. I've been in football a long time now, and at some clubs you see that some of the older, more experienced players can become self-obsessed and feel that they are above working with the youth players, but guys like Erich were the opposite to that – they would make a football club tick and help it progress, particularly when money was tight and the club relied on bringing young players through the ranks. I was very fortunate to grow up in that environment. Dumbarton always had a good mix of big players who had played at a higher level and young kids coming through.

"We had tremendous respect for Erich. Here was a guy that had played at the highest level in the world. He'd played against top, top-class players, been at the World Cup in 1974 and had been part of the Hibs team of the Seventies that was one of the best we had seen in our country. There's no doubt; he was a terrific player.

"His approach to football and training was an example to us all. He took real pride in his fitness levels, and it was working alongside players like Erich that inspired me later in my career, as I went on to play until I was forty when I was player-manager at St Johnstone. I was fortunate as a young impressionable player at Dumbarton working alongside guys like Erich and Pat McCluskey with that mentality. It may sound a cliché, but Erich was a supremely fit athlete who was ahead of his time. We were living in an era in British football where it was the norm for players to train and play, then fill in some of the rest of the time by spending the day in the bookies or the pub, but here was a guy who took a great deal of pride in his appearance and his life as a professional footballer."

Other up-and-coming young players at Dumbarton were right-back Ray Montgomery and Allan Moore, who has become a promising manager with Morton. Moore recalls, "I remember his leadership qualities. I had signed from Possil YM and thought that my chance of professional football had gone because I was twenty, especially as I was quite small, but I got the chance to go to Dumbarton. Erich was a help in that respect, because he wasn't the tallest of full-backs, but he showed you didn't necessarily have to be tall – you could make up for it with passion and determination for the game. He was one of the senior pros at the club and his attitude, work-rate and commitment rubbed off on the younger players like myself."

One of the frustrations for Erich Schaedler at Dumbarton, aside from the travelling, was that they were a part-time club. For the fitness fanatic, the sessions would come nowhere near the level of training he craved. To top-up his Dumbarton training, Schaedler therefore fixed himself up with extra sessions with Meadowbank Thistle and threw himself into gym work at the Edinburgh Club.

"We trained twice a week – at the local park and Boghead – but the sessions were high intensity," says Moore. "It probably didn't help that we trained on the pitch as well, and it used to have quite a reputation, but I actually remember it being a decent surface to play on, especially for me as a winger. We looked up to Erich because he had played at a very high level. We had a good blend of seasoned professionals who had been around in the game for many years and had a lot of experience to share, and younger guys starting out. It's about finding the right mix, and it's something I've done as a manager. People might have wondered what a player like Erich Schaedler was doing at Dumbarton at the time, but it was a good club to be at and the kind of experience that he had is invaluable. We also had big Donald McNeill at centre-half, Mark Clougherty – the whole back four was packed full of experience and we were a good side as a result of that."

The club captain, Clougherty, was one of few Dumbarton players who was a similar age to Schaedler, and he tells how they bonded before the season had even begun, when the club took the players away on a sunshine break to energise them for the season ahead. "I knew Shades had played for Hibs and done very well there, but I knew him better from his time at Dundee when I played against him a few times," says Clougherty, who went on to become Dumbarton manager. "He came to us in 1985 and that coincided with Sir Hugh Fraser taking over the club. I suppose it was the dawn of a new era at Dumbarton and Sir Hugh quickly got us all onside by taking us on a pre-season trip to Majorca.

"We were there for five days pre-season and I got to know Shades well. I had known from playing against Dundee that he was a hard, hard player, but when he came to us and we went on that trip it was immediately obvious he was a really nice guy. He didn't smoke or drink and he was dedicated to keeping himself fit. He could always be seen at the front at training. It's often the case at clubs that the defence gel as a unit on and off the pitch, and that was the case at Dumbarton. I was the sweeper, Donald McNeil was the centre-half, Shades was left-back and Graeme Sinclair or Ray Montgomery would play right-back.

"You might think of footballers going away on a trip to Majorca as a recipe for disaster but it worked wonders for team morale. The senior players – there were four or five of us – took the lead on that trip and Erich loved it. He was a bit of a joker and liked all the wee wind-ups that went on, and he kind of teamed up with me that way – we shared the same kind of humour. He was such a nice guy. He was a hard man on the park and would always get stuck in, but off the park he was just a real gentleman. In Majorca, Davie Wilson would have us up at eight for training, and he would work us hard, but there was no complaining and we would just spend the rest of the day lying around the pool. I remember on the final day the hotel manager telling us our behaviour had been brilliant and that he had only just found out that we were a football team – he couldn't believe he hadn't had any bother!"

After the trip to Spain and some pre-season training in Levengrove Park, Schaedler was immediately installed as first-choice left-back and despite a disappointing League Cup exit to Stirling Albion on penalties, Erich played his part in a strong start to the league season as Dumbarton won seven of their first nine First Division matches, keeping a clean sheet in five of them. Another two clean sheets followed in a 0–0 draw at Clyde and a 1–0 home win against Kilmarnock, before Erich picked up a knock in a 3–1 defeat at Brechin and had to be substituted. The injury forced Erich to sit out the following weekend's match, with Martin McGowan instead wearing the No.3 shirt in a 1–1 draw with Forfar at Boghead, and although he returned for a horrendous 6–1 thrashing at Hamilton, he again failed to last the ninety minutes.

On Saturday, 16 November 1985, Schaedler lined up for

Dumbarton against Montrose, a 2–2 draw in which top goalscorers Gerry McCoy and Stuart MacIver both scored. It was the last competitive game of Schaedler's life.

Clougherty remembers the numbing news being delivered to a hushed Dumbarton squad that Erich had been found dead. "We were in at training just after Christmas time when Davie Wilson came in and said, 'Look, lads, I have some really bad news. Erich Schaedler is dead.' He told us Erich had gone missing on Christmas Eve and that a woman walking her dog had found him in the woods. What could you do? What would you say? We were all absolutely devastated and we felt for his family."

Owen Coyle says, "The last time I saw him was when he arrived at training during the Christmas period. He had come along to training in his big Range Rover and had his two Dobermans with him. To learn a few days later he was dead . . . well, words can't sum up how we all felt. We were all very saddened at the time. He was someone I, and all the others, really looked up to. It was a real shock. There had been no warning signals and nobody knew of anything untoward in his life. He had come to Dumbarton and played an integral part in our success and our team spirit. We were all left in total shock because we'd not only lost a teammate but a friend as well. He had an aura about him and people really took to him. He was a real gentleman as well."

Allan Moore agrees: "His death was the biggest shock you could get. He was up front and open with anyone, so there was no indication. We were only part-time and trained twice a week, so we weren't seeing him every day, but he was a good guy and mixed very well and everyone had a lot of respect and time for him.

"He was a character as well, always full of beans. It was a shock, definitely. I went through the same later in my career with Paul McGrillen, who was the same kind of character. There was no indication whatsoever that it was going to happen. You do come across a few deep thinkers in football, guys who are quiet and keep themselves to themselves, and are guarded about their personalities.

But, to me, Erich was the exact opposite – he was always full of life and chatty.

"I suppose footballers sometimes try and put on a brave face when they come in to train and play; I've found that out through my own personal experiences. There can be a bit of an act – because you don't want to show any sign of weakness. But there are sports psychologists and a lot of professionals out there that can help with that now, which wasn't the case in the Eighties. A lot of footballers and managers can be chirpy and determined to keep the spirits up when they are in at the club, but then take the problems home with them. I was getting to the stage where I would go home, shut myself in a room and not have enough time for the wife and kids. It was becoming a problem for me and I recognised that. Danny Lennon [the St Mirren manager] gave me a book *Motivated Way of Life* and that has helped. I know how to cope with my emotions better and not to take the problems home with me.

"It's only natural. Football is full of ups and downs and when you are coming to the end of your career that is often the hardest thing to deal with. I didn't have as good a career as Erich, but I know it was hard for me when you realise you're getting near the end of it. It's difficult trying to find something to substitute it. But Erich was fit as a fiddle, and I'm sure he would have had a few seasons ahead of him. I think he would have made a great coach, because he was a likeable guy and people could relate to him. You could speak to him and unload a lot of your problems on him. He always made time to speak to the young boys in the team and impart advice if they asked for it."

Clougherty was perhaps the player closest to Schaedler at Dumbarton and he has constantly agonised over the years that he might have missed a warning sign that his friend was troubled. "I remember about late October, mid-November he took a bad cold and was off for about three weeks. When he was fit enough to train again he came back in a reserve game," says Clougherty. "I was down at the ground that night and I asked Davie Wilson if I could play too. But Erich had to come off during that game as he was still not feeling well and he went away home before the game had finished.

"I gave him a call the next day to see if he was okay, and to see if he wanted to come up to the house for a cup of tea and a chat. I called him at his house and then at the pub, and they told me there that I had just missed him. I still wonder what would have happened if I'd just phoned an hour earlier. I might have been able to catch him and managed somehow to lift his spirits – if they'd needed lifting. We just don't know how he was feeling at that time. There had been absolutely no sign that anything was up. I was just checking on him because I knew he must have been hurting at being unable to finish the reserve game. He took such pride in his fitness that he must have found it incredibly frustrating to first be out for a few weeks, then suffer a setback on his attempted comeback at getting himself fit to play for the first team again. He was a fit, fit person and because of that it might have pulled him down. It's very hard to say, as he could have had something else going on in his private life – but if he did, he gave absolutely no signal that there was anything up. It was shocking, we were all devastated."

Dumbarton had been due to play Alloa on 28 December, and the match was immediately postponed as a mark of respect. Robert Ryan, who worked for Dumbarton at the time and was the voice of the club's hotline, compared Schaedler's death to that of Gary Speed, the Wales manager who was found dead in 2011. Writing in his blog, Ryan said, "What drove Wales football manager, former successful club and international footballer and family man Gary Speed to hang himself? What kind of despair or unhappiness could drive a seemingly successful and happy guy to this ultimate self-harm? In the 1980s, I recall being the voice of the Dumbarton FC telephone news line (lots of clubs had them in pre-internet days). Dumbarton [and former Hibs and Scotland] defender Erich Schaedler took his own life, necessitating the cancellation of that week's game and an announcement to that effect. As club general manager Alex Wright and I discussed how to break the news, he looked at me and said, 'Why would he do it? – Ah mean nothing is that bad, is it?' Clearly something was indeed 'that bad'."

Interestingly, but very much in keeping with Scottish society in 1985, news of the death was kept low-key. Although the Alloa game was postponed, in the weeks that followed the club made only passing reference to the loss of Schaedler. Contrast this with the extensive club and media response to the tragic death of another Dumbarton player, Gordon Lennon, who died in 2009 in an off-road accident just weeks after captaining the club to promotion. Lennon's sad death, albeit in a vastly different age and in completely different circumstances, commanded two tribute programmes and spreads in virtually every national newspaper. But in Erich's case, Dumbarton programme editor Graeme Robertson explains, "The first issue after his death was for the visit of Morton on 1 January and was probably printed before Christmas. The following home game against Airdrie had a four-pager produced the day of [or day before] the game, as we thought it would be postponed. We then played Brechin City on 18 January, and the only comment is on page 14 in a column headed 'The Season So Far . . . December': 'The tragic loss of Erich Schaedler obviously soured the month for the club.'"

Robertson adds, "The Alloa game postponed on 28 December was eventually played on 4 February. The original programme was used with a one-page update, the first line of which read, 'Tonight's game was originally scheduled for Saturday, 28 December but was postponed because of the untimely death of Dumbarton player Erich Schaedler.' It had more coverage of Davy Wilson's resignation."

However, Ryan is correct when he stresses how the deaths of Lennon and Schaedler, and the subsequent reaction to them, are difficult to compare. "I think the Gordon Lennon comparison is a bit different. He was younger, had been at the club longer and had a baby son. Not to minimise the tragedy of Erich, but people have always been a bit uncomfortable with suicide – perhaps less so now, but definitely twenty-eight years ago," he says. "Alex Wright and I agonised for about an hour on what the wording should be on the club statement so as not to offend any supporters."

The updated history of Dumbarton FC by Jim McAllister certainly accords Schaedler a worthy mention of the role he played in his short but influential time at Boghead. McAllister writes, "By Christmas 1985, fortunes were on the wane, compounded by the tragic death of Erich Schaedler in a shooting accident. Thirty-five-year-old Schaedler had only joined the club in the summer on a free transfer from Hibernian, but his tough-tackling style had made him a favourite with the Dumbarton support."

Media coverage of Schaedler's death was also scant. "I think the difference was when somebody died in that way in that era, people tended to keep it as low-key as possible," says Clougherty. "Nobody had any answers – they still don't – and I think the feeling was that we should respect the family and allow them as much privacy as possible. Perhaps the press viewed it the same way."

And captain Clougherty had the added responsibility of getting the young grief-stricken Dumbarton squad through the rest of the season. "We all went to the funeral, dressed in our club blazers," he says. "There were people there from all of his clubs – Stirling, Hibs, Dundee and ourselves. It was obvious that wherever he had been, people took to him. The place was mobbed – it was a testament to how popular he had been and Iain Munro spoke for the family.

"The boys at Dumbarton were so close anyway that we just naturally pulled together. We would go on nights out together. Raymond Montgomery's dad had a pub down in Ayr so we would sometimes go down there and play darts and dominoes against the regulars. And we used to hold a couple of dances each year as well, so everyone got to know each other very well. Erich's death was shocking for us all, but we got through it."

Owen Coyle agrees: "There was total bewilderment and shock at his loss. He had so much ahead of him. But I think the team spirit we had in the dressing room helped keep the boys together during that period.

"Nobody knows to this day exactly why he died or the circumstances behind it, but if he had any kind of problem he was keeping it to himself; it may have been different for him nowadays. There was a different attitude in those days. People would often bottle something up than go to someone for help or for counselling. People can see now that there needn't be any stigma attached or anything at all wrong with going to someone for help. I have no doubt that if Erich did have something that was troubling him and had decided to seek some assistance, people would have been queuing up to help him – he was so well liked. There wasn't a great deal made of Erich's death nationally, as that was the era we lived in. If it had happened now, the tributes would be endless. Because it was 1985, he probably didn't get the send-off that he deserved."

Those who attended Erich's funeral in 1986 still remember the eloquent, glowing eulogy given by Iain Munro, something the Schaedler family are eternally grateful for. "I was close to him, but I think I was chosen because I had been with him for both spells at Hibs and I was the club captain at the time," says Munro. "It was probably the hardest thing I have ever had to do.

"It would have been hard enough to do for any teammate you have lost, but having become so friendly with him, it was really tough. I had got to know him so well on trips away, at training every day and in games. I just had to make sure I found the words that did him justice. He was a lovely lad and I felt sorry for him in the respect that he was either really high and super positive or down and lost in his own thoughts, sitting in the corner. He could withdraw sometimes, and when he did you left him to it. But he wouldn't have done anyone a bad turn, you could trust him with anything, and all the lads thought the world of him."

Janette Campbell, a lifelong Hibs supporter who worshipped Erich, was among the mourners and recalls, "My friend and I went along to his funeral which was packed out with superstars of the era in homage to Erich. It's always sad remembering this time.

"The fans have never forgotten him; he was such a likeable character who gave everything. A few years back I attended a function in the Forthview Suite in the Famous Five stand to commemorate Hibs winning the League Cups in 1972 and 1991. There was an empty chair between John Brownlie and John Blackley and I sat down next to them for a chat. 'That's Erich's chair, Janette. You can't sit there,' was what I was told by John Blackley. The pair of us just looked at each other and smiled!"

# 22

# WHY?

Popular, respected, charming, fit, and seemingly 100 per cent dedicated to self-preservation: so why on earth would Erich Schaedler want to kill himself? To die in such a macabre way, alone in a Borders forest, still doesn't make sense to those that knew him. No note, no clues, just a tragic sense of loss.

"Why" is the question that has haunted his family and friends since Christmas 1985, and after exhausting many leads they are no closer to establishing a cast-iron reason for Erich's tragic death. Found alone in his car and dead from a single shotgun wound to the head, the police concluded their investigations swiftly and understandably arrived at a verdict of suicide. There was no fatal accident inquiry, no inquest, and Erich was cremated in early 1986 – all of which his elder brother deeply regrets almost thirty years on. John Schaedler is far from convinced Erich took his own life. He is not in denial; he simply feels that there are way too many lingering unanswered questions to allow a line to be drawn under Erich's death.

When I set out to write this book I had hoped to get to the bottom of Schaedler's death, for his family's sake especially. The mystery is a source of constant torment to them. Surely he had said something to someone in the days and weeks before he went missing on Christmas Eve 1985? But no, not a single credible scrap of evidence emerged to prove Schaedler had been planning to take his own life. There were scores of good friends who would have done anything for Schaedler, but when it came to personal issues, he had a habit of putting the shutters up.

"He had lots of friends and was just a lovely, trusting guy. But if he had a problem he would usually bottle it up," says Hibs supporter and friend Frank Dougan. "He occasionally spoke about things on his mind, but it was only if there were two of us maybe alone in the afternoon in the Vicky [Victoria Bar] or at Shades. Erich was a very deep guy and he was a very personal man. He would be happy to speak to you all day and hear your problems, but he was far less comfortable when it was the other way round. He would rather speak about you than him."

Revisiting the days and weeks before Erich's demise, there is evidence that he was pre-occupied, troubled even. He had made a slightly agitated call to his Hibs supporter friend Frank Dougan, imploring him to come for a drink, then reacted moodily when Dougan was unable to take him up on his offer. An injury had sidelined him from playing for Dumbarton, and his attempt to regain fitness in a reserve game had floundered when he started to feel flu-like symptoms. Out of character, he had got changed and left the ground at Boghead before the full-time whistle and driven home to Musselburgh rather than sticking around to see the end of the game. Perhaps he had viewed this aborted comeback as a gloomy reminder that his football career could be approaching its expiry date. Schaedler was also finding it difficult to adjust to playing part-time, having spent almost his entire adult life as a full-time footballer, and although Dumbarton were a well-run competitive side, it must have felt like his best days were definitely behind him.

Gordon McDougall agrees that leaving Hibs, and full-time football, would have been getting Schaedler down. He had also noticed that his friend was having a drink – something he had never done before: "He had hated the travel between Dumbarton and Edinburgh but you would think that was a small thing. To go part-time, down a level, a few hundred folk in the ground compared to what you were used to. He was taking a drink, and Erich didn't drink. I'm not saying he was a heavy drinker, far from it, but he was having a drink more often. The number of folk who asked themselves, 'Could I have done anything?' I think he must have bottled it up, because I couldn't think of anything that was actually bothering him."

The feeling of rejection by Hibs must also have pervaded Schaedler's psyche. When he first left Easter Road in 1977, his departure was partly down to the unpredictable nature of Eddie Turnbull – the great Hibs manager had dispensed with the services of most of his Tornadoes team with similar ruthlessness. The blow of leaving Hibs then was also softened by a successful spell at Dundee, where he was constantly involved in promotion battles, returned to the Premier League, and reached a major Cup final while still in the First Division. However, leaving Hibs for a second time in the summer of 1985 emotionally floored Schaedler. John Blackley, his former Hibs and Scotland teammate and now his manager, had to deliver the bad news. He remembers how the proud Erich took it on the chin – testament to his character and professionalism – but while he may have displayed stoicism outwardly and adopted a stiff upper lip, there's no doubt that inside the rejection must have felt like a dagger to the heart. That feeling would have multiplied when a potential route back to Easter Road was slammed in his face by the board of directors. During his brief time at Dumbarton, he had volunteered his services to the club as a youth coach, more or less gratis, and had been deeply hurt when the gesture was snubbed. Although he was always a welcome visitor to the ground, on a professional level the door to his spiritual home had been closed.

At the age of thirty-six it would have been natural for Erich to fret over an uncertain future, the way most professional sportsmen do when the end of their career sneaks up on them. He had his pubs, but friends have told me that they too had started to drain his energy. Weeks before he died, Erich confided in one friend – who has asked not to be named – that a stock-take at Shades Bar had shown some glaring discrepancies, and while this hadn't crippled him financially, "he felt more let down than anything".

One of the more popular rumours surrounding Erich's death was that he had accrued substantial debts and was being chased for them, yet there seems to be strong evidence to contradict and dismiss that theory. Schaedler took a financial hit when he invested in a health club in Royal Terrace, but he had not pumped in more than he could afford and walked away from the venture still sufficiently solvent. When Erich's estate was divided after his death, he still had his flat in Musselburgh, a car and some modest savings. He did not own Shades Bar (he operated it on a lease) and he had his stake in the Victoria Bar in Leith Walk. He wasn't rich by any stretch of the imagination, but nor was he broke.

And then there was his personal life – undoubtedly a grey area, and the one that has been the subject of the most salacious gossip that has circulated since his death. Close friends of Erich say he was the type of person who could fall in love too easily, and in between his two marriages he had a steady string of relationships. There were break-ups too, of course, and divorces. He had also become estranged from his daughter Tracey – born in 1971 during his first marriage. His ex-wife had remarried and, according to his family, Erich accepted that he should back off and allow his girl to grow up with her new family. I was able to make contact with Tracey, but she has no lasting memories of her father. If Schaedler took any of these personal issues particularly badly then he was able to hide it from his friends and family. Admittedly, that does seem to have been one of his character traits, to bury feelings deep below the surface, but Schaedler's overriding nature was to take any of life's blows on the chin, dust himself down and get on with things the best he could. He didn't buy into the adage "a problem shared is a problem halved"; he was a one-man band when it came to maintaining and managing his emotions. If – as the police concluded – he committed suicide, then he took this guarded, intensely private side of his character to the ultimate extreme.

But while his close friends knew he was going through a turbulent few months, they insist there were absolutely no signals to indicate that he was so deep in the depths of despair. They have all asked themselves time and time again: "Was there anything I could have done to help him?"

"I think a combination of everything must have hit him at once," says Dougan. "His ties were finished with Hibs and he knew it and that really hurt him. When he first left Hibs he was absolutely devastated, but he was delighted when he returned – back to his spiritual home. I think that's what really hurt him, that the club didn't want him. He was a totally changed man. I wish I had spoken to him before he went missing, and I know his mum and his brother would have probably been feeling exactly the same."

Suicide rates soar around Christmas, of course, and any feelings of hopelessness or relationship problems can be magnified at this time. If Erich did choose to end his own life, it was probably no coincidence that he went missing at Christmas. But again, if he did have reasons for such drastic action, then any clues died with him.

His friend and former flatmate Jay Crawford acknowledges, "Christmas ties in with a lot of suicides, when people feel more lonely, but I can't imagine what's going through somebody's head to do that unless there's some real trouble. It was the same with the death of the Wales manager Gary Speed – sometimes you can't get to the bottom of it.

"I wish I knew what was going through his head," adds Crawford, who lost another celebrity friend in unexplained circumstances – Michael Hutchence, the frontman of Australian band INXS, who was found dead in his hotel room in 1997. "I asked a lot of people and a lot of players who were around at the time what the problem was with Erich and there were three or four theories. One was that there was financial problems, that he had got into problems with tax or he had been ripped off; another was that he was at the end of his career and that was weighing on him.

"The last time I saw him was only a few weeks before he died. I was coming up from Canonmills, heading to Radio Forth, and saw him in Rodney Street. I'd come up to the traffic lights and there's Erich sitting in the car next to me. I hadn't seen him for ages. I wound the window down and said, 'Give us a shout and we'll get together,' and he was saying, 'Yeah.' But a few weeks later he was dead. That always leaves you with a terrible feeling because you think, 'Why didn't I say "pull over" and have a proper chat with him?' But in those days you didn't have mobile phones at your fingertips and if you moved addresses a couple of times you could easily lose contact. I wish I'd said, 'Pull over or let's go for a chat or a coffee.'"

Dougan harbours similar regrets on not reaching out to Erich and taking him up on the offer of a drink days before his death. "It was the week before Christmas and I got a phone call at work and he said, 'Come and meet me for a pint,'" recalls Dougan, who was then a computer team manager. "I said, 'Erich, I can't. I've let all my staff away.' He was quite insistent; he said he would meet me after work. But it would have been eleven before the nightshift came on and eleven-thirty before I could hand over and I said I didn't want to go up town at that time. I said I'd phone him in the morning, but he said, 'Aye, whatever.' He was a bit agitated and humpty with me, which wasn't like him.

"I think he just wanted to talk rather than anything more sinister, but for a long time I thought, 'If I had spoken to him would it have made a difference?' and it really hurt me for a long time. But if you go through life thinking like that you are going to get nowhere. If somebody has reached that point where they are going to do that, it probably doesn't matter what you say. I just wish I had met him that night.

"Erich's death hurt everybody. It was horrendous for his mother.

That broke her in the end. It was tough for all of us, but her more so – not getting any answers or peace. I still miss him. Everyone who knew him does. He had a total winning mentality. He thought every time – 'I'm going to give the best I can.' That was him as a footballer, but on a personal level, he was so generous, a fantastic man."

George Stewart was another one of the last people known to have spoken to Erich shortly before his death. Together with Willie Allan, Stewart's partner in his pub The Chesser Inn, they had been out on a shooting trip days earlier.

"We went up shooting near Peebles with Erich. He took his dogs with him, and we had a good day out together. The police phoned me a week after, asking if I had an idea where Erich was. I told the police where we'd been and, believe it or not, that's where they found him.

"The policeman said that he thought Willie and I were the last to see him alive. That's why the police were so interested in us. Willie and Erich loved their shooting. He had come into the Chesser and arranged it with us: I would look after the dogs and we'd go for a bite to eat in Peebles, and then Willie and I just went home. Then I got the phone call. There wasn't anything to give us a sign or a signal. He was just his usual self.

"Willie was an ex-policeman and he asked a few questions, but we never got to the bottom of it. I heard a lot of stories afterwards, most of them nonsense, maybe one or two true, but it doesn't matter. Erich was a great guy, a lovely human being. And I'll tell you something, as horrible as it was, you've got have some guts to do what he did. God rest him."

Schaedler's former teammates were stunned by his death, although many believe there was occasionally a naïveté that left him susceptible to being taken advantage of by unscrupulous characters. "Maybe Erich was just a little too trusting," says Alex Edwards. "I think that was Erich's downfall at times; he couldn't see through anyone. With some of the rest of us, we could detect when somebody was up to no good or shouldn't be trusted, but Erich would think everyone was a nice guy."

As a few players have remarked earlier in this book, Schaedler undoubtedly was a deep thinker and prone to highs and lows. John Blackley says, "His attitude to life was full-on. His attitude to football was faultless. His attitude to his fitness was unbelievable. Honestly, he looked after himself. He was never a drinker, and my God, he was dedicated. But he was a complex fella. There was no middle ground with Erich – he was either up, high as a kite, or he was low. There was no middle area at all. He was kind of manic."

Several teammates have mentioned how Erich could retreat into quiet, brooding periods – and how they would just leave him alone with his own thoughts until he returned out of his shell. There is no clinical evidence to suggest Erich suffered from depression, but much of his behaviour and his mood swings could be considered consistent with some form of depression.

Robert Enke, the German international goalkeeper, committed suicide in 2009, and following his death his widow revealed that he had been suffering depression for six years and had been treated for the disorder. In Erich's era, however, there was an even greater stigma attached to depression, and the support network and understanding of the condition was nowhere near as developed as it is today.

Erich's former Hibs teammate Tony Higgins has helped a lot of footballers confront and cope with their off-field problems in his work with the players' union, the Scottish PFA, and now works for the international equivalent FIFPro. In his view Erich, while an enormously popular character in the dressing room, could be a complex, intense and private character. "I was astonished and shocked when I got the news," says Higgins. "Erich was always a bit of a loner; I think most of the guys would say that. He was never an integral part of the group socially, but he was liked by the players. He was a real smooth guy, a good-looking guy and an incredibly fit guy, but he would often go away and do his own thing. Erich also used to fall in love very easy. You would see Erich on trips perhaps holding hands with someone – more of a romantic than most of the guys, who had a more straightforward approach to members of the opposite sex.

"Suicides are very often out of the blue, in that there are no signs to predict what is going to happen. Take Gary Speed, for instance – there didn't appear to be any trail of desperation. Even after an inquest, it failed to establish exactly what the circumstances were that had led him to take his own life. I was completely shocked by Erich's death."

Schaedler's death was at the forefront of Higgins' thoughts when he set up a counselling service for players through the PFA, helping them to prepare for a life after football and the mental strain the end of their career can sometimes bring.

"When I took over the PFA Scotland job, obviously Erich's death was in my mind," says Higgins. "There were two or three other guys in desperate situations. I got in contact with them and I set up a counselling service. The former Grade 1 referee Dougie Hope and a great friend of mine, Jim Hossack, the football historian, were involved. I got to meet a lot of the greats of the game, English and Scottish, because of Jim's network. Some of them had moved on seamlessly to a new career, while others were really in desperate circumstances. I saw the impact at the end of a player's career – how a lot of players find it difficult to sustain the excitement, the glory, the spotlight that they had. So, I started thinking what can we do? The PFA in Scotland did not have a lot of money and we couldn't afford to start sending players to clinics for a week or ten days or to rehab centres, and a lot of clubs can't afford to do that either. So one of the things we set up with Dougie Hope was a counselling service that looked at three main areas: alcoholism, gambling and debt counselling.

"Jim and I used to speak at length. A couple of players we spoke to were struggling with depression – they would say to us, 'How do you recreate playing in front of 100,000 people at Wembley in a

Cup final? I don't get any excitement in life now.' Some guys are lucky, they maybe got a job as a coach or manager or might become successful in another sphere of sport, or go into business and be successful, but for a lot of guys it's almost like the end of a chute – they fall off somewhere and they find it difficult to ever be the person they were. We set up these counselling sessions and it has made a tremendous difference. Some have said it saved their life because they had been moving into a dark place."

Higgins accepts that the word "counselling" was an almost alien concept in 1985, and that Schaedler would have felt his options to reach out were limited. "Yes, it was a very different environment and even now it's difficult to get players to come forward, because they live and work in a very macho environment. You don't want anyone to detect any weakness. It's not like they go through their career in an atmosphere of natural empathy that someone will speak to them or take them aside. It's been difficult to break down those barriers. In Erich's day, it would have been far more difficult. Your best hope before then was maybe somebody at the club – like Tam McNiven or John Fraser – and if they'd detected anything different about Erich, they would have intervened.

"In the Seventies, the club doctor was often the first port of call. Our doctor at Hibs, Dr Ledingham, was very good. I remember one time we were playing a European game against Östers Vaxjo, and for a week I hadn't been feeling well, I had picked up a virus and felt very low. I shouldn't have played in Sweden but Turnbull was very keen for me to play. So for three or four days I felt really down and physically shattered. They presumed that I had a mental problem, so when I came to training one day, Tam McNiven said to me that the club had got me an appointment with the doc. I was a bit suspicious when I found out the club wanted me to go to his surgery, and started to put two and two together. So I went to see Doc Ledingham, who was a great guy. He was asking me how things are and asked me if anything was troubling me. I was playing along, and told him, 'I've got two women pregnant simultaneously!'

He was spluttering away and I spun it along for five minutes and eventually said, 'Look, Doc, the only thing that's up with me is that I've felt awful for the last ten days, blah, blah, blah. So I think he fed back to the club that having wound him up there was absolutely nothing wrong with my brain, it was a physical issue. That was the only time in my experience that they were keeping an eye on us behind the scenes, and their solution was just to send me to see the doctor. But nowadays, most players would not trust the club doctor not to reveal mental health issues – worried he might report it back to the manager. Now there is a mechanism where they can come to us.

"The service is fairly sophisticated now. The PFA is now working with the mental health organisations. What is sacrosanct is confidentiality. Occasionally you will get guys like Andy Ritchie who decide that they want to have their say, be it through the medium of a book or whatever, perhaps in an effort to offer encouragement to others. We need to signpost what we are doing, because at the end of the day we are not experts, but what I found is that if we could offer them that confidentiality and reassure them that they will get the best resources available they would be more willing to seek our help.

"I think part of the problem nowadays – and you see it perhaps with Paul Gascoigne to a degree – is that they all think the solution is a fifteen-grand-a-day rehab, which doesn't work for everybody.

"I remember thinking at the time of Erich's death, 'What could we have done? What could the game have done?' But it was very difficult in Erich's case. I would bump into him and saw him at Dumbarton shortly before his death, but I never knew anything was up. Erich probably took rejection quite badly – leaving Hibs then being denied a coaching post with kids – but how you could ever predict what was going to happen, as in the Gary Speed situation, I don't know.

"The PFA now go round the clubs in Scotland and they talk about it to the players, give them somewhere to come if they have problems. It's probably the same in any job. People are always worried what colleagues will say and about any stigma attached to mental health issues. Whether it will stop another Erich or Gary Speed is impossible to say. I'm sure there wasn't one sole reason in both of these deaths."

Just as has been the case in the death of Gary Speed, reasons for the death of Erich Schaedler remain thin on the ground, and his brother John doesn't believe that it was a straightforward suicide. While acknowledging Erich had a deep side, he is adamant his brother's death still does not make sense. "I accept that suicide is a possibility, but in my opinion there are a lot of unanswered questions and I can't rule out that he died as the result of foul play," says John.

Looking back to the time of the death, John adds, "He had been staying with my mother during the week leading up to Christmas and I did get the feeling that he had something on his mind. I wish I had got to the bottom of it, but although he seemed a little bit down that week, the last time I saw him when he came to see me while I was working at the hotel he was absolutely fine – quite chirpy if anything. He had wanted to go shooting with me, and while he was disappointed that I couldn't come, he accepted I was busy and said he'd see me later."

When the police declared Erich a missing person and initiated the search for him, John instinctively scoured all the old haunts that the two of them used to play together as children. "Where they found him was not somewhere we had ever gone, which was odd," says John. "What I found really strange was that his car had been completely covered with branches and foliage. Why go to all that trouble of covering the car? And another strange thing was that when we got the car back a few weeks after he died, there was absolutely no evidence that a gun had gone off in the car. No bullet holes – nothing – just a few little pin-sized holes in the roof lining. I am used to shooting, and I have to say it surprises me that there was not a lot more damage if a shotgun went off inside that car."

Erich's sister-in-law Beryl Schaedler shares her husband's suspicions: "The guy from the garage came to John after the funeral and said, 'I hope you don't mind me saying this, John, but I can't believe that someone would be able to cover the car with branches like that.' He said there was no mark on the driver's side whatsoever. He took the seat out, which was covered in blood, but he said that if someone had used a shotgun within the confined space of the car it would have damaged the interior – and yet there was no damage. We got the car back after it was cleaned and there was not anything to show that a gun had been fired."

John Schaedler says he was discouraged by the police from going to formally identify Erich's body after he had been found. He accepts this may have been to spare him from what would have been a harrowing experience, but despite his own insistence to identify the body, the police were adamant he shouldn't. John also says he was strongly advised to opt to have Erich cremated rather than buried. "I really regret that," says John, "but I wasn't thinking straight at the time, as you can imagine. I feel if he had been buried then at least there would be a chance of looking into his death further."

The Schaedler family were overcome with grief following Erich's sudden death. Erich's mother Leah never came to terms with the loss of her son and it blighted her final years. His father, Erich senior, was also distraught. The couple were separated by the time of Erich's death, and Schaedler senior remarried and settled in Perth. "He didn't mention it much, but you could sense he was hurting," says John. "Him and Erich had their run-ins, they were a pair of hot-heads and quite similar in some ways, but they were also quite close – the football tied them together, and my dad was always proud of what Erich achieved as a player. But Erich's death definitely hit my mother the worst."

Mrs Schaedler's ordeal worsened when she started to receive phone calls at her house. People purporting to be friends of Erich said they had information about how he died, and soon these calls were being made to John at his house too. "Sometimes it would be folk wanting to meet me in Edinburgh, telling me they had information about Erich's death. Other times, it would be people telling me to stay away, or just silence. A lot of them were time-wasters, a lot of them were being nosy, and some were genuinely people offering their help. Most of them were nuisance calls though," he says. "If someone said they had information then I felt duty-bound to go and check it out. So I would be going to and fro to Edinburgh, but I never did get any decisive answers. It just made matters worse, really, because I could feel the hope ebbing away.

"There are so many things that don't ring true," he adds. "Afterwards I would start to hear all the stories – that he's in debt, that he's involved with the wrong people, the things that he's running. People were contacting me and calling me up to Edinburgh. I got a call from an ex-CID officer. He was pushing it because Erich had helped his son in the hospital. He was told to drop it, but why were people higher up telling him to drop it?

"To be fair to the police, they looked into it, and there was a lot done. I felt like I was doing all the running about looking for answers, but unbeknown to me, the police did do quite a lot of investigating in the background. The police did come to me and say, 'John, if you ever need anything, we will try and help,' but they didn't seem to get anywhere either.

"What got me was that they seemed to know a lot more in Edinburgh, or at least claimed to know a lot more, things that we didn't know down here in Peebles. It was very difficult for my mother especially.

"I had been making regular trips to Edinburgh and asking plenty of questions when I got called into the Procurator Fiscal's office in Peebles and told to back off. He told me, 'Just leave it, John. I don't want to see you in a ditch too.' He had lost a daughter in London, who was killed, and he had never got to the root of it, and he said he knew exactly how I felt.

"One other thing that bothers me is that when we got the keys to

Erich's flat, it was suspiciously clean. It looked like someone had deliberately tried to move things around. It didn't look like Erich's place at all, and I had been in all of his flats over the years to do odd jobs. It was like somebody had gone out of their way to hide something – it didn't look like his usual messy bachelor pad.

"I know it all sounds very mysterious, but it has nagged me all these years that there is much more to Erich's death. One of my reasons for speaking about it now and helping with this book is that I might finally get some answers. I just want to know the truth and I don't feel I've ever fully had it yet. We are looking for some closure."

We may never know exactly why Erich Schaedler died. The evidence we have seems to point to a combination of events which led to him taking his own life as his football career stalled, his business ventures proved less successful than he'd hoped and he had issues in his personal life. He was also prone to keeping problems to himself, brooding on them rather than sharing them, and was perhaps also prone to depression, albeit undiagnosed. Perhaps there is one last piece of the Schaedler jigsaw still to be uncovered but, if there is, it remains elusive nearly thirty years after his death. What we are left with, however, is the memory of a much loved man – loved by his family and friends as a warm and generous person and by countless football fans as a player who had a fabulous career and worked incredibly hard to achieve his dream.

# 23

# TWENTY SHADES OF SHADES

Memories of Erich Schaedler and tributes:

**Gordon McDougall (friend and his former mechanic)**
He was the nicest guy in the world. I admired him as a footballer and as a person. Nothing was too much trouble for him. My kids looked up to him and he became like part of the family. He was fearless on the pitch, one of a kind almost, and it was just reward that he played for Scotland.

**Jim McArthur (goalkeeper and former Hibs teammate)**
Erich would have given you the sugar from his tea if you had asked for it. We hit it off, and although there were times he would go off into a world of his own, he had a great sense of humour and was loved by all the other boys. What an attitude he had to training, and it improved his game every step of the way. Seeing him line up with the rest of the Scotland squad for the World Cup said it all – he had got there thanks to his own hard work. It must have been the proudest moment of his life.

**John Blackley (Hibs teammate and manager)**
He was just super consistent. He wasn't flamboyant like John Brownlie – he was steady and dependable and as important to that Turnbull's Tornadoes team as any of the other lads. He also fully

deserved his place in Scotland's 1974 World Cup squad. He was a hard player, but he never flaunted what he had and was never violent. He just had that quiet reassurance that he knew he had it in his locker. When I was manager, I couldn't have asked for any more. He was the only one who knew what the gym was for.

**John Brownlie (Hibs teammate)**

When he first came in he really struggled at the start. I thought, 'What have we got here?' But he buckled down and he became a right good player for us. At the end of the day, you have to take your hat off to him. He was a laddie who had come from Peebles, more known for rugby than football, but he worked hard and got himself to the World Cup and got a cap for his country against his dad's country. He achieved a lot.

**Mike Aitken (*Scotsman* journalist)**

I thought of Erich Schaedler as the yin to John Brownlie's yang. On the pitch, the full-backs were a vital component of the Hibs side which flourished under Eddie Turnbull. While Brownlie was quick, gifted, stylish in attack, Schaedler was athletic, purposeful and intimidating in the tackle. Long before it became fashionable for footballers to put a premium on upper-body strength, the left-back took special pride in his physique. I'm not sure if his ferocious style of tackling would be tolerated in the modern game, which is in danger of becoming a non-contact sport, but he was a terrific professional and wingers must have trembled at the thought of taking him on. Off the pitch, I remember finding him a little intimidating – approachable enough but taciturn. He wasn't as elusive as, say, Gordon Smith had been in an earlier generation of players, but Erich struck me as a fearless, self-contained man with an added air of mystery.

**Sandy Macnair (Hibs supporter)**

I recall Erich really coming into his own a few years later, though as an integral part of that wonderful side we refer to as Turnbull's Tornadoes. We might have swooned at the sublime skills of the more silky ball players, but you couldn't have asked for a more effective counter-balance than a hard-as-nails full-back patrolling the penalty box. Overall, Erich was a great servant for Hibs and an integral cog in the marvellous green machine of the first half of the 1970s. Like every other Hibs supporter, I was saddened and shocked at the news of his untimely demise.

**Janette Campbell (Hibs supporter)**

I knew Erich as a player in the Turnbull's Tornadoes team and remember when he first came to Easter Road. He was quite unorthodox in the way he ran full pelt at defenders with the ball at his feet. He was very athletic and when tackled he used to just roll over, jump up and keep running, and the ball was still at his feet. Outside the club, I used to meet him and other players sometimes up town. Erich always had a smile for you and took the time to talk with the supporters on everything under the sun. I even used to meet him in Asda doing the weekly shop with his baby daughter in the seat of the trolley. Even in there he wanted to talk about Hibs. He just loved the club.

I used to go round after the games at Easter Road if we were to be playing Rangers the next week. We used to tell him to "kick" that Tommy McLean, their wee right-winger at the time, and sure as God up in the air the wee monster went and never bothered Erich again.

**Frank Dougan (friend and Hibs supporter)**

I remember at a game at Inverness he was winding up one of his long throws, but as he was stepping back, he went right over the wall and toppled right over it. He got a head knock in that same game, and as a precaution he was taken to hospital and kept in overnight for observation, in case he had a concussion. I went up to the hospital and took him in a carry-out from the social club.

Somebody had already been in before me with another, so that was about the only time I saw him a bit tipsy! Every one of that Hibs team could take care of themselves, but other teams were genuinely scared of Erich. They knew Hibs were hard, fit and would fight, but Erich was like the crème de la crème – he was the one they feared physically above all the others.

**Sean Allan (Hibs supporter)**
I would have been four years old and not yet started school when I first saw Erich play for Hibs. I don't recall anybody I knew having Shades as their favourite player. I don't recall anybody I knew not loving him almost as much as their favourite, though. Speak to anyone who followed Hibs religiously in the Seventies and I'll wager Shades would make everyone's top five. Everyone's. I remember his marauding runs from defence to attack, and how his tackles would raise a collective, "Ohhhh!" from the Easter Road crowd followed by an "Awwww!" as the opponent didn't need a stretcher after all.

**Jimmy O'Rourke (Hibs teammate and assistant manager)**
When Erich got picked for the 1974 Scotland squad we were delighted for him. In Erich's case it was the fulfilment of a lot of hard work. What he achieved for a laddie who had limited technical ability to get to that pinnacle of being picked to represent his country at the World Cup finals, it was all down to hard work and listening to his coaches. The total sum of Erich's good work was achieving the 1974 finals. You look at the squad, it was one of the best Scotland teams ever. I used to go down to Peebles quite often and people would always come up to me and speak to me about Erich. They always spoke about him.

**Ted Brack (author and Hibs supporter)**
Erich was one of these players who never let his standards slip. He was consistency personified. I can't remember him having a bad

game, although he must have done, but none sticks in my mind. His fitness levels were tremendous. He never stopped running throughout a match and was as fast and sharp in the ninetieth minute as he was in the first. He had real pace and was seriously solid. His tackles were bone-shakingly hard but always fair. His Tornadoes teammates are of the opinion that Jimmy Johnstone felt intimidated by him. Despite not being tall, he lost very few challenges in the air. He loved to bomb forward and, if he was less skilful than John Brownlie on the right, he was still very effective and could cross a great ball. Although clearly an excellent player, Erich didn't stand out in the Tornadoes team as so many of his colleagues were ultra talented. When he returned to Hibs late in his career for his second spell with the club, his teammates were less talented, and even at that stage of his playing career, Erich looked a class apart. I met Erich socially when I went with Jim McArthur and some of the other players to Erich's pub when Jim's first child was born. Jim was enjoying wetting the baby's head and Erich looked after our group very well. He was genial and welcoming and the perfect host – an absolute gentleman.

**Sandy Jardine (Scotland teammate)**
The team Erich played in was probably the best Hibs team since the late Forties/early Fifties. We always had some tough tussles with them, more so at Easter Road, because we seemed to hold our own against them at Ibrox. He was such a wholehearted player, who always gave 100 per cent.

**Scott Glenday (Dundee supporter)**
Myself and my mates who all supported Dundee and played for a Sunday pub team decided we would chip in for a trophy in his name and play annually for it against the Edinburgh Dundee Supporters Club. These games were keenly contested affairs played in both Dundee and Edinburgh; they were attended by some people who knew Erich, not least his close friend and colleague from his

Hibs days, Tom McNiven, and a former Dundee teammate from his time at Dens, Jocky Scott – he was manager of the club at the time that game was played and the presence of both men meant so much. Erich and the games played in his memory still get mentioned to this day.

**Donald Mackay (Dundee manager)**
When I heard Erich committed suicide in 1985 I was absolutely shattered to hear the news. I was living down in England then, as manager of Coventry City, and it just didn't make sense to me at all. He was always so full of life, although I've learnt through experience over the years that sometimes the more bubbly individuals can be the ones that are prone to mood swings – not that I ever saw any other side to Erich than a happy, smiling player who was an excellent professional and an example to others. He was always cracking jokes. Erich was exceptionally unlucky to get just one cap. He was a very good left-back, with a natural instinct for knowing when to get forward and when to defend, and when you look at the modern game, he would be worth his weight in gold nowadays.

**Bertie Auld (Hibs teammate and manager)**
Couldn't believe it. I *still* can't believe it. For someone who was so full of life, it just doesn't make any sense. Even now, once or twice things have happened that make me think about Erich, and I still wonder why it could end so tragically for someone who had so much going for him. He did have a deep side though. He was a chatty guy with the people he trusted and was close to, but if you went into the company of strangers he could withdraw a bit, like he was sizing someone up before deciding to open up to them.

**Kenny Davidson (former teammate)**
I broke my leg the week before the 7–0 game against Celtic reserves, two days before Christmas. Erich was staying in Peebles at the time and he used to stop at my house in Newtongrange and pick me up.

It was out of his way and not many people would have done that. My leg was in plaster, so getting to Easter Road myself would have been incredibly difficult. On those journeys into Easter Road we became quite pally and he really helped keep my spirits up. He would turn up in his wee white sports car with the roof down, wearing sunglasses – he was a bundle of fun. John Brownlie broke his leg against East Fife, the week after the 7–0 game. We had the same kind of break – a tibula and fibula compound fracture – which would keep us out for six months, so we went through our rehab together. We spent a lot of time with Tam McNiven as he helped us both on the long road to recovery. Tam was ahead of his time; we couldn't be in better hands. Erich used to pop into the treatment room from time to time to see how we were both doing. That was him in essence really, somebody willing to take the time to look out for others.

**Iain Munro (Hibs teammate)**
Erich and I had two spells at Hibs together and I considered him a true friend. We were very different characters but had a lot of things in common. We were both left-sided and both committed. He wanted to win every race, and so did I. The runs up Arthur's Seat were always keenly contested; we used to be the two that would tear ahead up the hill, but he was far crazier than me! His pal was Bobby Robertson and the two of them were mad on cars. They'd jump in their cars and race each other to training. They were a bit mad that way but good fun. I think even in those races to training Erich could not hide his competitive side. He would be the first to admit he was not the most technical player in the world, he was not silky in any way, but he made himself a player through hard work. He would dedicate every ounce of his body to bettering himself. Erich became an athlete through his strength and determination. He would just work at it and work at it until he was the fittest; he was incredibly driven that way. He wanted to be first in the gym and last out of it. The Seventies were great days for Hibs and we

were both privileged enough to be at a fabulous club. It was the best football side I ever played in. I won the treble with Rangers later in my career, and while they were a good team, that Hibs team was the best football team I was involved with.

**Alex Edwards (Hibs teammate)**
Even after he died, when we held any reunions for the Turnbull's Tornadoes teams there would always be a place laid for him. It showed the esteem he was held in, and he was always in our thoughts.

**George Scott (Hibs supporter and cartoonist)**
I grew up near Easter Road and we would wait outside the stadium to see the players coming out after training and after matches. Erich Schaedler was one of the guys who would always take time to stop and chat to us or sign autographs. His commitment and attitude on the pitch was excellent too. He was a player the fans could relate to – a 100 per cent man. I have drawn him twice, and have collected a lot of his memorabilia over the years, including his club blazer.

**Douglas Swan (researcher for histories of Tweeddale Rovers and Peebles Rovers)**
Erich never forgot his roots and he was a well-liked and highly respected figure in Peebles. The town is proud of what he went on to achieve in his career, and when an exhibition was held recently to celebrate sporting success over the years, one of the centrepieces was a display commemorating Erich Schaedler's football career and his international cap. He used to bring me back a programme from all of Hibs' matches in Europe, and nothing was ever too much trouble for him.

# APPENDIX: CAREER STATISTICS

(goals in brackets)

L = League; LC = League Cup; SC = Scottish Cup;
O = Others (including Europe)

**Stirling Albion**

| | L | LC | SC | O | Total |
|---|---|---|---|---|---|
| 1968/69 | 2 | 0 | 0 | 0 | 2 |
| 1969/70 | 13 (1) | 6 | 0 | 0 | 19 (1) |

**Hibernian**

| | L | LC | SC | O | Total |
|---|---|---|---|---|---|
| 1969/70 | 5 | 0 | 1 | 0 | 6 |
| 1970/71 | 17 | 8 | 0 | 5 | 30 |
| 1971/72 | 29 | 8 | 6 (1) | 0 | 43 (1) |
| 1972/73 | 32 (1) | 12 | 3 | 9 | 56 (1) |
| 1973/74 | 31 | 10 (1) | 4 | 7 | 52 (1) |
| 1974/75 | 30 | 9 | 1 | 6 | 46 + 1s |
| 1975/76 | 32 (1) | 8 | 6 | 2 | 48 + 1s (1) |
| 1976/77 | 24 | 0 | 3 | 4 | 31 |
| 1977/78 | 10 | 2 | 0 | 5 | 17 |

**Dundee**

| | L | LC | SC | O | Total |
|---|---|---|---|---|---|
| 1977/78 | 15 | 0 | 1 (1) | 0 | 16 (1) |
| 1978/79 | 27 (1) | 0 | 3 | 0 | 30 + 1s (1) |
| 1980/81 | 31 | 8 | 1 | 0 | 40 (1) |
| 1981/82 | 1 | 1 | 0 | 0 | 2 |

**Hibernian**

| | L | LC | SC | O | Total |
|---|---|---|---|---|---|
| 1981/82 | 23 | 0 | 1 | 0 | 23 + 7s |
| 1982/83 | 6 | 3 | 1 | 0 | 10 + 1s |
| 1983/84 | 29 | 4 (1) | 2 | 0 | 35 (1) |
| 1984/85 | 23 | 2 | 1 | 0 | 26 |

**Dumbarton**

| | L | LC | SC | O | Total |
|---|---|---|---|---|---|
| 1985/86 | 14 | 1 | 0 | 0 | 15 |

| | L | LC | SC | O | Total |
|---|---|---|---|---|---|
| **TOTALS** | 394 (4) | 83 (2) | 34 (2) | 38 | 549 + 11s (8) |